NEW IRELAND

Kavieng

Kimbe

ST

W BRITAIN

HERN

tta

3°

6°

wa

9°

150°

56°

rsity of PNG

© THE BAKER & TAYLOR CO.

# DEVELOPMENT
## and
# DEPENDENCY
## the political economy of
# PAPUA NEW GUINEA

Azeem Amarshi
Kenneth Good
Rex Mortimer

*Melbourne*
OXFORD UNIVERSITY PRESS
*Oxford Wellington New York*

*Oxford University Press*

OXFORD LONDON GLASGOW
NEW YORK TORONTO MELBOURNE WELLINGTON
NAIROBI DAR ES SALAAM CAPE TOWN
KUALA LUMPUR SINGAPORE HONG KONG TOKYO
DELHI BOMBAY CALCUTTA MADRAS KARACHI

*First published 1979*

NATIONAL LIBRARY OF AUSTRALIA CATALOGUING IN
PUBLICATION DATA

*Mortimer, Rex Alfred.*
   *Development and dependency.*
   *Index.*
   *Bibliography*
   ISBN 0 19 550582 4
   ISBN 0 19 550583 2 Paperback

   *1. Papua New Guinea — Economic conditions.*
   *2. Papua New Guinea — Politics and government.*
   *I. Good, Kenneth, joint author. II. Amarshi,*
   *Azeem, joint author. III. Title.*

   330.9'95

TYPESET BY COMPSET PRODUCTION COMPANY LIMITED
PRINTED IN HONG KONG BY HING YIP PRINTING COMPANY
PUBLISHED BY OXFORD UNIVERSITY PRESS, 7 BOWEN CRESCENT, MELBOURNE

# Contents

# A last word first

On Friday, 3 March 1978, in the national parliament of Papua New Guinea, the Prime Minister startled the public, the House and the Cabinet by an unannounced and emotional speech in which he proposed barring all top national leaders in politics and the administration, and the country's political parties, from engaging in private business.

The nation, Michael Somare declared, stood 'on the edge of disaster' because 'an increasing number of our top national leaders, both in politics and the public service, are getting too closely involved with foreign business interests for the good of the people', with the result that 'daily the temptations of personal gain and personal profit encroach on the responsibility and trust of implementing national principles' (*Parliamentary Debates*, 3 March 1978). Specifically, he proposed that Cabinet members, department heads and the Leader of the Opposition make a choice between their political positions and their business interests within three months, and that those opting to retain their posts divest themselves of their property either on the commercial market or to the state within nine months; also, that political parties dispose of their 'business arms'. In return, he promised substantial increases in salaries, expenses and pensions for those affected. He also expressed the hope of having these principles adopted by the provincial governments now coming into existence. As an indication of the importance he attached to his proposals, Mr Somare threatened to resign if they were not adopted.

The situation which Somare described with such concern is

no novelty, and is dealt with in some detail in the latter part of this book. But it was surprising that the Prime Minister should have raised the issue in such a dramatic fashion, consulting neither his Cabinet nor his party colleagues, nor even the Deputy Prime Minister and leader of the People's Progressive Party, Julius Chan. It appeared that the only ones who had advance knowledge of his intentions were a small group of close aides in the public service, and the Minister for Decentralization, Father John Momis.

Even more extraordinary was the fact that, in seeking to sever the close ties that have grown up between politicians and administrators, on the one hand, and overseas capital on the other, Somare was aiming to reverse a trend which he, as much as any other Papua New Guinean leader, had initiated and encouraged. As he stated in his speech, 'I own property in Port Moresby and Wewak. I have my own family business and two trucks for hire'. He might have said more. He has long had connection with Japanese interests, including one tycoon (Sasakawa) whose ruthlessness and imperialist outlook is a byword even by Japanese standards. In his autobiography, Somare reveals that he obtained financial support from these Japanese interests for his Pangu Party as early as 1972 (Somare, 1975: 83). Somare also serves on the board of Damai Pty Ltd, the business arm of the Pangu Party, of which the chairman and driving force is his intimate friend, Sir John Yocklunn, who has been instrumental in linking it with the Hong Kong banking and business world.

Somare, in fact, may fairly be said to have been a pioneer of the ideology of *bisnis* which captured the hearts and minds of Papua New Guinea's new élite and considerable sections of its people in the last decade of Australian rule. But politicians, like other people, may change their views, and there is no reason to doubt Michael Somare's sincerity in wishing to end practices which a short time before he zestfully promoted. One suspects that the men who conferred with him before his bombshell announcement, and who are known to regard the business mania afflicting their colleagues as a deadly virus, gave him such hard evidence of the corruption and abuse of office flowing from it that he felt impelled to take action to protect the political and financial viability of the country.

But it was too late to stop the rot. Realizing the odds against him, Somare in May deferred the bills and withdrew his threat to resign if they were not carried. In August, he acknowledged defeat and withdrew the bills from parliament. Few of his parliamentary colleagues or department heads relished his recipe for self-denial: the People's Progress Party, which has played the capitalist game with conspicuous success, was strongly opposed to the idea; the Leader of the Opposition, Iambakey Okuk, an ebullient Highlands capitalist, had overwhelming support in the National and United parties for his resistance to the proposal; and when it came to the test in parliament even the Prime Minister's own Pangu Party was less than enthusiastic.

To add to the Prime Minister's troubles, the Australian government, through its High Commission in Port Moresby, lobbied hard against his proposed leadership reform, contending that it was a socialist measure (!) and that it would produce political instability. Politicians and bureaucrats, still very much under the ideological influence of their former colonial mentors, and aware of Papua New Guinea's acute dependence upon Australian aid, did not view opposition from this quarter lightly.

Somare, then, was very much hoist on his own petard. When Iambakey Okuk declared that Somare's proposal would turn political leaders into 'rubbish men', whereas the people 'look up to men of wealth', he was expressing a modern consensus in the cash economy which the Prime Minister himself did something to fashion and which he is now seen to be trying to undermine, to some extent at least. Okuk could say, 'it is not our custom' to limit leaders' business ambitions or the ways they pursue them, because in the colonial and post-colonial era this is precisely how traditional ways have been adapted by outside capitalist forces and interpreted by the new rich peasants and bourgeoisie.

This was not the first occasion, however, on which Somare had sprung a political surprise of this order; he is prone to sudden changes of direction, which appear to reflect his ambivalence about the changes taking place in Papua New Guinea under his stewardship. He is only human in wanting the best of all worlds: on the one hand, foreign investment and foreign aid on a large scale, big resource projects, a thriving national economy, a high level of urban services, a powerful government and administration, and personal aggrandizement; on the other, the ideals enshrined in the government's Eight Aims — self-reliance, social and regional equality, rural development, honesty in public affairs, a Melanesian way of life. It is his ability to articulate these contradictory aspirations which has helped to make him such a successful politician in the country's transitional phase from colony to independent nation.

But Somare is running out of rope, as the failure of his appeal to clean up the government indicates. No one who has watched his shifts of policy, and has at the same time observed the inexorable manner in which the world capitalist system has tightened its grip on the country, can fail to sympathize with him in his dilemma. He and his fellow-leaders of Papua New Guinea are in a certain sense victims — until recently of a colonialism so influential over their lives, so powerful in its economic and social structures, and so insidious in its fostering of dependence among them, that they would have had to be Titans indeed to have overcome its legacy and struck out decisively for their own goals; and now, of a neo-colonial network that reaches out to them and appears to offer so much at so little cost by contrast with the sacrifices demanded by self-reliance. Each step on the road to deeper incorporation in the imperialist system is accompanied by a more contrived and hollow reaffirmation of the retreating Aims, while the structures of dependence set and harden in the economic system and in the mental universes of the leadership.

Hence, victims only in part; also collaborators and beneficiaries over many years and in many ways, as Somare belatedly and partially perceives. For those who will reap the bitter harvest of neo-colonialist policies and behaviour will not be the leaders, but the ordinary village people who, as he said in his speech on 3 March, were promised 'a society of equal opportunity, where every citizen is able to pursue his or her development as a human being'. The leaders may be induced to deny what is best in their society, but their personal loss will be assuaged by the well-known 'benefits of Western civilization'. For the mass of the people, the prospect is one of rising inequalities, more intense exploitation, chronic unemployment and insecurity, misgovernment, social disruption and blighted opportunity.

Just why this must be so — as we believe — is a lesson from history, and in particular the recent history of that great part of humanity we clumsily designate the Third World, for whom collaboration with the centres of world capitalism was said — by world leaders, social scientists and corporation executives — to offer the prospect of development, industrialization, modernization, welfare and democracy. Instead, the general outcome has been more of the rewards of the direct colonial phase — more underdevelopment, more impoverishment, more social trauma, more manipulation and repression. This, we argue, is no accident, but the direct consequence of the operations of a world system that feeds upon the weak, the vulnerable, the dependent. All these things Papua New Guinea is, more than most, and it would be naive indeed to expect that it will somehow escape the predicament that has befallen the rest, whose footprints loom before it. On the contrary, we try to show that the shape of what Papua New Guinea will become by continuing established policies is already writ large upon its present economic and social structures, ideas and conditions.

Many would deny that there is any alternative open to Papua New Guinea, and there is a sense in which this is largely true: looking at the objective structures of Papua New Guinean society, and the subjective experience and attitudes of its actual or potential leadership, it is hard to envisage circumstances (short of prolonged and severe crisis) which would induce a break from existing directions and current strategies. Those leaders and advisers who are trying to steer a course designed to obtain for the country the best that the world system can provide without its worst effects are not entirely in the wrong, even though in our view they are failing and will fail yet more decisively.

We have nothing to offer in the way of quick panaceas or easy formulae. We do not trip socialism off the lip, even though we believe that with all its failings it offers a potential for national development which dependent capitalism cannot possibly realize. Our contribution is a preliminary one, exploring the genesis of Papua New Guinea's present dilemmas right back to their early colonial source, following the process through the decades, and analysing the outcomes as they present themselves today. Any alteration in this course will emerge and become amenable to analysis only through the prolonged interplay of the classes being formed in Papua New Guinea at this time.

Azeem Amarshi
Kenneth Good
Rex Mortimer
Port Moresby and Sydney, 1978

# Introduction

This book grew out of our experiences as university teachers in Papua New Guinea in the mid-1970s. Our own need as social scientists to try and place the evolution of the society around us into a disciplined framework, and the obvious and urgent need of our students for a perspective to evaluate and build upon, encouraged us, first in a series of seminars, and now in this book to develop an introduction to the political economy of Papua New Guinea.

We say 'introduction' advisedly, because this is the first attempt to analyse the process of the country's incorporation into the modern world system,[1] and studies of some aspects of this process from a similar standpoint are just beginning to appear; it is certain that in coming years many gaps in our material will be filled in and many of our conclusions refined or vitiated. If this book helps to stimulate research of this kind, especially by Papua New Guinean nationals, it will have served a useful purpose.

For the most part, academic writing on Papua New Guinea has suffered from one or more of four main faults. Much of it has been what is called mere 'fact-grubbing', the assembling of data in a purely descriptive and empiricist fashion or with very limited analytical ends in view; this applies particularly to many of the highly detailed, small-scale anthropological studies and many of the histories. All too often, it has exuded a strong flavour of apologia for the colonial power, either because the authors were connected at some time and in some way with the Administration, or because the ideology of 'development' or 'modernization' to which they adhered, consciously or unconsciously, led them to find in the colonial project those beneficent effects which the ideology posits.[2] Even more common has been the view, explicit or implicit, that the historical relationship between Australia and Papua New Guinea has been in some significant way a unique one, and that therefore it could be studied in a discrete manner divorced from world developments and the colonial phenomenon generally. Finally, there has been a pervasive disciplinary myopia at work, so that little attempt has been made to integrate the economic, political, social and cultural aspects of social change into a dynamic whole.

We have borrowed heavily from these works, not hesitating to adopt interpretations as well as empirical data where they seemed consistent with our own views. But our general approach has been different in decisive respects. We seek to understand and explain Papua New Guinea's present condition, how it arrived at that condition, and what are the implications of that condition; and since we find the compounding elements in no crucial way unique, but rather a particular elaboration of a fate common to most of the countries that have passed through the colonial experience, we have had recourse to that body of theory which in our view best analyses the relevant processes, namely underdevelopment theory. Given that there are differing versions of this theory, it is as well that we state, in short and crude terms, the outlines of our approach.

The emergence of a number of industrialized states in the late eighteenth and nineteenth centuries led to the maturation of a world capitalist system which (despite the existence of a number of socialist states) remains fundamentally intact today. The ruling classes of the 'core' or highly industrialized states constitute the dominant element within the system, and through the exercise of their economic, political and military power they subject the economies and societies of the rest to their interests, principally through the enforcement of mechanisms of 'unequal exchange'. A larger group of 'semi-peripheral' states, while suffering the effects of this subjection, have been able to achieve some degree of independent development and some manipulation for their own benefit of the mechanisms of unequal exchange. The majority of countries, however — those loosely referred to as the Third World — remain on the periphery of the world capitalist system and are persistently 'underdeveloped' in their interactions with the core nations and those in the semi-periphery (Wallerstein, 1974; Amin, 1974).[3]

It follows that, in our usage, the term 'underdevelopment' has nothing in common with the static, 'value-free' usage of conventional economic and sociological theory. On the contrary, when we say that a country *is being underdeveloped*, we mean that it is subject to a many-faceted process inherent in the operations of the modern world system. Among the hallmarks of ongoing underdevelopment are: in the economic sphere, progressive dislocation of the economy, dualism between the domestic economy and the export enclaves, deepening divergence between domestic resources and domestic demand, an overwhelming export orientation, a stunted manufacturing sector, chronic dependence, the absence of an internal dynamic and coherence; in the social sphere, a perverse class structure shaped more by external than by internal pressures, characterized by extreme inequalities, and notable for the persistence of high rates of unemployment and underemployment; and in the political sphere, instability, acute dependence upon external forces, bureaucratism and authoritarian trends.

Papua New Guinea appears to us to conform closely to the postulates of underdevelopment theory. A congeries of more or less self-contained Melanesian subsistence societies on the very margins of the world economy 150 years ago, it was gradually drawn into the orbit of mercantile capitalism in the course of the nineteenth century. Direct colonization followed: imperial Germany annexed the northern half of mainland New Guinea and the smaller islands to the north and east in 1884; and, in response to Australian appeals, Britain in the same year planted the flag in the southern portion, known as Papua. Thriving copra plantations were established in the German colony, but poorer soils and rainfall discouraged the none too energetic efforts of the British and their successors, the Australians, to emulate them. Australia occupied German New Guinea after the outbreak of World War I, and retained it under separate administration as Mandated Territory of the League of Nations. Between the wars, little progress either in economic or welfare terms occurred; the plantation system, dependent upon indentured labour enrolled by the administration, remained the hub of the colonial effort, and it defined the master-labourer relationship characteristic of the whole caste-like society. Much of the country was only lightly administered or remained outside colonial reach altogether.

In 1945, Papua and New Guinea became jointly administered, and substantial economic change commenced in the 1950s, with the opening up of the populous Highlands and the introduction there of coffee, first as a plantation activity and then also as a peasant cash crop. Cocoa played a similar role in the fertile coastal zones, and tea and other commercial crops also made their appearance. As agricultural activity expanded, so did commercial and processing activity, with Australian Government aid providing infrastructure and administrative superintendence. The share that most Papua New Guineans obtained of this new-found wealth, however, was barely sufficient to pay their administration taxes.

In the 1960s Australia came under international pressure to provide the inhabitants with better health services, education, more economic opportunity and political representation. Its response was at first slow and grudging, but in the latter part of the decade the changes gathered momentum and education and urbanization began to stimulate moderate nationalist activities. At the same time, multinational interest began to focus on Papua New Guinea, symbolized by the establishment of the large copper mine at Panguna on Bougainville Island. Political parties and trade unions were formed, and Papua New Guineans manning the lower reaches of the public service became the standard bearers for greater political rights and economic opportunity. The Australian government now acted quickly to bring about political decolonization: in 1972 the first indigenous parliamentary cabinet took office; in December 1973 self-government was granted; and in September 1975 the country became independent.

None of these changes, however, has lessened the grip of world capitalism upon the country, or given any of its people, save small strata of politicians, administrators and rural capitalists, any degree of control over their affairs. The heights of the economy remain as firmly as ever under foreign domination, the country is overwhelmingly dependent upon foreign aid and investment for financial viability, and economic activity remains restricted almost exclusively to agricultural and mineral exports to world markets. The mass of the people have experienced change as a process by which their culture has been disrupted, their society made more unequal, their country become more dependent.

In short, Papua New Guinea has by a slow, lengthy and uneven process of colonization been incorporated into the world capitalist system as a highly dependent, underdeveloped entity, bearing all the features of the neo-colony. What is exceptional about Papua New Guinea is that for a long time its involvement in the world economy was so tenuous and marginal that it constituted what we have dubbed an 'ultra-peripheral' region, a condition which has produced variants upon the pattern of underdevelopment which are examined in the book. Apart from that, of course, being a living community, and not merely a category, Papua New Guinea has a history of its own within the broad confines of the analytical schema which alone makes the writing of this study a justifiable enterprise.

The book is divided into four parts, each tracing one major aspect of the process of its underdevelopment. Part I elaborates the economic history of Papua New Guinea, and the inheritance of economic structures and relationships which that history has produced. Part II looks at the changing global situation as it impinges upon Papua New Guinea, specifically in its relations with Australia and Japan. Part III examines the process and characteristics of class formation in the society, and Part IV looks at the role and nature of political institutions in the colonial and post-colonial period. The coverage is by no means comprehensive, nor is it intended to be; it selects those data which the authors, from their theoretical standpoint, regard as most crucial in determining Papua New Guinea's present situation and potential, and, in keeping with its avowed status as an introductory study, it leaves much to be explained which we hope others will not be slow to tackle.

We wish to acknowledge the assistance and encouragement of John Ballard, Helene Barnes, Peter Corris, Donald Denoon, Mike Donaldson, Peter Fitzpatrick, Sukhamoj Ganguli, David Hegarty and Hank Nelson. Many friends at the University of Papua New Guinea also contributed in various ways to the writing of this book, while Molly Pouru offered patient and efficient typing services. We bear sole responsibility for the book's final form.

## Note on the Papua New Guinean currency

Since 19 April 1975 the official currency in Papua New Guinea has been the Kina, which is divided into 100 toea. The Kina remained on par with the Australian dollar until July 1976, when it was revalued to a level where $A1.05 = K1. A second change occured in December 1976 when, following the devaluation of the Australian dollar, the Kina reached $A1.13 = K1. With some slight variations this level was maintained through 1977. A further minor revaluation in 1978 put the value of the Kina at $A1.26.

# I
# The economy:
# the development of
# peripheral capitalism

Azeem Amarshi

# 1
# The precolonial period, 1800-1880

The population of the Papua New Guinea region at the beginning of European expansion in the early nineteenth century consisted of a large number of very small-scale tribal societies. The basic system of production was 'a set of variations on the classic swidden or shifting cultivation system in which impermanent clearings are cropped for shorter periods in years than they are fallowed' (Brookfield with Hart, 1971: 88). This was combined with hunting, gathering and trapping, and in the coastal areas with lagoon fishing and collection of shellfish from reefs. The forces of production were those of a stone age culture and included a variety of stone tools, digging sticks, traps, fishing nets and dug-out canoes. These were made and used by the members of nuclear and extended families within clan and village societies. The ownership of the means of production and the distribution of the social product within the group were governed by the rules of the kinship organization.

However, the societies were by no means egalitarian. Along with kinship ties there existed patron-client relationships wherein the 'big man' — an accomplished fighter-leader who commanded more wives and wealth — possessed some limited powers in deciding production and distribution patterns; inherited leadership was not uncommon. These small-scale societies mostly existed as self-contained and largely self-sufficient units. The degree of specialization within societies — largely based on sex — and between societies, was limited, but certain restricted skills (canoe-making, sago making, pottery, magic and ritual) were well-established. However, extensive

3

trading networks existed, both in necessities and 'luxuries', products often being bartered in the context of simple commodity production, as well as for the purpose of customary gifts, reciprocity and compensations. To generalize, the production systems may be said to fall within the category of 'modes of production of the primitive community' (Amin, 1974: 139-40).

## The late arrival of capitalism

The South Pacific has been one of the most sparsely populated regions in the world and is one of the farthest from Europe, the centre from which global capitalism was beginning to unfold from the sixteenth century onwards. These two attributes help to explain the ultra-peripheral role which the Melanesian region assumed within the developing world system. European capitalism naturally tended to incorporate within its net the more accessible and promising regions first.

It was only after the establishment of a penal colony at Sydney in 1788, and the ensuing colonization of Australia and New Zealand, that the Melanesian islands began to become profitable to European capitalism. The development of settler colonialism in Australia and New Zealand gave rise to the establishment of trading routes between the South Pacific and the rest of the world — Europe first, then Asia and America. Melanesia was gradually incorporated as almost an ultra-periphery within the world system.

A number of factors contributed to the marginal role of these Pacific islands in global capitalist development. Australia itself remained a peripheral economy until well into the present century, and its mediation made for a slow penetration and low degree of capitalist development. The low levels of population and the distance from the centre continued to constrain capitalist penetration, and there were relatively few known or suspected resources of significant value. Lastly, the island of New Guinea in particular put up very substantial barriers to penetration by reason of its very difficult terrain, the prevalence of malaria, and the atomistic nature of the many hundreds of small-scale, self-contained societies. These

4

features increased the cost of penetration and control, so the economic returns were for a long time considered dubious. This explains why the New Guinea Highlands, a zone of very high population density by Papua New Guinean standards, became incorporated into the colonial economy only after World War II.

Nevertheless, 'the need of a constantly expanding market for its products chases the bourgeoisie over the whole surface of the globe' (Marx and Engels, 1970: 38); likewise the hunger for raw materials in Europe made its impact felt in Melanesia as elsewhere. And so Papua New Guinea was incorporated, however late. Beginning around the turn of the nineteenth century, Europeans and Australians began to open up barter exchanges with the more accessible coastal populations trading products of the reefs and forests, including bêche-de-mer, turtle shell, pearl shell and pearls for beads, axes, knives etc. 'Most early enterprise depended on individuals with little capital and small backing, who ... bought a schooner and embarked upon the risky but profitable business of inter-island trade' (Brookfield with Hart, 1971: 247). Sometimes missionaries were among the first traders. The products were sold to China where they were highly valued. In exchange, the traders brought back tea and other Chinese products valued by Europe and Australia but for which the latter country particularly had little to offer in return. Melanesians therefore helped to bridge the gap between supply and demand — for Australia-bound tea particularly — in the early and mid-nineteenth century, until plantations were established in Ceylon and other colonies (Shineberg, 1967: 215). From the late 1830s, in addition, whaling crews were frequently putting in to the Papua New Guinea coast for food and water; the local inhabitants again acquired industrial goods, some of their women had sexual encounters with crewmen, and men even joined the ships as crewmen.

In this phase, characterized by contact and exchange, the impact on the indigenous societies was perhaps not entirely detrimental, in spite of the unequal exchange and the excessive profits earned by the successful traders (Reed, 1943: 93). It is

5

possible the islanders were net beneficiaries in that the steel tools included in the traders' wares were technologically of great value to Melanesian agriculturists and fishermen (Salisbury, 1962). However, as will be seen, these relations of simple exchange were not to last very long.

Apart from the opening of trade routes, 'the timing of the invasion had much to do with the early and sustained interest in coconut products'. Vegetable oils had begun to supplant the use of animal tallow in the manufacture of soap and candles. '(By) 1840 West African palm oil, American cottonseed oil, and widely gathered coconut oil were all being imported into Europe.' Initially, the European traders purchased the village-produced coconut oil. However, with the development of suitable machinery for large-scale extraction of oil from copra in the 1850s, copra became the preferred commodity and the peasant-produced oil which tended to be discoloured and rancid, was phased out from the trade (Brookfield, 1972: 26).

This period was the turning point in the history of Melanesian economic relations with Europe. For the first time Melanesians were affected by European demand for an *industrial* raw material, so that Melanesia's relations with Europe began to be guided by the development of industrial capitalism as opposed to the trade relationships of mercantile capitalism. The substitution of copra for peasant-produced oil had a number of very important implications: it signified the beginnings of the disarticulation of the economy — the diversion of the productive forces from their roots in domestic consumption — and the redundancy of indigenous Melanesian technology associated with this process. It also meant that the value added in the processing of coconuts into oil was lost by the Melanesian producers to European industry. It eventually drove the independent peasant producers into wage-labour on European established plantations. And finally, it produced the conditions for big business to enter the scene.

The product improvement associated with the industrial extraction of coconut oil was followed by increased demand for copra. Britain and France having already established their vegetable-oil interests in West Africa — Britain's Unilever

6

monopolizing palm oil, and the French concentrating on peanuts — Germany found its haven in the South Pacific. Thus in the 1850s Godeffroy und Sohn of Hamburg, a large company, began to dominate the copra trade, beginning in Samoa where it established its headquarters and spreading outwards. By the 1870s the company had established a series of trading stations in the Bismarck Archipelago: '... the Godeffroy interests were realizing large enough profits from their New Guinea trade to warrant establishment of permanent stations in the Archipelago' (Reed, 1943: 43). This German trading enterprise was to have important consequences for the subsequent history of New Guinea.

In addition to the demand for copra, the region was also affected by the growth in demand and price increases for other raw materials, notably cotton and sugar, following the American Civil War. Plantations were established in Queensland, Fiji and Samoa to produce these commodities, and initiated the infamous labour trade in the South Pacific — 'blackbirding' — which lasted from 1863 to 1914, and involved the transportation of about 100 000 islanders to Queensland alone (Corris, 1973: 1). A substantial number of these were taken from the eastern Papua New Guinea region during the early 1880s. A rising Queensland company, Burns Philp, which was to become one of the most important colonial enterprises in Papua New Guinea and in Melanesia generally, pioneered the labour trade in the Bismarck Archipelago (Docker, 1970: 174).

Finally, two other major factors influenced the future of Papua New Guinea. One was the discovery of gold in southeastern Papua in the late 1880s, and the ensuing rush of prospectors and miners from Australia. The other was the scramble for colonies, which for Melanesia began with the annexation of western New Guinea by Holland in 1828, followed by the takeover of New Caledonia by France and Fiji by Britain. Germany and Britain (the latter power at the insistence, and on behalf, of the Australian colonies) respectively colonized New Guinea and Papua in 1884, the year of the partition of Africa. It is worth noting at this stage the role of the Australian

7

traders and trading companies in the early barter exchanges and blackbirding. Given the peripheral nature of the Australian economy then, Australian traders could be no more than merchant capitalists. In the trade triangle of the South Pacific (sandalwood, reef products), China (tea) and Europe (manufactured goods), Australians did not feature as producers of goods. They were essentially middlemen who cashed in on the profits that were to be derived from the trade with Melanesians. Together with blackbirding profits, and the super exploitation of Melanesian labour on Queensland sugar-cane fields, the surplus they garnered represented the primitive accumulation of capital which in part financed the development of capitalism within Australia. It was for Australia the phase of classical mercantile capitalism, Pacific-style. The role of Australian business still remains to some extent that of a middleman between the centre of the world system — Europe, North America and Japan — and the periphery of Melanesia. However, this role has undergone a significant qualitative change, now that Australia has risen to a semi-peripheral position within the global capitalist system.

# 2
# The plantation system

The first phase of the primitive accumulation of capital through trade and plunder in western Melanesia, mainly by German and Australian capital, did not involve a fundamental change in the mode of production in Papua New Guinea, nor did it result in great dislocation of the societies there.[1] However, the decimation of some communities through European-introduced diseases, and the strengthening of the position of some groups relative to others due to their monopoly access to European goods, did initiate social changes which prefigure the larger scale dislocations of the colonial period. The actual transformation of the mode of production may be said to have begun after the middle of the nineteenth century when traders established, firstly, stations employing wage labour to process peasant-produced coconuts into copra, and later, in 1882-83, actual plantations of coconuts, cotton and other crops in the Bismarck Archipelago (Robson, 1965: 128). It received added impetus in the late 1880s and 1890s when gold-mining concerns in Papua began to employ wage labour to extract gold in south-eastern Papua.

These developments inaugurated the social formation of peripheral capitalism in the final quarter of the nineteenth century, coinciding with the formal colonization of Papua and New Guinea in 1884, and the beginning of the second stage of primitive accumulation of capital in Melanesia, this time by Europe rather than Australia. The term 'primitive accumulation of capital' is used here in the sense defined by Samir Amin (Amin, 1974: 134-5).

9

International specialization has taken on a succession of varying forms: those that belonged to the prehistory of capitalism (the plundering of hoards, the slave trade, and so on) were succeeded by the 'classical' forms of colonial economy (trading-station economy and mining) and then its neoclassical forms (establishment of groups of light industries in the periphery, dependent on the heavy industries of the centre ... [During each of these stages], the relations between 'advanced countries' and 'underdeveloped countries' ... is actually a matter of relations between different social formations ... Analysis of these relations forms the essence of a study of accumulation on a world scale. It reveals the *contemporary forms assumed by the mechanisms of primitive accumulation:* unequal exchange, that is, the exchange of products of unequal value [due to the] allowing of different rewards for labour with the same productivity. (my italics)

The coincidence of the arrival of planters and miners and the establishment of the colonial state was not altogether fortuitous. The establishment of the colonial state — that is, direct colonization by annexation — was essential if capitalist activity was to transform itself from trading and blackbirding to plantation and mine production. The reason for this is that plantation and mining activities require land, which is an immobile and essential means of production, and continuous and large supplies of labour. Blackbirding entailed ruthless mining of labour supplies, threatening the exhaustion of the 'product'. The new situation called for the long term *management* of labour supplies (since both the land and the labour were to be obtained within the same political boundary) in which the active role of the colonial state was essential. In any event, the practice of blackbirding was becoming untenable both politically — slavery had been on the way out for half a century — and economically.[2] The fact that blackbirding into the Pacific extended into the twentieth century is another reflection of the late development of capitalism in Australia.

There are a number of interesting parallels between Australia and the United States in their regional political economy. Queensland — 'The Deep North' — corresponds to the 'Deep South' in the United States, both having been plantation regions depending upon imported cheap non-white labour. In both cases the pressure for the abolition of bonded slave-

10

labour (or slave-type, in the case of Queensland) came from the powerful and economically progressive interests of the industrialized regions — including white labour interests — although the political struggle in Australia was far less intense than was the case in the United States. To carry the analogy further, both the US southern region and Australia's north lie adjacent to island plantation colonies which were forced by the metropolitan power (Britain in both cases) to specialize in plantation products different from those of the settler colony. Within the South Pacific sub-system, sugar production was restricted to Queensland and Fiji, while the other Pacific islands were made to specialize in copra and mineral production. In the case of Papua and New Guinea, sugar production was actively discouraged, in spite of the fact that the sugarcane grown in Queensland originated in New Guinea.

Such a comparative analysis of regional sub-systems leads us to the concept of a four-tier sub-system which helps us to explain some of the peculiarities of Papua New Guinea today. Within the centre-periphery model, Wallerstein (1974: 403) has employed the concept of the semi-peripheral economy. This concept has proved useful in the analysis of sub-systems within the global system. Indeed the semi-peripheral role of Australia within the South Pacific region has already been referred to. However, our discussion on blackbirding and the Queensland plantation economy implies that 'national' capitalism within Australia was itself only just emerging in its semi-peripheral form in the latter half of the nineteenth century. In other words, Queensland's hitherto plantation-based economy was being absorbed into a more integrated national economy under the domination of the capitalist industry and agriculture established in south-eastern Australia. This integration could only take place by the ousting of the plantation system from the Australian economy. Queensland of course continued to remain a backward state economically, trailing behind the southern states. However, in the colonization of Papua it was Queensland which played the leading role, although Sydney played the role of the sub-metropolitan centre within the region as a whole.

The implication of the foregoing for our purposes is that the concept of the semi-periphery can profitably be extended further: if, instead of employing the term semi-periphery — or perhaps more accurately, sub-metropole — for Australia as a whole, we confine it to the south-eastern region of Australia, then Queensland is a periphery within the regional system. The status and role of Papua then becomes that of an 'ultra-periphery'.[3]

Such a conceptualization is pertinent: firstly, it connects the emergence of semi-peripheral (or sub-metropolitan) capitalism in Australia to that of the development of peripheral capitalism in Papua (and New Guinea later on); secondly, it enables us to explain the very uneven pace of economic growth of Papua and New Guinea; thirdly, it explains the particular form taken by peripheral capitalism in Papua (and New Guinea) which helps us to distinguish it from that of, say, Kenya or Nigeria. In particular, this analysis enables us to explain the extreme dependency of the colonial economy which has extended right up to the present.

## Papua from the 1880s to the 1940s: the case of the lethargic colony

Conventional historiography of Papua has tended to minimize the importance of economic factors in motivating its colonization, placing exclusive emphasis on the desire of the Australian colonies to secure protection from Japan and Germany (Biskup et al, 1968: 44; Mair, 1948: 69).

Before colonization, Papua's economic importance lay in the coastal barter trade. Then came the minor gold rush to Port Moresby in the late 1870s which involved individual Australian miners operating on a small scale, and finding little paying ore. By 1884 a small white community had been established in Papua. However, in contrast to New Guinea, no big business interests were yet involved. Large enterprises such as BNG Mining Co. and Woodlark Island Gold Mining Co. were attracted to the scene for the first time after gold prospectors struck rich deposits in the islands off the south-eastern tip of Papua in the late 1880s. By 1907 most of the 2000 indentured labourers in Papua were involved in carrying for individual miners and the companies. Because of the gold strike the exports of the colony jumped from about £6000 in 1888-89 to around £76 500 in 1904-05 (Legge in Ryan, 1972: 120). Gold continued to dominate the colony's exports right up to the outbreak of the 1914-18 war, after which the reserves dwindled, reviving for only a brief period in the 1930s.

The overriding importance of gold in the colony's first few decades was closely related to the very slow growth of the agricultural export sector. Up to about 1900 the second, third and fourth places in the export hierarchy were occupied by products of the coastal trade — pearl shell, bêche-de-mer and sandalwood respectively (Legge in Ryan, 1972: 120). The agricultural sector could develop either by the systematic encouragement of peasant export production, the establishment of large-scale settler (or company) plantations, or a combination of both. The last alternative, though not an impossible one, was not in fact a viable one due to the inherent conflict between the expansion of peasant production and the need of plantations for constant supplies of labour (see the next section on New Guinea).

The colonial state tried to evolve a strategy combining peasant production and plantations. The record of success was continually disappointing, both by comparison with the expectations of the state and the performance of estate agriculture in German New Guinea in the corresponding periods. The proportions of alienated plantation land under cultivation were 26 per cent and 55 per cent in Papua and New Guinea respectively in 1940, and Papua had less than one-fifth of the total plantation acreage of the two colonies combined.

The lack of success of agricultural export production in Papua may be attributed to the relatively less favourable ecology there. At the same time it also reflected the weakness of Australian capitalism and unsound policies, both on the part of the metropole and its colonial apparatus in Papua. There was insignificant demand within Australia for tropical raw materials and, therefore, insufficient pressure to secure

13

supplies from its colony (especially as north Queensland constituted a tropical region within Australia itself). On the other hand, since Australia itself depended upon metropolitan Britain for capital, markets and immigrant labour, neither the state nor private enterprise had extensive resources to spare for economic development of any kind in Papua. In general, opportunities for would-be settlers, investors and speculators were more certain and favourable within Australia itself. In particular, during the first decade of the 1900s the reorganization of the sugar industry was an important priority for the Queensland government and also provided significant openings for settlers. Between 1901 and 1905 the number of cane-growers in Queensland increased from 2601 to 3422, nearly all the increase being on small holdings. And 'in the six years from 1902 to 1908, in an effort to clear Australia of the Pacific Island labourers ... the Commonwealth Government spent £1,356,908 in the form of bounties to Queensland growers producing sugar using all white labour. It took over thirty years for the Commonwealth Government to spend such a sum in aid to Papua' (Power, 1974: 160-1). Thus little capital was available to the colonial state for infrastructural development necessary for the establishment of an agricultural export economy, and settlers with private capital were reluctant to come for this reason as well.

In the face of all this, and in spite of efforts by the state to subsidize colonial private enterprise, the record remained poor, partly because of the ill-directed nature of the subsidies. The Burns Philp Company, for example, a growing commercial and shipping enterprise based in Queensland, had extended its influence throughout Melanesia in the 1880s and was granted a contract for shipping between Queensland and Papua under an Australian government subsidy. For the period 1901-34 this subsidy amounted to 'just over £1,000,000 .... or about the same as the total subsidy to the Papuan Administration for the same period!' (Power, 1974: 149n). Rather than assisting capitalist development within the colony, this arrangement contributed only to the profitable growth of Burns Philp, whose shipping monopoly imposed intolerably high freight

14

costs for importers as well as exporters.[4] Thus plantations as well as peasant export agriculture tended to remain stifled.

In addition to the shipping subsidy, the colonial state provided almost unlimited acreages of alienated land on lease, and a free surveying service. In 1934, during the Depression, it paid out a subsidy of £8000 to copra planters, most of whom at that time were considering going out of business (Mair, 1948: 81).[5] Nevertheless, capital was generally lacking both for direct productive investment and for the development of transport, marketing and research infrastructure, so that agricultural development of any kind — plantation or peasant-based — could not have progressed very far.

Initially, in 1884, the British declared Papua a protectorate; this status was changed in 1888 to that of a British colony; and a further change in 1906 transferred full responsibility to Australia. These changes gave rise to a good deal of uncertainty, particularly in defining economic policy, and inability to reconcile the ambition for white settlement with the interests of the native population.[6] In this climate little plantation development took place.

In 1906, the Royal Commission of Inquiry into Papua's 'development' settled on a strategy for export agricultural development involving the establishment of plantations by European settlers. Previously, efforts had been made to compel villagers to plant coconuts for marketing, but these had met with little success. With a clear policy formulated on the role of private capital and Papuan labour, a minor land boom followed and the number of plantation holdings increased from ten in 1906 to seventy-six in 1907. Also in the latter year a Planter's Association came into being.[7]

By 1914 there were 230 plantations and the industry employed some 11 000 indentured workers. The outbreak of the 1914-18 war, however, brought a fall in commodity prices and an enormous increase in the already very high freight charges, at a time when a large proportion of the plantations had just begun producing. After the war ended, although prices rose substantially, freight charges remained high (see below) and many marginal plantations were threatened with bankruptcy. Then in the early 1930s the Depression finally spelt an end for many planters whose holdings, one by one, came under the ownership of the large trading companies. For these reasons, total plantation cultivated acreage rose only slowly in the period 1914-20 from 43 000 to 62 000 acres and froze at around that level for the next twenty years (Mair, 1948: 79). The late initiation of the plantation industry therefore turned out to be very inopportune.

By 1918, Hubert Murray, Lieutenant-Governor of Papua, had become very concerned about the failure of the colony to achieve budgetary self-sufficiency, due to the sluggish growth of plantation-based export agriculture. For this reason, and perhaps also because the shortage of labour was beginning to give concern, the colonial state in 1918 introduced the Native Plantations Ordinance and the Native Taxation Ordinance. These regulations comprised a two-pronged strategy to induce the Papuan villagers to earn cash, either by paying tax to the state from wages earned in capitalist enterprises or by compulsorily providing labour for a set number of days on communal village plantations, the proceeds of which were to be divided between the state and the labouring villagers. While the Head Tax accounted for some 10 per cent of state expenditure up to 1939, the attempt to compel establishment of village plantations resulted in no more than token success. The insensitivity of the administration to local land tenure customs and the villagers' motivation to work (Crocombe, 1964); the expropriation of a substantial proportion of the product by the administration; its failure to provide an adequate marketing and transport infrastructure all contributed to continuous disappointment with the performance of peasant export production (Power, 1974; Mair, 1948).

Finally, the policies of Australian mercantilism contributed to the failure of export agriculture to take off. Foreign-based capital — even of British origin — was not encouraged to invest. In 1898 an application for extensive tracts of land for plantation development and a proposal to establish a shipping line by the large British consortium, New Guinea Development Syndicate, was declined by the colonial authorities. The

16

Syndicate was

financed (by) eminently respectable London sources, similar in many ways to the German New Guinea Company ... [MacGregor] was prepared to let the Syndicate import labour from India and the Pacific Islands [and] ... to allocate the Syndicate 250,000 acres of land at a purchase price of two shillings an acre. [However], the scheme was shelved. The Australian [settler] colonies were not prepared to accord such rights to an English company at a time when a purely Australian administration for British New Guinea was in sight. (Burnet, 1967: 21-2)

Similarly, a request by the German-based 'Long Handle Company' for trading rights was refused. Nevertheless by 1915 two British companies were among the biggest and politically most influential capitalist enterprises in Papua (Power, 1974: 169-70). Except for these two companies, though, most of the capital was Australian or raised locally through profits from trading. While in the medium term, that is up to the 1939-45 war, these mercantilistic policies on the part of the administration may seem to have been short-sighted, in the long run they paid very handsome dividends to Australian capital which (as will be seen in later sections) benefited enormously from the tight monopoly it held in Papua New Guinea in the post-war period. In any case, this aspect of mercantilism was not of great importance in holding back capitalist development in Papua. British capital in particular — which enjoyed much greener pastures elsewhere in the imperialist world, including Australia itself — very likely would not have invested heavily in Papua. The fact that the Colonial Sugar Refining Co. and two other Australian companies, Burns Philp and W.R. Carpenter, predominated in the British colony of Fiji is perhaps an indication of the general disinclination of British capital to invest substantially in the region (see Rokotuivuna, 1973).

A more significant aspect of Australian mercantilism affecting Papua (and New Guinea) was the application of the Commonwealth Navigation Act to both the colonies in 1921. The Act effectively barred non-Australian vessels from transporting the colonies' produce. The result was that all imports and exports had to be transhipped at Sydney, despite the fact that almost all the exports went to Europe and the bulk of the colonies' imports of manufactured goods and rice originated from Europe and Asia respectively. Burns Philp, which had enjoyed a monopoly in shipping, charged 90s. a ton to transport copra to London, 'whereas it was asserted that it could be shipped direct for 60s. or 70s' (Mair, 1948: 80). Brookfield (1972: 68) records an even more staggering difference: 'the Papuan government plantations . . . reported that it cost £19.00 per ton to freight rubber to London via Sydney in 1924 . . . but only £8.82 per ton by direct service in 1928'.

The Act was withdrawn from the colonial territories in 1925 following insistent representations and protests from plantation interests and the colonial administrations. The damage had been done, however, particularly in Papua which, as we saw, was also affected by the inopportune timing of the development of its plantation industry.

To mitigate the effects of World War I and the Navigation Act — and perhaps also to secure raw material supplies for developing Australian industry — the Australian government accorded preferential treatment to the colonies' exports of coffee and desiccated coconut to Australia, later including rubber as well; bounties were offered to encourage production of a variety of products not competing with Australian agriculture and which till then had not been produced on any significant scale in the colonies.[8] As well, Australia stepped up its annual subsidy to Papua from £30 000 to £50 000 to enable the territory to weather the effects of the slump in the copra and rubber markets. However in the face of the world-wide depression which set in only a few years later, these efforts to stimulate the development of colonial agriculture came to nothing. Indeed, Papuan agriculture had hardly begun to recover from the worst effects of the Depression by the time the 1939-45 war broke out.

Papua's record of economic development therefore accords with the conceptualization of the colony as an ultra-periphery. As the gold reserves began to dwindle in the early years of this century, a small and relatively unprofitable plantation sector developed. The industry produced copra and rubber which remained the mainstays of the capitalist economy, with the exception of a short-lived period in the early 1920s when copper accounted for 29 per cent of the colony's exports,[9] and another equally brief and limited boom in gold mining in the depressed 1930s, encouraged by the high prices for the metal. Overall, however, the extent of capitalist enterprise remained very limited and the development of infrastructure was minimal.[10] Peasant production of marketed surplus remained pitifully small throughout the period.

## New Guinea up to the 1940s: the case of the classic colony

New Guinea's colonial history opened in ways markedly different from Papua's in several respects. It was colonized by a metropolitan (industrial) European power, with a substantial economic empire, which had been expanding in the Pacific since the 1850s (Firth, 1973). Large-scale financial, industrial and trading interests, situated within the centre itself, were interested in the colonization and exploitation of New Guinea. Subsequently, following the defeat of Germany in the 1914-18 war, the Australian administration capitalized upon the strong base created by its German predecessor, putting plantations in particular, and capitalist interests in general, above all else. This continuity and relative dynamism stood in sharp contrast with the situation in Papua where, although Hubert Murray ruled for the whole period from 1906 to 1940, the emphasis of the administration's policies continually shifted between 'native' rights and plantation development with great lack of success in both spheres. However, certain similarities with Papua also obtained, arising out of the common experience of the Navigation Act, the Depression, the 1939-45 war and, above all, the weak colonial master that both shared after 1915.

In the 1870s, about a decade before formal colonization, German companies had begun to enter the New Britain Archipelago (later renamed Bismarck Archipelago), trading in copra with coastal villagers and, later on, blackbirding for

19

German-owned cotton and copra plantations in Samoa. The pioneering firm was the Hamburg-based Godeffroy und Sohn, which in 1878 went bankrupt and was absorbed into D.H. & P.G., or the 'Long Handle Company'. It was followed by another Hamburg-based company, Robertson and Hernsheim (later Hernsheim & Co.). Then Germany annexed New Guinea during the scramble for colonies in the 1880s. A consortium of powerful financial and political interests in Berlin played an active role in the annexation and persuaded the German Imperial government to grant its colonial enterprise, New Guinea Kompagnie,[11] a monopoly over land and a charter to administer the colony.

Thus, in contrast to Papua, where the economic interests at stake were those of small-scale traders and where the early instigator was peripheral Queensland, the annexation of New Guinea was carried through by powerful interests originating in industrial Germany.[12] And in spite of an initial phase of 'unprofitable imperialism' by the New Guinea Kompagnie (Firth, 1972), it eventually learned from the success of coconut planters in the New Guinea islands and built up the thriving plantation colony that Australia seized in 1914.

The initial activity of the New Guinea Kompagnie was in land speculation, the alienation of land for subsequent sale to settler-planters, most of them German immigrants in Australia. After the expected inrush of settlers failed to materialize — presumably for the same reasons as in Papua — the Kompagnie redirected its resources to plantation development. However, with the copra market in a serious slump between 1883 and 1901 (Firth, 1973: 15), the Kompagnie decided to develop tobacco, coffee and cocoa plantations on the mainland (Kaiser Wilhemsland), for which purpose it set up two subsidiary companies. From the very beginning, the plantation industry in New Guinea was constrained by shortage of local labour. The New Guinea Kompagnie's plantations were in areas where capitalist enterprise had not penetrated before and colonial control had not yet been established; at the same time the extensive alienation of land had aroused intense hostility among the local inhabitants in many areas, where the German establishments experienced frequent attacks. Only small supplies of labour could be recruited from the Archipelago.

In order to alleviate the problem, the Kompagnie arranged to import Malay, Javanese and Chinese coolies from the Dutch East Indies and Singapore in the early 1890s. But the experiment with coffee and cocoa production failed in the first year and was abandoned, and the tobacco ventures ended in failure by 1896, mainly because of extremely high death rates (from diseases and other causes) among the coolies. Moreover, the Dutch and British colonial regimes were reluctant to export large supplies of labourers to an imperial competitor, particularly when death rates were so high. 'By 1893 over 7,000,000 Marks had been sunk into the [New Guinea Kompagnie] enterprise, more than had been invested in any other German colonial firm, but it brought nothing except losses'; and 'half the plantation labourers died during 1891 and 1892'. In 1899 the Kompagnie was freed from its obligations to administer the colony and received from the Imperial Government, in compensation for its 'pioneering work', 50 000 hectares of land and M4 000 00 in cash (Firth, 1973: 21).

Meanwhile smaller companies, mainly operating as copra traders in the New Britain Archipelago, had been far more successful, and the New Guinea Kompagnie, following their example, diverted its resources to the copra trade. After the end of the slump in the copra market at the turn of this century, very substantial capital was invested by the Kompagnie in copra plantations in the Archipelago aided by the infrastructure established by the colonial state. A head tax was introduced in 1907 to stimulate greater supplies of labour for the plantations; an extensive road system was built in the plantation regions and agricultural research stations established; a competitive shipping service was available direct to Europe and Asia, so that the cost of imports — and therefore production costs — were lower,[13] and export returns higher, than those obtained by enterprises in Papua. The subsidy from the German government was twice as large as that paid to Papua by Australia.[14] Moreover the presence of the Chinese ex-coolies and immigrants provided cheap skilled and semi-skilled labour,

21

as well as an extensive trading network within the colonial economy. By 1912 the Chinese owned 207 businesses in New Guinea (Firth, 1973: 22). This class of middlemen was typical of classical colonial situations elsewhere — for instance in East Africa and South-east Asia, and played a very important role in extending commercial relations within the colonial economy. (Such a group of petty businessmen operating in isolated regions on very low margins was prevented from entering Papua due to the 'White Australia' policy, though the weakness of the colonial economy was perhaps an equally important factor.)

The cultivated plantation area rose from some 6000 acres in 1899 to 38 000 acres in 1907, and by 1914 it stood at about 85 000 acres, almost double that of Papua. The number of indentured workers employed at the time was some 20 000. The value of exports rose from £A19 235 to £A393 404 over the period 1890-1913, the corresponding increase in Papua being from £A6455 to £A128 016 (Burnet, 1967, Appendix). The Kompagnie owned a quarter of the plantation acreage, most of the rest being owned by six large plantation and trading companies, including D.H. & P.G., Hernsheim & Co. and E.E. Forsyth & Co. ('Queen Emma'). Thus after a period of experimentation and failures, the colony ceased to be the trading frontier that it was at the turn of this century and by 1914 was firmly established as a classic, monocrop plantation economy[15] under the hegemony of a handful of large, mostly German companies.

When the 1914-18 war broke out, German New Guinea surrendered to Australian forces in the first year of hostilities and a military government was established in New Guinea. The development of German colonialism was thus abruptly arrested. The Australian military establishment, however, allowed German capitalist enterprises to continue operating, pending the final outcome of the war. Indeed, the latter were provided with every encouragement to carry on as before, although repatriation of profits to Germany was prohibited. In these conditions, the German planters, confident of victory in Europe, continued to produce copra and reinvested their surplus to expand plantation lands, which by 1919 had risen to some 135 000 acres. The plantation labour force correspondingly increased to approximately 30 000 workers; and copra production went up from 14 000 to 30 000 tons.

Following the end of the war and the defeat of Germany, New Guinea came under Australian rule as a mandated territory.[16] An expropriation board, set up in 1920, took over all non-mission German assets by 1923. Australia thus inherited a thriving plantation colony at very little cost. In 1926 the properties began to be sold to Australian ex-soldiers on generous terms. The latter, however, lacking in capital, were financed by large Australian trading houses, particularly Burns Philp and W.R. Carpenter;[17] the combination of lack of expertise on the part of the ex-soldiers, and the onset of the slump in the copra market during the Depression, ruined many of the small planters and the properties fell into the hands of these trading oligopolies (Reed, 1943: 195).[18] W.R. Carpenter was able to acquire the assets of the New Guinea Kompagnie, while Burns Philp obtained other properties as well as the main shipping service, together with a subsidy and a guarantee of trade (Brookfield, 1972: 67).[19] The large trading companies acquiring the properties were particularly fortunate since a substantial proportion of the holdings planted to coconuts in 1920s were just beginning to mature. In 1938, of the 'total estimated capital value of coconut plantations [of] approximately £A5,000,000, the large companies [held] outright or in part over £1,500,000 worth of expropriated properties alone' in New Guinea (Reed, 1943: 196). And 'in 1937, B.P.'s and their eight subsidiaries had a total of £1.5 million [worth of plantation interests] including £0.5 million as mortgages; Carpenters had £1.9 million' in the two colonies (Power, 1974: 168n).

The expansion of plantation acreage continued at a steady pace in New Guinea and the 1940 acreage was almost double that of 1920. In contrast to the experience of Papua, the plantation economy of New Guinea expanded production during the difficult periods of the Navigation Act and the Depression, due largely to the vastly better foundation established in the German period, which meant among other things that a far higher proportion of coconut trees was bearing during these difficult years. The volume of copra produced in 1937 was 76 400 tons compared to 22 700 in 1920.[20]

By the outbreak of the 1939-45 war, the large trading houses — particularly the trio of Burns Philp, W.R. Carpenter and Steamships — had established a solid grip over the colonial plantation and trading economy. These large corporations became the core of the economic system. They were based in Sydney but developed Pacific-wide, multinational linkages 'in order to operate in their role of agency houses, growers, traders, shippers, and de facto bankers. Vertical integration has been the key to their success ... and [at all times] they ... exercised considerable political influence, if not power (Brookfield, 1972: 13). However, originating as they did in the sub-metropolis of Sydney, these Pacific-wide multinationals were essentially merchant capitalist corporations, more in the style of the East India Company than that of Euro-American colonial corporations such as Firestone, Brook-Bond, Unilever, and Tate and Lyle. They were powerful corporations within the Pacific, but no match for the truly global corporations originating from the centres of capitalism.

Herein lies the real significance of Australian mercantilism in Papua New Guinea. Australian manufacturing interests, for instance, stimulated the production of rubber in Papua, all of whose output was accorded preferential treatment and imported into Australia; and the rubber plantations that were established tended to be larger in scale than their coconut counterparts. Nevertheless, the industry was under-capitalized, backward in technology and inefficient in the face of competition from such producers as Goodyear, Dunlop and Firestone operating plantations in South-east Asia and Africa. The copra producers also faced international competition, but survived because technological change in the industry was minimal, and the continually advancing labour frontier enabled wage rates to remain exceptionally low until well after the 1939-45 war. As late as the 1960s the minimum agricultural wage in Papua New Guinea was among the lowest in the Pacific region, being $A16.42 per month (cash equivalent) compared with $20 in the

Solomon Islands, up to $32 in the New Hebrides, $50.60 in Fiji, and $95 and over in New Caledonia (Brookfield with Hart, 1971: 143).

In contrast to the dynamic growth of the plantation sector, the peasant production of marketed output — mainly copra again — stagnated as in Papua, in absolute as well as relative terms. While in 1886 the Tolai of East New Britain alone sold some 2000 tons of copra, total New Guinea peasant production in 1922 was only about 6000 tons compared with 19 000 tons produced on plantations (Power, 1974: 170). In 1914 almost half the copra export from New Guinea was accounted for by peasant production — so-called 'trade copra' — but by 1940 this share was down to a very negligible proportion.[21] On the other hand, the number of labourers increased from approximately 20 000 (including 2500 'casuals') in 1914, to around 43 250 (including 2400 'casuals') in 1938 (West in Ryan, 1972: 845). These two features — the stagnation of peasant-marketed output and the expansion of the wage-labour force — are closely related. While in Papua the colonial regime — in a situation where capital was generally scarce — could afford to be ambiguous about native policy, in New Guinea the native was more clearly seen as a provider of labour to capitalist enterprise. With the acute and continuous shortage of labour that the New Guinea capitalists suffered, a significant alternative source of income for the peasants, competing with wage labour, would have been fatal to the colonial enterprises.

Such logic was by no means peculiar to New Guinea. In colonial Tanganyika also, for example, where sisal plantations depended upon migrant labour for almost all their labour requirements, 'peasant production of sisal was discouraged and obstructed by the estates with some help from the colonial administration' (Lawrence, 1975: 104). Similarly, in colonial Nyasaland, African cash crop production suffered because 'the settlers, who feared that they would lose their labour supply if Africans had their own source of cash income', opposed peasant cash crop production (Morton, 1975: 7).

Although 'trade copra' was highly profitable during the plantation establishment phase — indeed it was the most im-

25

portant source of accumulating capital for subsequent plantation development — profits from plantation-produced copra
were far more lucrative:

> Given the right conditions, above all adequate supplies of labour, a high
> proportion of mature palms, and a favourable world price, plantation
> copra was much more profitable per ton than trade copra, since the
> benefits to the trader of a higher world price were diminished by the
> competition of other traders willing to pay more to the indigenous pro-
> ducer.

Like buying-out trade competitors, 'planting was a step
towards rationalising production and reducing the number of
uncontrollable costs' (Firth, 1973: 14, 27). Given the
oligopolistic structure of the plantation and shipping sectors,
the drastic fall in copra demand during the Depression acted as
a further discouragement to peasant production, since planters
and the oligopolies naturally gave priority to their own produce
in order to minimize their losses.

In New Guinea, the Depression was also accompanied by the
development of gold production following the Bulolo gold
rush of 1926, with important consequences. The pioneers, as in
Papua earlier, were small prospectors and miners, but already
by 1927 mining was entering a new phase dominated by big
business which bought out the small operators with the bless-
ings of the state. One of the two major companies was the
Bulolo Gold Dredging Co., initiated by a small Canadian-
based firm, Placer Development Ltd, whose original capital in
1926 consisted of Can$100 000.[22] The other large company was
New Guinea Goldfields Ltd, a subsidiary of Russo-Asiatic
Consolidated Ltd, which was developing the Mount Isa field in
Queensland. NGG's nominal capital was announced as
'£5,250,000, the largest recorded for any mining organisation
in Australia up to that time' (Healy, 1967: 34).

The onset of the Depression provided an urgent incentive to
develop the goldfields at Edie Creek and Bulolo. The crash had
a near-fatal impact on the colony's copra industry, copra
prices declining from £22 per ton in 1925-26 to £3.64 in
1933-34. As well as subsidizing the planters and creating a

26

Marketing Board to rationalize marketing, the colonial government introduced 'strong' deflationary measures applied especially on the wages of indigenous workers where cuts of an order quite inconceivable in metropolitan countries were imposed' (Brookfield, 1972: 81). The colonial government therefore had a great interest in obtaining higher revenues through the exploitation of the goldfields. Meanwhile, the slide in the export prices of Australian produce had begun to create an enormous trade deficit in Australia, which was finding it increasingly difficult to raise long-term loans abroad. The resultant pressure towards export of gold placed Australia in a critical situation at a time when the value of domestic gold production had fallen to a mere £1.8 million per annum (Healy, 1967: 91); the Australian pound was devalued by 20 per cent in 1931. In this situation Australia was sufficiently interested in developing gold mining to waive income tax payment by the New Guinea gold companies.

The collapse of currencies during the crash pushed up gold prices high enough to make private capitalist interests — at a time when profit rates and investment opportunities elsewhere were at their lowest — obsessed with bringing the New Guinea goldfields into production as quickly as possible. Australia could not spare the resources to build a road for bringing in to the gold field capital equipment and other supplies from the coast. Nor was there time. Private capital therefore transported thousands of tons of materials and many thousands of passengers by air. The rapidity and scale of operations in developing the gold mining industry were outstanding, and of such a kind as to be a dress rehearsal for the establishment of the Bougainville Copper mine some thirty-five years later.

The decision to opt for air transport in place of road was to have a very great long-term impact on the future pattern of transportation and economic development within Papua New Guinea. For while air transport proved to be economical in the short-run, from the long-term, social point of view the neglect of surface transport was to result in a very high cost structure within the economy.[23] Here again Australia's weak, sub-

27

metropolitan capitalism continued to restrict development within its periphery.

If gold production was of great value to an Australia suffering the effects of the Depression,[24] it was also a tremendous boon to the colonial economy, where the slack in production and employment in the copra industry was more than taken up by the immense increases in output, government revenue and employment resulting from gold mining.[25] The greatest benefit, however, went to the Australian and other investors, who reaped unprecedented levels of profit. The intense exploitation of the mine workers is demonstrated by the case of the Bulolo Gold Dredging Company, for whom 'throughout the 1930s the [5 per cent] royalty payments exceeded the annual wages bill'. Between 1934 and 1941 each $5.00 share in BGD realized a total dividend payment of $21.00, an average rate of return of $2.625 per share per annum (Healy, 1967: 94, 108).[26] The similarities with Bougainville Copper Ltd's operations in the 1970s, as will be seen, are stark indeed.

The Japanese invasion during World War II prompted the Australian military to destroy the Bulolo infrastructure. The industry found it not worth its while to restore production fully after the war, particularly as ore reserves had begun to decline and handsome compensation was forthcoming from the Australian government. In the immediate post-war era, Placer, in an attempt to diversify, invested in a large plywood factory at Bulolo in partnership with the Australian government, the latter's urgent interest in the project stemming from severe plywood shortages in Australia. In spite of this, however, the decline of gold production left the Wau-Bulolo region, in the post-war period, with little to show for its pre-war prosperity but rusting dredges and large stones by the roadside which dredging operations had discarded.

The inter-war crises had begun to establish a trend towards increasing state intervention in economic life in both colonies (subsidies, tariff protection and assistance in marketing have already been mentioned), setting the stage for even greater state involvement in the post-war era. In addition, a new set of circumstances encouraged the integration of the entire popula-

28

tion and geographical area of Papua and New Guinea into a single political unit. Hitherto, colonial economic activity and control had been established on the islands and along the coastal regions; the central Highlands region with its large population was outside the colonial system. Frenetic prospecting for gold in the late 1920s and in the 1930s led to economic penetration of this region for the first time though Lutheran missionaries preceded the prospectors.[27] Furthermore, the hegemony of the same three plantation-trading oligopolies in both colonies, and the changed circumstances of the post-war period, set the stage for a new phase of the development of peripheral capitalism in Papua New Guinea in the 1940s.

## Economics of the plantation system

One of the most important instruments of capital accumulation in the modern era has been the plantation, which has continued to operate within the colonial system ever since it first emerged in the West Indies in the sixteenth century. The peculiar feature of the plantation system, however, is that, for all its importance in capital accumulation on a world scale, it has persistently discouraged domestic capital accumulation of a kind which promotes the economic development of the host economy itself (Beckford, 1972). This is borne out historically by the fact that, with the exception of Brazil, no country that began its career within world capitalism as a plantation economy has managed to emerge from the periphery.[28]

There are a number of theoretical and empirical explanations for this anti-developmental bias within plantation economies. Plantations have invariably been metropolitan-owned and have operated parasitically within the colonial economies, transferring their surpluses to the metropole. The parasitic relationship, however, goes deeper than this: it involves a dual process of unequal exchange and exploitation. As was the case in many African colonies, the plantations in Papua and New Guinea depended for labour supplies upon indentured migrant labourers who were deemed to be single men both by the planters and the administration. They were paid extremely low wages which barely covered the bare subsistence needs of the single man. Capitalist plantations, therefore, did not have to bear the cost of the reproduction of labour power (in other words, the upkeep of the worker's family); they only paid for the immediate production of labour. Thus as long as the bonded migrant labour system operated, the pre-capitalist sectors continually subsidized the capitalist sector. At the same time, however, the benefits did not necessarily all accrue to the capitalist planters. Where the values of commodities are reckoned in competitive international markets, the tendency is for the rate of profit to equalize internationally and the prices of commodities to equal their prices of production (Emmanuel, 1972; Amin, 1974, vol. I). In other words, the exploitation of the pre-capitalist societies by the plantation sector is manifested in unequal exchange at the international level, where manufactured products from the metropole exchange for primary commodities whose prices reflect only a part — that which the planter actually pays — of the full cost of production. This implies the continual transfer of values from the pre-capitalist formations on the periphery to metropolitan capitalism, where costs tend to fall and surplus value tends to mount.

Papua and New Guinea have been among the last frontiers of bonded labour within international capitalism. The indentured workers in the two colonies were particularly exploited, since the small-scale and scattered nature of the copra plantations had the effect of pushing up fixed costs and transportation costs and depressing wage levels to the absolute minimum. (Brookfield, 1972: 51). The planters could continue to maintain very low wage rates for long periods because the labour frontier could be pushed further and further inwards and outwards from the coastal plantation centres, labour itself was bonded, and there was no competition for labour supplies.

Any growth in the productivity of peasant agriculture would have put pressure on plantation wages to move upwards, but in fact it tended to remain stagnant, partly due to the impact of the plantation system on land use and labour supply, and partly due to the neglect of peasant cash crop production and of subsistence production by the colonial authorities. Although there were qualitative changes in the structure of agricultural output due to the introduction of new food crops, this was paralleled by a decline in the diversity of production of handicrafts. Reed (1943: 255) laments the decline in the artistic quality of artifacts produced by men in villages due to the indentured workers often leaving their villages at the very age when they traditionally learnt many of the skills. Even women's skills were not immune because 'when the men return they bring bolts of calico, iron pots and empty kerosene tins as presents to their wives and sisters, thus striking at the manufacture of both tapa clothing and pottery'. Also, an extensive deterioration in agricultural practices has been observed (Brookfield with Hart, 1971: 122). After the initial spread of steel axes and knives into rural Papua New Guinea there were few significant technological changes which would have resulted in increased productivity. Indeed even steel tools did not result in increased productivity (Salisbury, 1962), but rather in the diversion of labour from subsistence production to other activities.

However, the innovations did give rise to higher productivity within the total system, by enabling specialization. Bairoch's (1975: 34) observation, based on exhaustive time-series analyses of a sample of twenty-four Third World countries, confirms the assertion about the relationship between plantation production and subsistence agriculture productivity: 'Productivity in subsistence agriculture is generally higher in countries where plantations are relatively unimportant ... The difference is explained by the fact that plantations (or export crops) have monopolised the best land. We should realise moreover that the more productive methods used on plantations do not seem to have had an apparent influence on subsistence agriculture'.

The plantation system affected the pre-capitalist economy in other respects as well. Alienation of land for plantations in Papua and New Guinea has been a small proportion of total land area, but the extent of 'effective' alienation (that is, as a proportion of arable land) is much higher.[29] In localized regions such as the Gazelle Peninsula — a volcanic zone and one of the most fertile regions in the country — alienated land as a proportion of the total is as high as 40 per cent. The crucial question, however, is not how much good land has been alienated, but to what use the land is put and what are the effects of that utilization. Up to the time of the outbreak of the 1939-45 war, most of the plantation land was planted with coconuts, one of the lowest-value plantation crops. Their low value and their perennial character have meant that large areas of very good land, often in densely populated regions (such as the Gazelle), have been seriously misallocated. Since the land had been acquired originally almost free of cost, this mattered little to the capitalist planter, but the perennial character of the crop not only meant that the misallocation was more or less permanent, but also that it had serious effects upon the productivity of the 'shifting agriculture' system upon which the peasantry depended for subsistence. The result was that over time the peasantry became increasingly dependent upon the capitalist sector in order to maintain its subsistence standards (Power, 1974: 60).

Thus the plantation system has the effect, within the rural economy, of producing unevenness of regional development between the plantation centres and the labour-supplying peripheries;[30] and causes a general decline in productivity and skills in subsistence production, thereby imposing on the peasant an increasingly marginal existence. While in the plantation region subtraction of good land accounts for the decline, in the labour-exporting region it is the subtraction of able-bodied men that hits subsistence production. Rowley (1965: 109) provides a horrifying account of the plight of villages on New Ireland in German times as a result of uncontrolled recruitment of men.

Apart from these effects, a number of biases operated at the macro-economic level which prevented the development of an integrated, self-sustaining capitalist economy. The plantation system gives rise to a fracturing of the economy manifested in: (i) the peasant base and the export enclave following their own divergent paths in spite of the interdependence of the two sectors and (ii) a progressive divergence opening up between domestic resources and domestic demand. Because plantations are foreign-owned, often by large corporations vertically integrated into metropolitan industry, the growth of the colonial economy is either arrested because of the drain of surplus to the metropole or, if growth does take place, it is dependent on export demand, thus reinforcing the economy's external domination and erratic performance.

The combination of foreign ownership of capital and the export orientation of production and accumulation continually militates against any 'spread effects'. In particular, there are few linkage or multiplier effects, both of which are highly important for integrated, self-sustaining economic development. Capital goods for the export sector tend to be imported from the metropole, while product elaboration, such as coconut oil and soap manufacture from copra, also happens within metropolitan industry. On the other hand, wages and profits generated from plantation production tend to dissipate into import consumption rather than leading to the domestic production of consumer goods. The oligopolies monopolizing the plantation, shipping, export-import and commercial sectors within vertically integrated structures are more interested in maximizing the profits from their total operations than in building up a healthy economy locally.

In view of the fact that the colonial administration derived most of its internal revenue from import duties on manufactured goods, it was not in the interest of the state to favour industrialization. In East Africa, for example, it was common for the colonial administration to manipulate railway rates and taxes in order to discourage new industries (Zwanenberg with King, 1975: 125-6). The metropolitan governments also restricted the growth of industries within the colonies in order to protect their own. Thus, while Australia provided preferential treatment for Papua's rubber, it discouraged the development of a coconut-oil based margarine industry within its colonies for fear that it would threaten Australia's dairy interests (Gadiel, 1973: 75). The colonial economy therefore becomes increasingly dependent on metropolitan imports not only for manufactures but even for food for labourers. The linkage and multiplier effects for the most part are felt within the metropolitan rather than the peripheral economy.

The development of an indigenous manufacturing sector is still further inhibited by the characteristics of the wage labour force that the plantation system produces. Plantation workers, particularly in an industry such as copra, develop few technical skills. Even if the plantation enterprise innovates to increase the productivity of labour in response to labour shortages and/or international competition, the low productivity of subsistence agriculture and the lack of trade union organization among the bonded plantation workers ensure that whatever productivity gains are made through technical change are transferred to the metropolitan consumers of the plantation products (Beckford, 1972: 201). This tendency perpetuates the relationship of unequal exchange and inhibits the growth of effective demand to stimulate the development of a domestic consumer goods sector. By the outbreak of the 1939-45 war the only industry in Papua and New Guinea worth mentioning consisted of preliminary processing of primary products (e.g., copra drying, plants producing desiccated coconut and rubber sheeting, a few small sawmills) and plants producing aerated water and bread for the urban, mainly expatriate, markets. The urban centres were tiny and mainly concentrated along the coasts where, for the most part, economic activity took the form of cargo handling. The extreme primary-product and service orientation of the economy are evident in the following statistics for capitalist sector employment (under indenture) in New Guinea in 1939:

| Type of employment | Number engaged |
|---|---|
| Plantation | 20 885 |
| Mining | 7189 |
| Shipping, Commerce & Industry* | 7511 |
| Domestic Service | 4477 |
| Administration Service | 1747 |
| Miscellaneous | 70 |
| Total | 41 879 |

Source: Reed, 1943: 218

*Although separate employment statistics for Industry are not available, the great majority of workers in this category worked in the shipping and commerce sectors (Reed, 1943: 227-30).

Finally, the external orientation of the economy promoted a transport and communications network geared solely to the needs of foreign enterprise. The pre-colonial trade networks gradually ceased to exist and in their place each region either separately or through a nearby port became directly linked, as an appendage, to the metropolitan economy.[31] Thus the established colonial economic structures not only failed to realize the potential of pre-existing patterns of specialization and exchange but actually destroyed those structures and substituted patterns of production, exchange and communication which were to produce an economy chronically dependent and almost totally lacking in any internal dynamic or coherence.

# 3
# The transformation of peripheral capitalism, 1945-1978

The combined effects of the Depression and the 1939-45 war created in Papua New Guinea — as in the capitalist world as a whole — radically different patterns and rates of growth compared with those of the inter-war period. Important factors in shaping Papua New Guinea's postwar economy were the merger of the two colonies, the far greater degree of state intervention in the economy, and the incorporation of the populous Highlands region into the commercial sector.

However, capitalist development within the colonies has always been determined fundamentally by factors external to them: in particular, the state of commodity markets and the availability of capital in the metropolitan zones. Consequently, in order to understand the causes and nature of change within peripheral capitalism, it is necessary to survey briefly trends in the capitalist world as a whole.

The most important feature of the economies of the industrialized states, and particularly those of western Europe and Japan, was the very high rates of growth they maintained for twenty-five years after the end of the war (Ashworth, 1975: 239). This was accompanied by an even higher rate of growth in international trade and investment. The demand for primary commodities increased greatly, especially during the Korean war boom (1950-53). Thus in the period 1948-70 the value of exports from non-communist Third World countries rose by a factor of 3.25 (Bairoch, 1975: 93).[1] More significantly, however, because of much greater metropolitan investment in the Third World economies, manufacturing output in those

36

economies experienced a very rapid increase, the average rate of growth being 7.2 per cent in the period 1953-70 (Bairoch, 1975: 65).[2] The metropolitan powers also increased their 'aid' to the colonies for social and economic infra-structure to complement private metropolitan investment. These expanded subsidies also reflected changes in metropolitan ideology, in which a concern for 'development' and political decolonization began to materialize. Classical colonial exploitation, based mainly on plantations and mines, was giving way to the neo-classical form of imperialism characterized by limited industrialization, metropolitan state 'aid' to the colonies and ex-colonies, the advance of industrial over merchant capital (Kay, 1975) and the hegemony of industrial multinational corporations and United States-dominated financial institutions such as the World Bank (International Bank of Reconstruction and Development) and the International Monetary Fund.

These changes within the world capitalist system inevitably had their impact upon the South Pacific region. Australia, the junior partner of Western imperialism in the region, shared in the unprecedented growth in the capitalist economies and experienced its 'second boom'. Given these conditions, Papua New Guinea's capitalist economy responded in much the same way as those of other small Third World countries, albeit with certain peculiarities arising from the fact that the metropole was weak, and geographically situated very close to the colony. World markets for primary commodities improved, and Australian subsidies to the colonial state were greatly increased from $A95 000 (or £A42 500, given to Papua only) in 1940 to $A505 480 in 1945-46 and $A4 037 346 in 1946-47, a 42-fold increase over the pre-war level. By 1970 the level of subsidy stood at $A99.27m and increased to $A143m in 1975. The impact of these Australian grants has been so great as to make state expenditure the 'leading sector' in post-war capitalist development, relegating export production to a secondary position.

The parochial liberalism of many an Australian economist and historian has prevented them from viewing this development within its fundamentally imperialist perspective. Thus for

Biskup (1968), Australia's gratitude to Papua New Guineans for their 'sacrifices' to save Australian lives during the 1939-45 war was an important factor in this massive increase in the Australian subsidy to Papua New Guinea. Similarly, Fisk and Tait (1972) believe that it is 'sheer altruism' on the part of the Australian state to grant such massive subsidies since, they claim, the levels of these subsidies far exceed any returns to Australia. These explanations make little sense in historical terms. Australian aid represents, and has always represented, primarily a means of fuelling and transforming peripheral capitalism in Papua New Guinea so that it may perform more adequately its role as a secure and profitable centre for the expansion of Australian commercial, agricultural and industrial capital. Asking whether the Australian government obtains equivalent returns from its subsidies is as misleading as asking whether it obtains an equivalent material return from the construction of ports, roads and other infrastructure in Australia itself; in these respects, the state acts as the service agency and co-ordinator for the capitalist structures. The simple fact was that the colony could not be held or incorporated into the metropolitan economy on a scale demanded by the times without relatively high injections of 'aid'. The returns have to be measured, not merely in terms of the entire operations of Australian capitalism in Papua New Guinea under colonialism, but also in terms of the continuing dependence of the country and its leaders upon Australia to the present day.

The immediate concern of the plantation owners at the end of the war was to rehabilitate their devastated plantations, in New Guinea particularly.[3] The post-war boom in commodity prices gave them an urgent stimulus. However, labour supplies had dried up considerably. Severe demands on labour by the military during the war and the need to rehabilitate the villages themselves made the peasants particularly reluctant to sign up for plantation work. To make things worse for the planters, the Labor Government in power in Australia had cancelled all labour contracts in 1945, with the result that most of the workers went home and the economy came to a standstill (Mair, 1948: 210-11). The Australian government, in the same

38

year, also raised the minimum cash wage to 15 shillings per month, reduced the working week by a fifth, increased rations and promised to do away with indenture. Almost overnight the cost of labour went up by 100-150 per cent in New Guinea over the pre-war level (Mair, 1948: 218).

Capital, however, was not a problem; it was abundant in relation to available labour. While the New Guinea coastal plantations were able to secure workers from the traditional source, the Sepik region, the Papuan rubber plantations and the gold mines in Morobe Province were particularly badly hit by shortages.[4] Relief was finally obtained by tapping the newly incorporated Highlands region in the late 1940s. Very quickly the Highlands became the most important labour reserve for the expanding colonial economy. The government instituted the special Highlands Labour Scheme in 1950, through which numbers of indentures increased dramatically from 2100 in 1953 to 15 400 in 1968. Highlanders made up 62 per cent of the total 'Agreement' labour employed in the primary sector during the latter year (Papua New Guinea Department of Labour, 1969),[5] making a very substantial contribution to the coastal plantations. The increased supplies of labour and capital, and favourable market conditions, enabled rapid expansion of cocoa production — a more labour-intensive and valuable crop — which could be profitably interplanted with coconuts. Cocoa output increased from about 1000 tons (valued at £A526 000) in 1954-55 to more than 14 000 tons (£A2.956m) in 1962-63 (IBRD, 1965).

Unlike the traditional labour reserves, however, the Highlands region did not remain solely a labour reserve for the plantation economy. Indeed, it became a new and profitable area of colonial capitalist development in its own right. The boom in coffee prices during the Korean war period and the existence of fertile valleys in the Highlands were sufficient to attract several hundred settlers with capital into the area.[6] Empty land was by no means unlimited, however, and the colonial state, which by and large was not as sympathetic to plantation interests as in the pre-war period (Mair, 1948), did not alienate land indiscriminately by evicting or dispossessing the

Highlanders. Those settlers who had wished to convert the region into Papua New Guinea's 'White Highlands' discovered that the times were not on their side. Given that profitable opportunities were available to entrepreneurs elsewhere within the economy (see below), the administration's policies did not result in a showdown between the state and the capitalist settlers.

Although the post-war administration was much less committed to plantation development than its predecessors, it was by no means uninterested in the expansion of agricultural production for export. With Morobe's goldfields in serious decline, and the colonial economy's imports rising rapidly, the administration was firmly committed to a rapid increase in exports. Given the massive subsidies from Australia and the changed political and ideological environment, the administration opted for a policy of encouraging peasant as well as plantation-based export production. Since the newly incorporated Highlands population made up some 40 per cent of the country's total population, the conflict between peasant production and labour supplies for plantations, so important in the pre-war era, was not immediately threatening to planters. Even if the planters wanted to oppose the administration's policies — and they did for some time — they were no match for a government which was far more powerful and hence much less dependent upon the planters for political support than it had been before the war. The 'Big Three' (Burns Philp, Carpenters and Steamships), which had been politically very influential, were sufficiently diversified and resourceful to convert the new emphases of the colonial state to their advantage. The massive state expenditures greatly boosted their shipping and commercial sections and provided opportunities for expansion into new areas, including manufacturing, based in the rapidly expanding urban centres.

In the event, the planters discovered that, rather than their interests being threatened by the expansion of peasant production, substantial profits could be made by processing and marketing the peasants' output. Thus the state and the planters acted in partnership to encourage peasant production of export crops. Peasant production of all the major export crops, with the exception of rubber — that is, copra, cocoa and coffee, and later tea, pyrethrum and oil palm — expanded quickly. Peasant coffee production in the Highlands was a particularly important success. 'From an active beginning about 1954, plantings by indigenes soon exceeded those of Europeans in the three main districts, so that by 1961-62 over 60 per cent of all coffee acreage and about 43 per cent of the output was under indigenous control' (IBRD, 1965: 101).

Peasant incomes from export crop production increased greatly from a negligible sum in the pre-war period to an estimated K55m in 1975-76. With the total value of crop exports in that year being K110m, the plantations and the peasant sector each produced exactly 50 per cent of agricultural export output (Papua New Guinea Central Planning Office, 1976: 80). A very rapid quantitative increase in agricultural export production and, perhaps more significantly, a dramatic change in the structure of commercial agricultural production had begun. The rural export base became much more diversified than in the pre-war period, and the plantation sector declined in importance. This decline was only relative initially, but became absolute in the immediate pre-independence period as planters sold out to local groups and companies.[7]

The development of the Highlands region displayed a classic unevenness in the growth of incomes. The labour frontier moved further and further into the interior as the peasants in more accessible regions, especially near the plantation areas, began to engage in coffee production themselves. Other districts specialized in the export of labour and as a result suffered the backwash effects (reduced local output of both subsistence and marketed goods and services) of export production. In the coastal regions also the growth of peasant export production occurred in the areas which had previously been dominated by plantations, while the traditional labour–supply areas like the newer highland areas continued to stagnate. In the mid-1970s, therefore, substantial parts of districts such as Western, Gulf, Southern Highlands, Chimbu, West Sepik and South-east New Britain remained poor, and suppliers of cheap, unskilled labour to the rest of the economy. Districts such as East New Britain (Gazelle Peninsula), New Ireland, Bougainville, Morobe, Milne Bay, Eastern and Western Highlands, and parts of East Sepik were relatively prosperous because of export sales (see Wilson, 1975). At the same time, the broad mass of the peasantry, whose function had been largely to supply labour to the capitalist mines and plantations, were now beginning to differentiate into poor and rich peasants and even rural capitalists. The latter two groups increasingly began to build a stake in the agricultural export economy (see Good, below).

While exports of the agricultural and fisheries sectors were increasing at a phenomenal pace — rising in value from approximately $A19.6m in 1954-55 to $A143.5m in 1974-75 — the production of food for the rapidly increasing domestic market virtually stagnated. Food imports into the economy rose from $A9.4m to $A71.5m during the same period. (Exports of food products increased from about $A17m to $A90.2m during the twenty-year period.)[8] Throughout the period, therefore, roughly half the export receipts from the agricultural and fisheries sectors were used to finance food imports. The government's obsession — boosted by the recommendations of the IBRD Mission in 1963 — to step up exports in response to its huge import bills, was an important factor contributing to the structure of production (and consumption) implied in these statistics.[9] However, the oligopolistic structure of the commerce, shipping and manufacturing sectors was perhaps equally, if not more, important in perpetuating such extreme divergence between domestic resource use and domestic demand. The IBRD Mission characteristically understated the problem when it suggested that 'There were indications that some of the trading groups have discouraged local production of items that might be in competition with those imported on grounds of quality, unreliability of production, costs, etc'. (1965: 214).[10]

The further distortion and transformation of the economy have proceeded hand in hand during the post-war period. The fact that the expenditure of the Australian state had catapulted it into the role of the 'leading sector' within the Papua New Guinean economy has already been noted. The ramifications of this development were far wider than simply increased agricultural exports and the transformation of the peasant economy, in which the state's policies and expenditure undoubtedly played a very important role. The big Australian subsidies were also giving rise to an extremely large state machine, stimulating a rapid increase in the rate of urbanization and quasi-industrialization. There was a dramatic increase in the numbers of the employees engaged in the public service, mostly in the urban centres;[11] and their wages and salaries encouraged imports and a domestic consumer goods manufacturing sector; furthermore, state expenditures on the creation of social and economic infrastructure stimulated a large construction sector, which employed approximately one-tenth of the enumerated wage labour force in 1972. Employment in secondary industries as a whole increased four-fold from about 4000 in 1960 to around 16 200 in 1973, and the value of production within the sector rose from $A6.4m to $A69.4m (at current prices) over the period (Dixon, 1974).[12]

Because most capital goods had to be imported, and there had been little increase in the production of materials (including food) for the domestic market, the output of the manufacturing and construction sectors had a very high import content. Of the total non-labour inputs in the manufacturing and construction sectors, $A74.67m worth were imported while only $A53.6m worth were domestically supplied in 1970. In addition, payment to expatriate labour in these sectors totalled $A15.33m compared to $A23.91m paid as wages to indigenous workers in the same year (Parker, 1973: 2). The value of imports increased greatly, from $A41.6m to $A228.8m during the period 1960 to 1973. Because of this high degree of dependence on imports, the foreign trade deficit grew from around $A4m in 1949 to $A129.2m in 1972.

In summary, while agricultural export production was increasing at a rapid rate, the economy's growth and diversification were really reliant upon the expenditure of the state sector, which grew at a still higher rate. Thus overall, dependency was aggravated: the super-imposition of a huge, highly para-sitic bureaucracy upon an economy which was unable to sustain it without external subsidies signified a new aspect of economic dislocation — one which has become a major concern of planners and politicians in the post-colonial period.

Despite the spread effects of state expenditures through the operation of the multiplier, linkage effects and skills transfer, these spread effects (due to the nature of the economy and the state's expenditures, and the rate of increase of these expenditures), were necessarily limited. Very substantial leakages occurred because of the dissipation of peasant and wage incomes into import consumption and the transfer overseas, and particularly to Australia, of much of the expatriate-controlled surplus in the form of savings from salaries as well as dividends. Since the major part of both state and private capitalist investment was of a highly capital-intensive nature, backward linkages to stimulate a capital goods sector were not possible.[13]

On the other hand, the high degree of capital intensity also implied that the share of profits in the value of production was extremely high, particularly since wages had remained very low up to the early 1970s. In 1960-61, the distribution of incomes between wages (indigenous workers), salaries (expatriate workers) and foreign capitalist surplus was as follows:

|  | Wages | £A'000 Salaries | Surplus |
|---|---|---|---|
| Primary sector | 3867 | 2814 | 2441 |
| Secondary and tertiary sectors | 851 | 6578 | 6140 |
| State sector | 3043 | 8046 | — |
| Missions | 380 | 1092 | — |
| Totals | 8141 | 18 530 | 8581 |

Source: White, 1964: 98

As can be seen, the rate of exploitation of indigenous workers was extremely high in the secondary and tertiary sectors because of the combination of very low wages and high capital intensity. The minimum urban wage was $A6.00 per week in 1960 and had risen to only $A7.00 by 1970. In the latter year the income distribution between wages, expatriate salaries and foreign capitalist surplus was as follows:[14]

| | Wages | $A'000 Salaries | Surplus |
|---|---|---|---|
| Plantation sector | 7170 | 2090 | 14050 |
| Secondary and tertiary sectors | 26720 | 46850 | 54120 |
| Totals | 33890 | 48940 | 68170 |

Source: Parker, 1973: 2

With such a pattern of income distribution, the operation of the multiplier was stifled very considerably. For the most part, the spread effects of Australia's subsidies and resulting investments in Papua New Guinea were felt within Australia itself.

The industrialization that resulted in Papua New Guinea was for the most part merely final-stage processing of luxury-type consumer goods[15] (usually of low value and high volume), some export-crop processing, metal fabrication and concrete moulding, saw-milling and joineries, furniture manufacture, printing, and engineering works for repairs. Most of the establishments are foreign-owned and located in the two coastal cities of Port Moresby and Lae, and in the export regions. There is no textile mill, sugar mill or cement factory in spite of sufficient demand within the domestic economy.

While the industrial and state sectors were expanding, the traditional colonial sectors, especially plantations, began to run down, particularly after 1970. Plantation employment reached a peak with some 48400 workers in 1970, but declined from then on and stood at approximately 32100 in 1973.[16] A combination of relative unprofitability and political insecurity led foreign investors to withdraw from some of the traditional colonial sectors. This usually implied takeovers by local

45

capitalists, business groups and companies. In 1974 foreign capital withdrew investments of $A1.88m in the agricultural sector. Similarly, retail trade saw an outflow of foreign capital investment totalling $A7.79m between 1972 and 1974, while in 'Transport, Storage and Communication' the total amount was $A10.44m for 1973 and 1974 (Papua New Guinea Bureau of Statistics, March 1976). These disinvestments by foreign capital are reflected in corresponding increases in investment by small-scale local capital in 'PMVs' (small buses), trade stores and plantations.

Together with the sectoral shifts, there have been significant qualitative changes in the structure of ownership and competition within the economy. Although the 'Big Three' expanded and diversified considerably during the post-war period, their virtual monopoly over the economy has been under pressure from several directions. Small-scale local businesses are increasingly making bids to enter coastal shipping, plantations, retailing, real estate and — of lesser concern to the 'Big Three' — urban transport. On the other hand, the state sector, through its Investment Corporation, has been buying up minority shareholdings in foreign enterprises, including one of the three, Burns Philp Ltd. These trends may not be entirely detrimental to the interests of these companies, however. Over the long term they would prefer some state participation, and diversification away from activities now becoming less profitable due to greater competition and higher wages. Burns Philp Ltd is consciously attempting to reduce its holdings in order to expand its base in Australia (Gottliebsen, 1976).

## The multinationals: from copra colony to copper neo-colony

More significant over the longer term, however, is the competition from the larger multinational corporations — representing the real metropolitan industrial capital — which have come on to the scene since the 1960s. These global enterprises have entered into all the major sectors by establishing subsidiaries and branch plants. Their activities include copper mining (Rio

Tinto Zinc), oil palm nucleus estates (Harrison and Crosfield), cigarette manufacture (Wills, Rothmans), construction (Hornibrooks, Dillingham Corporation), car hire (Avis, Hertz) and a number of others.

Since the early 1970s a further significant structural transformation has been in evidence in Papua New Guinea which undermines the old Australian imperialism as represented by the essentially commercial activities of the 'Big Three'. In the longer term, this transformation also promises to shift the dependency relationship away from Australian state finance towards multinational corporations. From 1956-57 to 1975-76 the Australian state subsidy to Papua New Guinea increased from $A18.89m to $A186.4m. Although this represents a large increase in absolute terms, the proportion of this subsidy to total government revenue has decreased from 70 per cent to about 40 per cent. The reasons for this include the introduction of income tax in 1960 for the first time and the progressive increase in the rate of taxation; the rapid growth of the economy over the period and the establishment of large-scale projects for natural resources exploitation by multinational corporations, symbolized by the giant Bougainville Copper Company.

These changes in the 1970s signify yet another qualitative transformation in the character of peripheral capitalism in Papua New Guinea. On the one hand, there is a relative, and perhaps even an absolute, decline in the importance of Australian private (mainly commercial) and state capital investment in the economy.[17] On the other hand, the level of investment by multinational corporations and lending by international financial institutions have been increasing rapidly. Whilst in 1956-57 all foreign assistance was accounted for by the Australian grant, in 1975-76 and 1976-77, Australian subsidies accounted for about 90 per cent of total foreign aid, while IBRD and Asian Development Bank loans accounted for between 7 and 8 per cent. The non-Australian loans are mainly for the purposes of infrastructure and export projects, such as roads, ports, hydro-electric power, telecommunications, oil palm nucleus estates and livestock projects. The Australian subsidy over recent years has increasingly been channelled to

47

finance budget deficits for current (i.e. consumption) government expenditures, while the infrastructural and directly productive investments are being financed through tied loans and metropolitan capitalist investment.

These new investments reflect the increased attractiveness of Papua New Guinea to metropolitan capitalism and are eagerly welcomed by the neo-colonial government, which is planning future economic development on that basis. Although in the view of the government such a transformation implies (budgetary) self-reliance, in reality all it means is a movement of dependency away from the Australian state to multinational corporations and international finance agencies. In this, of course, Papua New Guinea is travelling a well-trodden path, guaranteed to perpetuate its underdevelopment in the context of a continuing, though changing, peripheral capitalism. The structural changes may imply increased reliance of the economy upon a single export product. In 1975 about 59 per cent of total exports were accounted for by copper ore alone.[18] A second large copper prospect, Ok Tedi in the Star Mountains, if it were to come into operation in the mid-1980s as is hoped, could further increase the share of copper in total exports to 65-75 per cent of the total. Papua New Guinea would then have come a full circle where, from having been a *copra colony*, it would turn into a *copper neo-colony*.

# 4
# Consolidation of the neo-colonial economy

Structurally, the major transformation now taking place is the growth of capital-intensive copper mining, and forest and fisheries exploitation. In sectoral terms, the non-agricultural primary sector is expanding dramatically, with a corresponding relative decline in agriculture, manufacturing, construction, transport and communications, commerce, finance and other services. By 1975, copper alone accounted for more than half the total value of exports ($A236.67m out of $A423.9m).

These new factors, together with its reliance upon foreign subsidies and loans, makes the Papua New Guinea economy one of the most open and dependent in the world. Fully one half the value of the economy's output goes to satisfy foreign demand, while an even greater proportion of the gross domestic demand is met through imports, subsidies and loans. What is even more significant and unusual, however, is that this divergence between domestic production and domestic demand has greatly increased since the war. This is evident from both the increased export dependency and the relative decline of those sectors which have hitherto produced goods and services for the domestic market: manufacturing and construction, commerce, transport and communications.

The other natural resources that metropolitan (mainly Japanese) capital has become heavily involved in, apart from copper, are fisheries and timber. Fish and timber exports have been rising rapidly and stood at $A10.4m and $A10.99m (plus $A4.6m worth of manufactured wood products)[1] respectively in 1975. The domestic markets for (mainly canned) fish and

49

wood/paper manufactured products had to be supplied by imports worth $A5.5m and $A9.4m respectively.[2] The fish market situation is particularly anomalous; Papua New Guinean-produced tuna is exported to Japan and Japanese-processed mackerel pike imported into Papua New Guinea. (Even bourgeois economists in the country have been reluctant to defend this reality by resorting to the usual 'comparative advantage' argument.) Together with a chronic dependence upon food imports, observed earlier, these recent developments in peripheral capitalism in Papua New Guinea have forced the country into a pattern of specialization which is producing a degree of economic dislocation from which any recovery and subsequent planning, towards integrated development would be extremely painful.

The disarticulation of the economy as already suggested arises largely from a pattern of investment and production which results in extreme inequalities in the distribution of productivities and correspondingly in the distribution of incomes. While it would be foolish to argue that an economy should adopt a uniform intermediate technology — a practical impossibility, in any case — and although it is highly plausible that a hierarchy of technologies is essential for successful economic development,[3] the structural characteristics of the Papua New Guinean economy are such that its hierarchy of technologies cannot sustain, or form the basis for, a nationally integrated economy. Such a pattern of economic development is especially improbable under the dynamic of peripheral capitalism whose tendency, as we have shown, has been to disintegrate the economic system, and whose *raison d'être* is to provide cheap raw materials, gullible markets and surplus for metropolitan capitalism.

Within Papua New Guinea the extreme disarticulation of the economic system is all too apparent and has been commented upon by the most casual observers. Even the so-called 'informal sector', so much romanticized in recent development literature, is conspicuous by its virtual non-existence, so that even the appearance of continuity between the subsistence and modern sectors is absent. We have noted the highly capital-

50

intensive nature of investments in the post-war period: in manufacturing, construction, electricity, air transport, tea and oil palm nucleus estates, and various service industries.[4] The most extreme instance of high capital-intensity is Bougainville Copper Company — a subsidiary of Conzinc Rio Tinto (Australia), itself a subsidiary of the British-based Rio Tinto Zinc. The very high productivity at the mine, achieved through the use of such technology as 100- to 200-tonne computerized trucks, is evidenced by the fact that in 1973-74, some 4000 workers produced a value of production amounting to $A264.5m (Lepani, 1976b). In contrast, the entire subsistence output — to feed, clothe and house some 2.5m people — was estimated at $A159.5m in the same year!

Rather than the development of technology being rooted in a dynamic equilibrium between domestic resource use, production and consumption (Thomas, 1974), where spread effects from the indigenous adaptation of technology extend to the mass of the producers in the form of transferred skills and increased productivity, the structure of the Papua New Guinea economy is such that any transfer of technology between different sectors — in particular, from the capitalist to the subsistence sector — is minimal. Since the widespread adoption of steel tools and certain new crops in the latter sector in the pre-war era, little transfer of technology into the subsistence productive base has taken place. The same goods are produced with, if anything, decreasing productivity.[5] Since few technological inputs, in the form of fertilizers, insecticides, mechanical equipment and the like are used to increase productivity in peasant export agriculture most of the increased production of export crops takes place simply by the more extensive use of labour and land, frequently at the expense of subsistence production. However, since peasant export crops tend to be tree crops, this results in virtually permanent reduction of land area for food production with the consequence that the fallow cycles become shorter and land productivity declines. This, coupled with a rising population, results in a decline in subsistence production. Thus increases in peasant export production and increased malnutrition in rural areas (Korte, 1975)

51

represent a very important contradiction within peripheral capitalism. The transition 'from tribalism to peasantry' hardly represents a situation of 'terminal development' (Howlett, 1973); rather, peripheral capitalism in rural Papua New Guinea dynamically creates and recreates underdevelopment.

Technological stagnation in the rural economy is of course not accidental. As Bairoch (1975) has shown empirically, the decline in agricultural productivity has been a generalized phenomenon in most of the non-communist Third World. This follows the logic of capital accumulation under peripheral capitalism. While in the case of mature metropolitan capitalist development, increases in agricultural productivity were an essential pre-condition for the release of rural labour to allow the accumulation of capital through industrialization, under peripheral capitalism the exact opposite holds true. Rooted, as it is, in the exploitation of cheap labour and unequal exchange of values at the international level, the development of peripheral capitalism prompts the release of rural labour by means of a *decrease* in its productivity and, therefore, its opportunity cost. An urban proletariat is eventually created as a result of this process and, although the onset of political independence and trade union militancy may result in an increase in urban real wage rates, this development only succeeds in further depressing the relative opportunity cost of rural labour, with a consequent increase in rural-urban migration and urban unemployment. The latter phenomenon functions to arrest significant rises in real urban wages.

In a closed capitalism characterized by large agricultural and manufacturing sectors producing for a domestic market, low wages may hinder further developments in these sectors, so that at some point increases in real wages become necessary for the markets to expand and for continued domestically-based accumulation to take place. In Papua New Guinea, the commercial food-producing sector is very small; and the manufacturing and construction sectors (which have experienced buoyant growth rates) are becoming relatively less important as foreign investment channels into large-scale projects to exploit the copper, timber and fisheries resources. In theory, the spread effects of an industry such as timber can be very great, and this has been true, in practice, for Sweden — a small economy, incidentally (Rostow, 1960: 56). However, given the highly dislocated structure of the Papua New Guinea economy, and the *raison d'être* of multinational investment to produce for export, such spread effects as are generated occur in the metropolitan economies rather than the periphery.

The operation of an export-oriented, natural resource-based economy is such as to discourage any generalized increase in productivities. It is well known that the linkage and multiplier effects of capital-intensive mining are very limited indeed (Bairoch, 1975). While some multiplier effects may occur through the channelling of tax revenues into the economy by the state, these are necessarily limited. In Papua New Guinea 'the ratio of administrative costs to visible services (such as schools and aid posts) is among the highest for any developing country' (Papua New Guinea, Central Planning Office, October 1976: 4), and the power of the bureaucracy ensures that this will continue. Furthermore, government revenues from copper mining are for the most part used to finance government consumption expenditure rather than productive investment. The copper-mining sector in Papua New Guinea even lacks smelting and refining operations so that the very minimum of value is added to the ore before export to the metropoles.

Rollins (1970: 198), in considering the relationship between mineral development and growth in underdeveloped economies, has cogently argued that 'the effect of growth on costs of production for the mineral industry is ... immediate, and detrimental ... Mineral producers have ... in a very real sense, a vested interest in the continued backwardness of the economy in which their production operations are carried on'. This, he argues, is because economic development involves, firstly, an increase in productivity in the economy generally, leading to increased wages; and secondly, it is initially at least associated with a high-cost industrial sector, protected by high tariff walls. Both these adversely affect the mining industry's cost structures. Since mining by multinational corporations usually uses the most advanced and capital-intensive

53

technology available, there is little scope for substitution in response to factor price movements. Increased productivity of labour in other sectors, and the initiation of industrialization are, therefore, detrimental to the mining industry whose profitability ultimately relies upon the availability of cheap local labour and cheap imported inputs.

This theory is confirmed by Bairoch's (1975: 578) empirical analysis of rates of growth of the manufacturing and extractive industries for nineteen underdeveloped countries for the period 1958-70. He concludes that 'among the countries registering a considerable expansion in the mining sector, most show only slow growth in manufacturing industry, and vice versa ... There is a correlation between high rates of growth in the extractive industry and low rates in manufacturing industry'. Little wonder, therefore, that Reno (1970: 81, 82) should say about the Caribbean countries, which 'produce the ore for half the capitalist world's aluminium, [that] out of every four urban workers, at least one is unemployed [and] in their countrysides, underemployment is universal and chronic'. This was in spite of the fact that 'government revenues have more than doubled over the past ten years'. The situation in the copper-exporting countries is little different.

The effects of large-scale mining at the local level are little better. A number of studies have shown, for example, that the social and environmental effects of copper mining on Bougainville island (North Solomons Province) have been highly adverse (West, 1972). A study by Makis Uming (1976) on the impact of the mine on local businesses shows that almost all are service-oriented, highly dependent upon the mining company for markets, management skills and often the initial capital, and are unlikely to survive independently when the ore begins to run out towards the end of this century.[6] He concludes (page iv):

> [the Bougainville Copper Company] ... merely directs businessmen into business opportunities that lie under [its] wings. This in the long run results in the denial to these local enterprises of the basic independence they desire and hope for. In the main these enterprises become mere appendages of the giant Octopus — Bougainville Copper. The majority of them are a sort of one act play, aiding to fulfil the *raison d'etre* of the

54

Business Advisory Services as Bougainville Copper's shock-absorber, and when taken together they make an excellent puppet show. [The 'Business Advisory Services' is a section within the company.]

Since government revenue from Company dividends and taxes[7] have so far been used largely to finance government consumption expenditure,[8] the accumulation of capital is left, for the most part, in the hands of the foreign-owned companies. Large mining companies such as BCL are highly unlikely to reinvest their surpluses within the domestic economy, their priorities being determined by world indicators. The result is that most of the surplus is drained away overseas in the form of loan repayments or dividends. In the years 1972, 1973 and 1974, income payable overseas by foreign enterprises in the country amounted to $A37m, $A88.2m and $A205.7m respectively. The latter amount represented 24 per cent of the monetary sector GDP, and far exceeded the Australian subsidy in that year. The amounts attributed to the mining industry — that is, virtually Bougainville Copper — during the three years were $A16.7m, $A74.9m and $A188.8m (Papua New Guinea Bureau of Statistics, March 1976). In the same three years, the inflows of foreign private capital investment amounted to $A169.8m (of which $A143m were invested in the Bougainville Copper mine), $A29.2m and $A96.3m. The reality of dependency and exploitation in Papua New Guinea is too stark to belabour the point further, except to note that had substantial proportions of the surpluses been reinvested, that would only have meant the further entrenchment of the multinational corporations through locally generated finance, and the mortgaging of the economy in the longer term.

Foreign domination of the economy is not, however, total. The government since 1971-72 has been financing national participation in large-scale enterprises through its Investment Corporation, usually in the form of minority shareholdings. These holdings range from various manufacturing enterprises to commerce, taxi service, hotels, cattle and poultry. In addition, the state directly holds (usually minority) shares in export enterprises such as the Bougainville Copper mine, timber projects and oil palm nucleus estates. But this cautious economic nationalism merely reinforces the essential structures of the peripheral capitalist economy. The Investment Corporation, for instance, operates on the basis of short-run profitability. Rather than pioneer new, untried ventures in an attempt to restructure the economy, it has so far only bought into existing profitable enterprises. That the enterprises are more than adequately profitable is reflected in the rates of return on average capital: 28 per cent, 23.5 per cent and 14.7 per cent in 1974, 1975 and 1976 respectively, the latest rate of return 'reflecting the very low level of economic activity in Papua New Guinea in common with the world generally' (Papua New Guinea Central Planning Office, October 1976: 145). Inevitably the state capitalist sector in Papua New Guinea is no more than a subsidiary of metropolitan capitalism.

The government has so far demonstrated little interest in, or understanding of, a strategy for industrialization. It is assumed that many basic industries cannot be established because market size is limited and/or production costs will not be competitive. The fate of the industrial sector has been left more or less to the whims of foreign investors whose investment policies are determined by the structure of their world-wide interests. The industrial sector represents a perverse capitalist industrialization typical of that found in ex-colonial economies elsewhere. Its features include (Rweyemamu, 1974: 103):

> the establishment of a productive structure that is biased against capital goods industries, thus limiting industry's contribution to the production of farm equipment and transport facilities, (b) utilizes relatively more capital intensive techniques of production ... thus compounding the problem of the urban unemployed, (c) has limited linkage effects, especially with the traditional sector, (d) fosters lop-sided development both in terms of geographical location within the country (especially the concentration of industry in the export enclave) and sectoral distribution of consumer goods output, favouring luxuries, and (e) sets up uncompetitive, oligopolistic structures.

Clearly, neither the natural-resources export sectors nor the industrial sector possess the dynamic for a nationally integrated economy based upon the continued accumulation of capital for domestic enterprise and the conscious use of spread effects within the economy.

# 5
# Conclusion

The foreign bourgeoisie undoubtedly created significant productive forces in Papua New Guinea, both through the accumulation of surplus from within the economy and the import of capital from abroad. The essential logic of peripheral capitalism means, however, that such productive forces, because they are foreign-created, foreign-directed and foreign-owned, are not for the long-term benefit of the indigenous economy and population. Rather, such capital accumulation represents no more than the extension of metropolitan capitalism, whereby the people of the periphery provide cheap labour to supply cheap raw materials to the metropolitan economies. It is for this reason that the development of productive forces within the numerically largest sector, the subsistence economy, was rudely arrested after the initial transition 'from stone to steel' (Salisbury, 1962),[1] and that the vast majority of the productive citizens of Papua New Guinea remain poorly-paid wage workers and even less well-off peasant producers.

The conquest of Papua New Guinea by metropole-dominated capitalism destroyed the extensive trading networks of the relatively self-reliant societies of western Melanesia; it made redundant much of their indigenous technology, handicrafts production and even agricultural skills.

The socio-economic transformation that took place gave rise to a stunted capitalism incapable of fostering the progressive social formations characteristic of metropolitan capitalism. The exchange economy that was established is almost wholly externally-oriented. Although the peripheral capitalism was a growing one, its rate and pattern of growth have been and remain wholly dependent upon metropolitan market conditions and supplies of metropolitan private capital and state subsidies.

Although a manufacturing sector was established after the war, it could never become the leading sector of the economy. Indeed, with increased metropolitan investment going almost exclusively to export production, the tiny manufacturing sector shows every sign of stagnation. Similarly, as agricultural export production increases, the importing of food to feed both rural and urban populations, rises also. Outside the subsistence sector few of the material needs of the citizens of Papua New Guinea are met within the country.

A century of capitalist development has failed to spread specialization and commodity relations throughout a society which numbers less than four million people. The new social formations that have evolved are extremely fragmented. The pre-capitalist formations survive, but in a distorted and weakened form, in the face of a creeping capitalism with which they have few historical or economic linkages. While the proportion of Papua New Guineans in the exchange economy increases, so also does the proportion that is malnourished and without employment. There is little reason to suppose that as commodity relations continue to spread the mass of the population will enjoy a fate any better than that of the pauperized peasantry and the chronically unemployed which characterize most of the non-communist Third World.

The economy of Papua New Guinea, notwithstanding the wishful thinking of many colonial apologists and politicians, exhibits the same structures of underdevelopment as do other countries of the Third World, particularly most of Black Africa. It is characterized by: an exchange economy dominated by mining, plantations and peasant production, whose output is almost wholly destined for the satisfaction of metropolitan market demand; a limited, perverse industrialization lacking an internal dynamic, and characterized by final-stage processing of imported raw materials to produce, for the most part, lux-

58

ury goods for an overwhelmingly urban market; a badly underdeveloped but expensive internal transport infrastructure; extreme differentials in productivities between sectors, geographical regions and individual producers, with corresponding inequalities of incomes; almost total absence of linkages between sectors or of economic inter-dependence between geographical regions; underdevelopment of skills among the population and a complete reliance on foreign sources of technology; almost total foreign ownership of the 'commanding heights' of the economy; lack of mobilization of domestic savings for productive investment, and massive export of surplus appropriated by foreign corporations; absence of an entrepreneurial class capable of mobilizing resources for self-sustaining economic development; an overdeveloped state machinery which is both parasitic upon the domestic economy and heavily dependent upon metropolitan subsidies and loans; and so on ...

If Papua New Guinea presently lacks the conditions of abject poverty which exist in many parts of Asia, Latin America and Africa, that is simply because capitalism was late in arriving, and sub-metropolitan Australia was incapable of exploiting its resources and people as thoroughly as were the classic metropolitan powers. As was seen above, however, metropolitan capitalist interest in Papua New Guinea has been growing over the last quarter century.

It is not unlikely that over the next quarter century, if the second (final?) Great Depression of the century does not occur, multinational corporations will penetrate further, encouraged by Papua New Guinea's relatively virgin condition, rich natural resources and the receptivity of the neo-colonial state.

To raise the productivity and material well-being of the mass of the population would require a frontal attack on the structures perpetuating dependency and underdevelopment. However, the neo-colonial state has so far put its faith firmly in the country's rich natural resources and accepted heavy reliance upon multinational corporations to develop the economy. It has shied away from economic planning and adopted, for the large part, the post-war model of economic growth. 'Sound economic management' is the operational motto and consists of creating a 'favourable investment climate', reducing 'aid dependency' and maintaining the exchange value of the currency. However:

> Development is not a matter of dressing in other people's clothes and imitating their way of life but of using the instrument of technology to achieve an honourable style of existence. It is not a matter of escaping from one's society and one's history, but rather of creating a society capable of inventing a history (Jean-Marie Domenach, quoted in Currey, 1973).

# II
# The changing global context

# 6
# The development of Australian capitalism

## Kenneth Good

The development of capitalism in Australia is of importance to an analysis of the political economy of Papua New Guinea in two main ways. First and most obviously because of Australia's nearness, relative dynamism and position as main colonial power; for a century and a half no other country has had such an impact on Papua New Guinea. Yet Australia itself has been a colony and dependent country on the periphery of the world system. For this reason growth in Papua New Guinea has been related to the tempo, direction, and intensity of capitalist development in Australia. Australian colonization of Papua New Guinea largely coincided, for example, with recession in Australia — the 'Long Trough' from 1890 to 1940. It was Papua New Guinea's fate to be the colony of a colony, not of a burgeoning industrial giant, and the detail of Australian development is relevant to that of Papua New Guinea.

Secondly, because Australia has arisen from a peripheral position it once shared to some extent with Papua New Guinea, its experience constitutes a comparative model of capitalist development. Overall, however, it is the peculiarities and difficulties of this experience which seem most outstanding. Australia's industrialization this century has been based on its special advantages as a settler colony, advantages not experienced by an administered colony like Papua New Guinea. Australia's success, moreover, is still limited, and its weakness relative to the core of the capitalist system — the United States, Japan, and the European Economic Community, for example — is perhaps increasing. It is because of Australia's international weakness that control over the relatively assured Papua New Guinean market is important to it, which in turn provides Papua New Guinea with leverage over Australia if the newly independent state wishes to use it.

## The creation of a settler colony

Australia's colonial origins were unpromising. As with so many other colonies of far-flung empire, the country was settled primarily, according to Blainey (1966: 34), 'to serve the supply lines of war'. For some thirty years after 1788, while Britain concentrated on war with France — its imperial archrival — the colony remained a backwater. This situation changed, however, with the defeat of Napoleon's forces and Britain's emergence as the world's most powerful nation. It was the first to enter the process of industrialization, and its dominance was based on its leading position within the colonial world (Hobsbawm, 1969). Even Britain's internal problems were to some extent favourable to independent capitalist development in Australia. Early industrialization and contact with revolutionary France caused social upheaval in Britain, and in the repression which followed more convicts flowed out to Australia, followed by free settlers.[1]

In this movement of settlers, Britain at the core of the capitalist system and Australia on the periphery developed complementary interests. For reasons of cheapness (in an empire stretching from Canada, through Australia and New Zealand, to India and to South Africa), Britain was ready to encourage the growth of local merchant and agricultural capitalism (Rowley, 1972b). Not that such concessions were unlimited or quickly granted. Australia's commerce had been linked to Asia and the Pacific during the first thirty years (Blainey, 1966), but imperial restrictions prevented direct trade with China until 1834, thereby reducing the profits to be gained by Australian merchants from sandalwood in the Pacific (Shineberg, 1967: 1-15); further, Britain retained the Navigation Acts until 1849, only then ending its monopoly of

Australia's coastal and foreign trade (Blainey, 1966: 174-6). However, the beginnings of Australian agriculture and the needs of expanding British industry were soon linked in a dynamic and mutually profitable relationship. Between 1830 and 1850 the Australian colonies established their ability to meet the requirements of the British textile industry in both quantity and quality, ousted earlier suppliers, and gained an assured market.

## Agricultural capitalism and light industry

If agricultural exports have come to be a mark of dependency and underdevelopment across the Third World, agricultural capitalism can also serve to 'initiate and sustain growth on a large scale' (Boehm, 1971: 66), as in Australia, if the broad characteristics of the colonial political economy are favourable. The colonies of white settlement such as Australia seem to have been in a qualitatively better position than the general run of directly administered colonies such as Papua New Guinea.

It is useful to consider the range and strength of the material and social resources for capitalism in Australia:

(i)   Land was abundant and was ruthlessly seized from the Aboriginal people who had occupied and used it for thousands of years. With the ideology of 'sacred trust' totally absent, the Australian land was soon producing agricultural resources (wool, meat, etc.) and minerals, especially gold in the early period. Self-sufficiency in food production — a notable absence in most colonial situations — was quickly attained and was merely one stage in a move towards far greater productiveness. In particular, gold and wool 'enormously increased' the demand for Australian manufactures and farm products, stimulated commerce and infrastructural development, and multiplied jobs (Blainey, 1966: 145). And the large-scale exploitation of the products of the land — raw materials and foodstuffs, minerals, pastoral products and grains — gave Australia 'its special role in relation to the maturing British economy' through the second half of the nineteenth century (Butlin, 1964: 4).

(ii) Labour — its quantity, mobility, and range of skills — is also necessary for successful capitalist development, and in Australia the situation was favourable. The bloody annihilation and ruthless exclusion of the native population (as in the settler colonies in North America), solved the problem of rebellion which has faced colonies of settlement in Africa. The nomadic nature of Aboriginal society also meant that, unlike most Third World countries including Papua New Guinea, Australia had no heritage of non-capitalist economic and social relations — communal land-ownership, absence of wage-labour, multiplicity of small-scale, decentralized societies — as barriers against successful capitalist development. And the inflow of settlers from Europe greatly supplemented the growth of the white population from natural causes, and served to provide the country with the basic social resources for independent development. With gold there was a massive inflow of white settlers, and the population trebled to reach some 1.2 million in the 1860s; it attained 3.8 million at Federation in 1901 and, with 4 million immigrants arriving between 1947 and 1966, the population passed 12 million in 1970 (Boehm, 1971: 40-3; Clark, 1975: 54). Immigration, not natural increase, has made the greater contribution to the growth of the skilled and semi-skilled work force in recent years (Boehm, 1971: 64).

(iii) Capital and investment funds were a third resource available for capitalist development in Australia. By 1860 agricultural and mineral production had attracted a prolonged inflow of British capital and labour. The Australian colonies were a very important market for British foreign investment during the height of the 'Long Boom' (1850-90). They constituted 'the most important single borrower' of British capital, 1875-83 (Clark, 1975: 56), and the inflow of British capital, 1860-90, was greater than locally-raised savings by a significant margin (McFarlane, 1972: 44). 'More than any other growing new country of the time, Australia depended on the transfer of British resources ... British funds dominated financing of pastoral assets and were a major part of the finances required for communications development' (Butlin, 1964: 5).

(iv) A fourth advantage for development lay in the nature of the settler society. There were external as well as internal aspects to this important sociological factor. The metropole was inclined to see the settler colonies in a quite different light from other colonies. In British thinking throughout the nineteenth century, Canada, Australia, New Zealand, and the Cape Colony were 'the natural, as well as the most rewarding mode of imperial expansion', the 'most loyal and energetic partners', with the 'supreme virtue of being self-propelling' (quoted in Good, 1976). Because of this, Britain was ready to encourage, at least initially, capitalist development in the settler colony, and the Australian colonists displayed their loyalty in the enthusiasm and relative numbers with which they joined imperialist wars in Sudan and South Africa.[2] Internally, not only were the settlers (unlike missionaries, planters, administrators elsewhere) especially ready to exploit the resources that lay to hand to the utmost, but they did so in a particularly unified way.

As in other settler situations, there was an important sense in which a growing Australian working class and bourgeoisie were, despite all differences, 'in it together' in the long-term development of the new homeland. 'The tendency of colonial life is to annul the prejudices of European society', wrote John West in 1852, 'and to yield to every man the position which may be due to his talents or virtues' (quoted in Inglis, 1974: 29). Capitalism without the heavy exploitation of the working class which Europe and other countries experienced was possible in Australia. The working classes 'shared in Australia's general prosperity' in the formative period of the 1860s; living standards were 'the highest in the world', with per capita income and consumption levels 50 per cent above those prevailing in America and 100 per cent above those in England, and they 'continued to rise steadily until 1890' (Rowley, 1972b: 22-3). Workers held a strong position in relation to capital and the bourgeoisie in the decades after the discovery of gold, specifically because of the strong demand for labour (Turner, 1965: 1-2). It was out of this background of social cohesiveness that the class structures emerged.

This settler society was therefore able to push for broad,

integrated development out of the early agricultural economy. Manufacturing industry grew out of import substitution to meet local demands for food and drink, clothing, furniture, building materials, agricultural implements, railway equipment and machinery (Rowley, 1972b: 22) and, in 1860, economic growth that was 'sustained, large-scale, and complex' was begun (Butlin, 1964: 3). Boehm (1971: 67-9) has indicated the main ways in which the export of raw materials by a settler colony to its metropole can contribute to the achievement of diversified and integrated economic growth:

> The backward linkage effects in the pastoral and agricultural industries meant, in particular, investment in the clearing of land and in the provision of agricultural machinery, fencing, building materials, and fertilizers. The forward linkages involved the development of the processing industries (such as, with wheat, flour milling for both local consumption and export) and the service industries handling the sale and distribution of commodities. Thus there was substantial investment in the development of financial enterprises and in road and rail transport and port facilities. The growth of base metal mining . . . also had important linkages: backward in the demand for mining equipment and fuel, and forward in needing railways and smelting plants at or near the mine, or port of export.

Even at a time (c. 1860-90) when Britain received over three-quarters of Australia's exports and supplied the same proportion by value of the country's imports (Clark, 1975), Australia's growth was rapid and sustained, and GNP expanded at an average rate of 4.9 per cent per annum — a rate twice that of England's at the time and outstripped only by the United States and Japan (Rowley, 1972b: 23). Industrial activity in the Australian colonies was only 5 per cent of total output in 1860, but it had risen to 10 per cent by 1891 (Butlin, 1964: 181-2). It is thus possible to speak of an imperial-settler colonial 'partnership' (Clark, 1975: 58) for the development of agricultural capitalism, and in commerce, light industry, and the building of infrastructure during the 'Long Boom' to 1890.

## Limitations of late industrial capitalism

Imperial and settler colonial interests and capacities diverged, however, over the development of heavy industrialization in Australia. By the end of the nineteenth century, Britain no longer possessed the most advanced industrial and military technology, and its earlier dominance in the colonial world was under increasing challenge from Germany, France, the United States and Japan. The established exchange of colonial agricultural and mineral resources for imperial capital and labour was disrupted thereafter by recurring crises at the core of the world system. Intense international competition exposed the vulnerability of Australia's position and weakened its advance towards industrial capitalism and secure semi-peripheral status. At the same time, other agencies of development grew in importance.

An early strategy was the establishment of an active and interventionist state. The Australian colonial states were active in developmental works to such an extent that almost half the capital inflow in the 'Long Boom' went to public agencies, and government capital outlays accounted for a third to a half of total capital outlays: as communications grew, government became the largest single employer of labour and the leading entrepreneur (McQueen, 1970a: 49; Butlin, 1964: 6). Through the present century the state has performed a crucial function 'providing the economic infrastructure without which private capital could not operate profitably, and sustaining aggregate demand' (Rowley, 1972a: 278).

More unusually, the state also assumed, from the end of the nineteenth century, important functions in the whole field of industrial relations, thereby making a special contribution to 'the shift of capitalist economic power from the rural to the urban sector' (Sorrell, 1972: 249). The arbitration system, for which the trade unions themselves had strongly pressed, probably 'facilitated the growth of unionism and made it more complete' (Turner, 1965: 34),[3] but at a certain price. The workings of a complex and legalistic system also served to bureaucratize the workers' movement and to incorporate it further into the capitalist system; the unions became in effect

69

'part of the apparatus of state' (Sorrell, 1972: 255).

Another agency of late capitalist development in Australia was the protective tariff system. From 1856, the colonies (with the exception of Western Australia) had 'considerable control' over their own tariffs, but only Victoria deliberately attempted a policy of encouraging domestic industry (Patterson, 1968: 1 and 164). Beginning in 1908, however, high tariffs effectively protected a large part of manufacturing industry from foreign competition through most of this century. The very introduction of such a system was a consequence of Australia's position as a 'self-propelling' settler colony, and an indication of its capacity for relative economic independence and strength; to an extent Britain 'allowed' Australia to introduce tariffs in a way that no directly governed colony would have been able to do (McFarlane, 1972: 50). As a result, between 1900 and 1928, the share of British imports into Australia (mainly manufactures) fell from 74 per cent to 56 per cent, while imports from the United States rose from 15 per cent to 31 per cent (McFarlane, 1972: 42). The process went further following the Depression; while the value of imports represented 18 per cent of GNP in 1928, it had been reduced to around 13 per cent in 1937 (Schedvin, 1970: 377).[4]

But the costs of these gains too were high. Australian industry assumed a high-cost and undynamic character which greatly limited the competitiveness of its manufactured goods on international markets. The development of industrialization under such controlled conditions was partly based on the exploitation of the country's agricultural and minerals sectors; since world capitalism wanted mainly raw materials from Australia, this had to be done if the country was to escape from extreme dependency. But the costs were not least for the working class. Tariffs had a political significance similar to that of the arbitration system. Through the principle of the basic wage, they linked the interests of the working class closer to Australian manufacturers in resisting the competition of British manufacturers (Clark, 1975: 62). Protectionism, the provision of jobs and a decent wage all went together and carried with them the lesser importance of strike action as a corollary.

70

The negative consequences of the imperial link have grown through this century of intense competition and disruption. The British capital which earlier flowed with productive effects represented, in the 1920s, severe external dependence — a 'heavy burden' of national debt and a 'major structural weakness'; in the early 1920s, the servicing of the overseas debt required 20 per cent of exports and four per cent of GNP, and grew sharply in the first half of the 1930s to require 39 per cent of exports and 6 per cent of GNP (Boehm, 1971: 115-16). Despite the diversification and growth of manufactures which occurred during and immediately after World War I, the Australian economy was caught between the smallness of the domestic market and the limitations imposed from the core of the capitalist system. British finance capital in Australia was concentrated in agricultural production, and its owners were reluctant to support industrialization (Cochrane, 1976: 22-3). When in 1929-30 a large fall in earnings from agricultural exports coincided with maturing heavy interest commitments to London, British banking capital resisted Australia's break with the gold standard and the devaluation of the Australian currency. The country's vulnerability was shown by the fall of total gold holdings for monetary purposes from £46m, at the outset of the crisis, to £16m by December 1930 (Cochrane, 1976: 30-6), and a rate of unemployment, in 1932, as high as 28 per cent (Clark, 1975: 67). Only through such experiences did the Australian ruling classes move, with hesitation, towards a more independent economic position.

Significantly, heavy industry, which had begun in World War I, was the sector which led the country out of the Depression, beginning in 1932, and the enforced break with the international economy encouraged the shift of resources into manufacturing (Schedvin, 1970: 11, 372). While agriculture remained the most important sector until 1939, industrialization expanded rapidly thereafter. During World War II, a leading role was played by the development of iron and steel, machinery and engineering, motor vehicle assembly and chemicals and fertilizers, and the importance of manufacturing since then marks Australia as 'one of the most highly in-

71

dustrialized countries in the world'; manufacturing reached 29.4 per cent of GNP in 1959-60 (Boehm, 1971: 7-9). In this decade Australia again experienced a heavy inflow of foreign capital and new settlers.

The vulnerability of Australian capitalism has nevertheless continued into the 1970s, and in crucial respects become more serious. Before then, what remained of the old direct links with Britain had given way to a general incorporation into the global system and association with a number of powerful capitalist states and corporations. United States involvement in Australia increased to some US$1100m by 1962, of which half was in manufacturing (McFarlane, 1972: 53). More recently, however, foreign investment has concentrated more in mining and in commerce and banking, than in manufacturing (Moore, 1972).

Such significant shifts did not strengthen the international competitiveness of Australian industry. It remained hedged within the limits of the domestic market where, given the direction of foreign investment and moves towards the reduction of tariffs, it now faced increasing competition from foreign manufacturers. Internationally, and as far as the big capitalist powers were concerned, it was reliant still on the production and export of raw materials (agricultural and mineral). At the same time, the largest percentage of total manufactured goods (perhaps upward of 69 per cent) in 1970-71, and almost all of its exports of consumer goods and capital equipment, were exported to weaker countries near or on the periphery of the system — South Africa, New Zealand, South-east Asia, and Papua New Guinea (Moore, 1972). In 1974-75, Australia's trade with so-called developing countries was only slightly lower in importance than that with Japan, which was by far the most important single market for Australia — $2367m to the former grouping and $2401m to the latter country (Australian Department of Overseas Trade, *Annual Report*, 1975-76: 9). Only to the Third World and peripheral nations did Australia export a fuller range of its products. Papua New Guinea specifically, with its colonial and neo-colonial status, its small population and largely peasant society constituted, in

72

1976, Australia's third largest market for manufactured goods (e.g., *Post-Courier*, 11 November 1976).

Yet few markets are really assured to Australia even within this regional or peripheral system, as witnessed by the fall in automobile exports from some 20 per cent of total vehicle output in 1973 to a mere dribble in 1976, in consequence of the closing of the South African and New Zealand markets to the sort of cars produced by the foreign-owned corporations in Australia (*Financial Review*, 16 August 1976: 27).[5] And by this time the position had deteriorated further, through the combined effects of tariff reductions and very strong overseas demand for raw materials — wheat, coal, uranium — to the point where the very existence of an Australian industrial capacity came into question.[6] The importance of the small but relatively assured Papua New Guinean market for Australia has therefore not declined with the years but rather increased. But there are few reasons to think that Australia would be able to compete successfully against Japanese competition even in Papua New Guinea given, that is, a reduction of political constraints on the former colony and sufficient determination on the part of the Japanese to penetrate the Papua New Guinean market.

## Limitations placed upon Papua New Guinea

Both Australia's capacity for external colonialism and its interest in development in Papua New Guinea were limited from the start. Early trading contacts occurred, but Australian colonialism was established in the country during the 'Long Trough' of 1890-1940, a period of low growth in Australia. The settler society's own great need for capital and labour left little aside for capitalist development in Papua New Guinea. Australia's rather low level of development, and its wealth in raw materials for export to the British metropole, meant that it was unnecessary to seize and disrupt Papua New Guinean society to get the raw materials of that country. Such an undertaking would have been difficult anyway, given the formidable nature of the country's topography and societies. The weakness of Australian colonial capitalism up to World War I is seen more clearly when contrasted with the vigour of German colonialism — a metropole with a strong and expanding industrial capacity — in New Guinea (see Amarshi above).

Development in Papua New Guinea was usually in competition with development in Australia which was given priority. Potential export crops, such as sugar or bananas, which could compete with Australian products, 'were always actively discouraged by Australian interests'.[7] These policies were continued even as Australia acquired an industrial capacity; various Australian governments, in the 1940s and 1950s, sought to prevent commercial sugar production in the colony. A minister of the reformist Labor government expressed, in 1945, what appears as little short of consistent long-term policy: 'It would be wrong to encourage the production in the territories of goods which would be competitive with commodities produced in Australia' (quoted in Langmore, 1972: 4). The recent strong emphasis upon peasant-based coffee production in the Highlands (which is considered below) is of course not competing with Australian agriculture. Finally, to some extent a nakedly exploitative relationship also existed, in that profits made by Australian interests in Papua New Guinea sometimes served as a not insignificant increment to capital inflow into Australia: Burns Philp, for example, has invested the profits from its operations in the Pacific islands, over most of the years, to assemble in Australia 'the largest portfolio outside the major life offices' (Gottliebsen, 1976: 59); and there were the high profits quickly obtained from gold mining at Wau and Bulolo at the critical period of the Depression in Australia (see pages 26-8 above).

Australia's broad impact on Papua New Guinea has been determined by the fundamentals of the settler society, and specifically by the nature of relations with Britain and the weakening international position of that country. The loyalty of the settlers has already been referred to, and it was such that Australia did not ratify the Statute of Westminster — passed by Britain in 1931 to give full autonomy to the white dominions — until 1942. Despite long constitutional and formal dependence upon Britain, however, Australia in fact sought to obtain an independent and strengthened military capacity from around the turn of the century, and it expressed this aim not least through its expansion into the Pacific; as Meaney (1976: 12) says:

> Australian governments primarily sought to defend their vital interests by extending their territorial boundaries into the Pacific, thus keeping potential enemies as far as possible from their shores while at the same time endeavouring in co-operation with their empire partners to build up a Pacific defence force ...

The military uncertainties of the earlier period were, after 1905, replaced by a 'fear of Japan', and this governed Australian policy until well after 1945. For Papua New Guinea, as the assigned and helpless defence buffer, the between-wars period was largely one of stagnation when Australia sought little other than 'the exclusion of foreigners' from New Guinea (Radi, 1971: 80). But when war did come it brought 'great destruction' to certain areas, and the Tolai population, for example, fell by perhaps one-third between 1941 and 1946 (Brookfield, 1972: 93). Today, with a greatly changed configuration in existence in East and South-east Asia, the Australian government has stated that the defence and military relationship with Papua New Guinea is a matter of 'high importance' to both countries (Defence Minister Jim Killen, quoted in *Post Courier*, 24 February 1977: 1); other Australian sources go much further and believe that Papua New Guinea 'could well become a problem area of worrying proportions',[8] and speculate about circumstances in which 'it may well be necessary either to deny [it] to an enemy for purely selfish strategic reasons or to be able to carry out retaliatory operations there'.[9] The impact of Australia's military policies upon Papua New Guinea is clearly not at an end.

Such fixed military considerations were accompanied by policy changes, during the period of the 'Second Boom' following World War II, when the Australian colonial state, more than Australian capitalism *per se*, became the agency for limited growth in Papua New Guinea. In this respect Australia duplicated its own earlier experience with Britain and followed the precedents set by British and French colonialism in Africa. Yet Australian subsidies to Papua New Guinea remained modest in relation to overall capitalist development within the Australian metropole. Papua's grant from Australia was only $90 000 in 1939; Papua New Guinea's grant was $4m in 1946-47; $6m in 1948-49; $10.5m in 1951-52; and some $110m near the end of the decade: the significance and generosity of the final figure should perhaps be considered in relation to the fact that the state of Queensland, with a population of about 1.75 million, had a state budget of $1000m in 1969 (Hudson and Daven, 1971: 152). At this same time, great inadequacies still existed simply in basic infrastructure in Papua New Guinea. The failure to extend the road system and improve coastal shipping services faster was 'particularly serious' (Langmore, 1972: 11).

The international weakness of Australian capitalism defines the role of Australian state aid (and much else) in Papua New Guinea. With Australian interests dominant within the economy, the country has been a net exporter of capital since the late 1950s; the transfer of savings and profits by Australian individuals and companies 'must contribute to this movement' (Langmore, 1972: 21). As already noted, Papua New Guinea is of importance to Australia as an assured market for Australian manufactures; in a situation where about 50 per cent of Papua New Guinea's total imports are supplied by Australia, the Papua New Guinea-Australia Trade Agreement of 1976 (the first of its kind for the independent country), included a guarantee that Papua New Guinea would not discriminate against Australian products.[10] It is also of significance as an outlet for Australian private investment overseas; in 1967-68, Papua New Guinea received 61 per cent of total Australian private investment overseas, and in 1970-71, the figure was still 55 per cent (Moore, 1972: 39). Given all this, the Australian grant appears as the necessary and not unreasonable cost of retaining economic domination and political and military influence in changing circumstances.

The process of decolonization since the 1960s has meant —

specifically in the recommendations of the World Bank — the opening of Papua New Guinea to economic contact with other capitalist states. Australia's impact has been such as to ensure that real political change, however, will be minimal. As will be seen below, both the educated petty bourgeoisie who now control the post-colonial state, and the state itself, are predisposed to maintain the Australian connection. Proposals for import rationalization that would have favoured Japanese suppliers came to nothing in 1975 precisely because, in the words of a government statement, they threatened to undermine Papua New Guinea's relations with its traditional (i.e. Australian) suppliers (see chapter 15).

None of Australia's programmes and initiatives, including the grant-in-aid, are however backed by the industrial strength which Japan commands as a purchaser of Papua New Guinea's copper and other resources and a potential supplier of cheap manufactures. Both Australia's economic dominance and the broad political influence on which this stands seem likely to decline, even if slowly, over time. It is most unlikely, however, that Papua New Guinea will achieve integrated capitalist development as a result. Australia's own experience in economic growth, with all the advantages it enjoyed relative to most other colonies, would seem to preclude the possibility of a strong capitalist future for Papua New Guinea.

# 7
# The Japanese connection

## Rex Mortimer

While Australia remains by far the most important influence shaping the economy of Papua New Guinea, formal independence has accelerated the tendency for the core nations of the capitalist system to play an increasingly active role in the country's future. The Somare government is assisting this process by its economic policies: sometimes troubled by its dependence on Australian aid and the disruption it would face if that aid should suddenly be cut off or heavily reduced, but being unable or unwilling to venture upon austerity and greater self-reliance, it has opted for a fairly open strategy of economic growth fuelled by foreign investment. The result is that the only prospect it can offer for reducing dependence upon Australia is one that will involve an equal or greater degree of dependence upon greater capitalist powers, of which the most interested and active is Japan. Copper, timber, and fish are the key resources in the Papua New Guinean government's medium-term strategy for balancing its budget, and the major customer for these commodities is, and appears likely to remain, Japan.

Just how much the future of the Papua New Guinean economy is tied to the Japanese connection is implicit in income and expenditure projections worked out in 1975 by Ross Garnaut, an economist attached to the Papua New Guinea Department of Finance. Put in tabular form, Garnaut's estimates give a budgetary outlook of this order for the fiscal year 1982-83 (figures at constant 1974-75 values):

| INCOME | $Am |
|---|---|
| Domestic revenues from taxation and other non-investment sources | 175 |
| Receipts from Bougainville copper project | 90 |
| Receipts from timber resource projects | 30-50 |
| Receipts from fishing leases | 3-4 |
| Direct government investments | 10 |
| Total | 308-329 |
| EXPENDITURE | |
| Total government expenditure | 480-500 |

Source: Garnaut, 1975: 10-11

Garnaut concedes that his forecasts are based upon 'rather low estimates of expenditure needs and rather hopeful estimates of revenue'. On the expenditure side, for example, he has assumed 'no growth at all in per capita expenditure on any but a few high priority government activities, and five per cent per annum per capita growth in the expenditure of the education, agriculture, health and business development departments'. Garnaut's paper was written before the introduction of provincial government, which is bound to place a considerable but as yet unquantified burden on government expenditures by adding an extra tier of government to the system, and there are other cogent reasons for doubting the ability of the government to pursue a fiscal programme of such austerity over any but a short period of time. The collection of domestic revenues on the level estimated by Garnaut assumes an efficiency and probity in the public service which is not likely to be realized, while receipts from foreign-financed resource projects necessarily imply a high level of international economic activity and a control over these operations by the Papua New Guinean government of which Garnaut himself is dubious (15-18). The income estimates for the Bougainville copper mine seem grossly inflated. The figure of $90m was achieved in 1974, before the impact of the world economic crisis was felt; in the following year government receipts from the mine fell to $36.5m.

79

Recovery in world copper prices is expected to be very slow (the *Australian*, 16 January 1976) and the government is committed to reserving part of the income from good years to tide it over lean ones. Its Central Planning Office estimates allow only a K60m average income from the Bougainville mine (*National Development Strategy*, October 1976: 16). In the National Expenditure Plan adopted in 1978, another income and expenditure projection is presented. The details are unimportant, but the general conclusion that viability will require 'very buoyant revenues and therefore favourable economic conditions including a substantial level of new investment' indicates the general picture (NPEP, National Planning Office, Waigani, February 1978: 23).

Nevertheless, even accepting Garnaut's optimistic parameters, the government would still be faced in 1982-83 with a gap of about K170m, compared with the Australian grant of K150m in 1974-75 (all in 1974-75 values). In other words, by the early 1980s Papua New Guinea will still require at least as much Australian aid input as it was receiving at independence. This itself is a vivid commentary upon the 'developmental' impact of Australian aid and the merits of the present Papua New Guinea government's economic strategy. Part of the shortfall could notionally be made up by new borrowing abroad in 1982-83, but as Garnaut again points out, 'further borrowing would contribute positively to net resources available to the government in 1982/83 only if borrowing was discontinued or reduced in intervening years. The continuation of recent levels of borrowing is likely to add as much to debt servicing as to gross resources available by 1982/83' (page 11). In fact, since Garnaut wrote, the Papua New Guinea government has continued to negotiate considerable amounts in new loans from the World Bank, the Asian Development Bank and other international sources (for details see National Public Expenditure Plan, 1978: 42).

The Papua New Guinea government's dilemma arises from the uncertainty of Australia's future aid commitment. At present, Australia is committed until fiscal year 1978-79; it will probably be prepared to continue aid after that date, but on what scale and terms no one can predict, since it depends on political factors operating within and between Australia and Papua New Guinea at the time. Papua New Guinea in the meantime is compelled to try to reduce the cost of its inordinate import bill by diversifying supply sources away from Australia — but this in itself undercuts one of the motivations behind Australian aid. So, if Papua New Guinea is to maintain its accustomed standard of spending — and the government has decided that it will — then it has to seek large-scale income-generating inputs.

The government has made it abundantly clear that it has put most of its eggs in the mineral resource basket, counting upon the opening up of a number of major resource projects by the early eighties to cover its budgetary deficiencies. Immediate hopes and attention are focused upon known copper deposits in the Ok Tedi, Frieda River and Telefomin areas of the western mainland. Kennecott, the American giant, originally held an option to prove and exploit the Ok Tedi field, but this was terminated by agreement in 1974. The Papua New Guinea government decided to pay for the final exploration stage itself; meanwhile it induced the Broken Hill Pty Ltd of Australia to form a consortium with USA and West German partners to work the field, although unofficial reports in late 1975 suggested that the Australian corporation was showing no great haste to plan operations, in all probability waiting upon more informed assessments of the future world market situation before committing itself too heavily (*National Development Strategy*: 5). Present estimates are that the mine is not likely to commence full operations before 1985; the Papua New Guinea government will hold an equity in the project, probably of the order of 20 per cent. Across the Star Mountains at Frieda River, a member of the Japanese Sumitomo group is financing the evaluation of another copper deposit, having bought into a prospect held by Mt Isa Mines Ltd of Australia (Garnaut, 1975: 14). There is little information on the progress or prospects of this venture.

Whatever combination of multinational interests owns the copper projects in combination with the Papua New Guinea government, the principal market, as will be apparent below, is assumed to be Japan.

Hopes are also held out for the discovery of oil and natural gas deposits in the Gulf of Papua. A number of international corporations have been drilling intermittently in the area for many years, and geological strata are said to be favourable. Esso, which has already spent some $A40m in the area over the past four decades, began new drilling operations towards the close of 1975 (*Post-Courier*, 6 October 1976). Substantial success in this field would of course launch Papua New Guinea into a new stage of resource-based growth, but so far there are nothing but hopes to build upon.

Finally, there is the alluring promise of harnessing the vast hydro-potential of the Purari River in the Gulf Province. This project, which if fully developed would dwarf the Snowy River Scheme in Australia and could 'smelt the whole of Japan's aluminium requirements' (Garnaut, 1975: 18), is only at the early exploratory stages, with the Japanese and Australian governments helping to finance a joint feasibility study of a dam site at Wabo. This is at best a very long-range prospect, and opposition to its formidable environmental implications has already obliged the Papua New Guinea government to emphasize that 'at this stage the Purari study is just a study of potentiality. No decision to proceed with a dam has been taken' (Programmes and Performance, 1975-76: 123).

On the available resource and exploitation data, then, the likelihood is strong that by 1985 or thereabouts the economy of Papua New Guinea will be heavily dependent on one product, copper, and upon one key buyer, Japan. Even then, her reliance upon Australia for aid will not have disappeared, since none of the projects now in the pipeline, alone or in combination, will generate anything like the minimum figure of K170-200m (1974-75 values again) she will need to balance her books. The World Bank has quite correctly emphasized that a high level of Australian aid will be essential to maintain the country's external viability for the next decade at least (*Post-Courier*, 30 March 1978).

Japan relies far more than any other highly industrialized

country upon the import of industrial raw materials and food (Kaplan, 1975: 223). During her massive growth phase in the 1960s and early 1970s, when the Japanese GDP growth rate averaged better than 10 per cent a year, her demand for these imports became insatiable. But being a later developer among capitalist powers, she had little ready access to secure markets of her own; the available supplies were effectively in the hands of other major powers, particularly the United States. In any case, up to the end of the 1960s, Japan had little excess capital to invest directly in overseas sources of supply; her own booming industries had a voracious appetite for capital and loan monies, and imports ate heavily into foreign currency reserves. Consequently, most of Japan's supplies of vital commodities like oil, coal, iron, copper and foodstuffs, were bought through long-term trade arrangements made with the companies or countries producing for export. She had no particular difficulty obtaining these supplies during most of the boom years, as production and the opening up of new sources of supply followed the demand. How much longer this will be the case, however, is another matter. One Japanese expert body has estimated that if Japan's growth rate had continued undiminished throughout the 1970s, by the end of the decade she would have required the total anticipated world export surplus of a wide range of raw materials merely to fuel her economy (Halliday, 1975: 285). Since this would have left other importers out in the cold, it is unlikely, to say the least, that Japan's burgeoning needs could have been met by conventional means. No doubt it was an appreciation of the crisis potential of this which led a number of critics of Australian resource policies to warn that if raw materials supplies were not made freely available to the Japanese, they would be compelled to seize them by force.

The extent of Japan's resource requirements can be vividly illustrated by reference to the two major products with which Papua New Guinea hopes to establish its financial viability. In 1950, Japan imported 20 per cent of her copper consumption; in 1970, the figure had grown to 73 per cent (Kaplan, 1974: 234). By volume, Japanese imports of copper grew from

320 000 tons in 1960 to 833 000 tons in 1970, or at an average rate of 10 per cent per year (Yoshino, 1974: 253). Her share of world copper imports was rising astronomically — from 21.5 per cent in 1972 to 27 per cent in 1973 and the first half of 1974 (Garnaut 1975: 3). Even on the assumption that Japan's growth rate falls to about 6 per cent in the 1980s, and that her ratio of resource use to unit of GDP decreases appreciably, it was still estimated before the world economic crisis that her import requirements of copper would rise by the year 2000 to almost three million tons (Kaplan, 1974: 239).

As for timber, Japan accounted for 59.2 per cent of the growth in world trade in the commodity between 1965 and 1969, and a further 17.5 per cent between 1969 and 1971. Her share of world imports of non-conifer logs, the main exports from South-east Asia and Papua New Guinea, rose from 44.1 per cent in 1965 to 53.2 per cent in 1972 (Garnaut, 1975: 3).

An increasingly tight situation so far as resource supplies, then, was causing Japanese industrialists and politicians serious concern by the early 1970s. At the same time, other conse-quences of Japan's rapid growth began to assume crisis pro-portions. Exports had to be increased at a high rate in order to pay for raw materials imports, a necessity made all the more imperative by the fact that her competitiveness was sustained by relatively low wage rates which restricted the internal market for her products (Halliday, 1975: 262). Inflation, fuel-led by labour shortages and the elaborate and extended credit structure of the Japanese economy, outran that of any other major industrial country, reaching a level of 20 per cent just before the onset of the world economic crisis in 1974 (Halliday: 280). Environmental deterioration in Japan's congested in-dustrial centres, where protective measures had been neglected in the interests of higher profits and lower costs, had assumed dangerous proportions and given rise to major political con-flicts (Halliday: 280-1).

These problems came to a head in conflict with the United States in 1971-72. Following on the shock experienced by Japanese leaders at America's reconciliation with China, they were hit hard by United States pressures designed to limit

Japanese penetration of the American market and to open up Japanese industry to US investment (Halliday: 287). In an agonizing appraisal of their situation, Japanese policy-makers linked the balance of payments problem to urgent issues of environmental pollution, labour shortages, inflation and long-term resource supplies. Japanese industry, it was concluded, must 'concentrate on the production and export of knowledge-intensive goods, making lesser demands on natural resources, unskilled labour and the domestic environment. More raw materials were to be imported in processed forms'. Direct Japanese investment in developing countries was to be stepped up and directed towards developing exports of labour-intensive and resource-intensive commodities. 'The level of foreign aid was to be increased and it was to be provided on more liberal terms' (Garnaut, 1975: 3-4). Some steps were taken in this direction following the government-instituted reappraisal, but it is doubtful that such a degree of economic transformation could be realized except over a long time span. Some of the effects, moreover, proved less than welcome to Japan's trading partners in South-east Asia. The riots which greeted the then Japanese Prime Minister, Tanaka, in Jakarta and Bangkok in January 1974, while reflecting longstanding resentment against the Japanese and their dominant role in the economies of these countries, were incited particularly by the establishment of locally-based Japanese manufacturing industries which both displaced indigenous business and labour, and catered to the luxury tastes of unpopular ruling elites (Yoshino, 1974: 270).

Before Japanese renovation could proceed very far, the country was overtaken by the global economic crisis of 1974. Japan was hit particularly hard by the recession, partly owing to the inordinate impact on her of the oil price rises of that year. From a growth rate of 10 per cent in 1973, Japan crashed to an absolute decline in production in 1975. The effect on her resource suppliers was severe: in the case of the new copper industries in Indonesia, the Philippines and Papua New Guinea alone, shipments were cut back by 15 per cent at the end of 1974 and further cuts imposed in 1975 (Garnaut, 1975: 6). There was no growth in petroleum or timber demand, fish prices fell, and Japanese investment in timber and fish production slowed down to a trickle (Garnaut, 1975: 6).

The worst of the crisis now appears to be over, and Japanese production is beginning a slow climb back as world markets expand again. It is more than doubtful, however, that Japan will revert to the extraordinarily high growth rates of the 1960s and early 1970s. Even before the crisis, Japanese economists were predicting that the country's growth rate would slow down to about 6 per cent by the 1980s (Kaplan, 1974: 238). General world conditions are not expected to favour high growth rates by the major industrial countries in the foreseeable future, and long-term unemployment and continued inflation are expected to persist. If some economists are right, and the world capitalist economy has entered one of its protracted 'troughs', then the pace of growth is likely to be considerably slowed.

Japan can confidently be expected to step up her raw materials purchases from the levels to which they dropped during the crisis, even if the rate of growth in imports slows down somewhat by comparison with the boom years. The resumption of her economic growth and export drive depends upon these resources, and there is no way in which the Japanese can reduce their high coefficient of consumption of natural resources per unit of GDP within a short time span (Kaplan, 1974: 238).

The emphasis is likely to shift steadily towards direct investments in resource extraction, as opposed to the long-term purchasing agreements with foreign governments and the multinationals which were characteristic of the pre-crisis period. Even before the crisis, direct resource investment had begun to figure more prominently in Japanese industry's priorities, when its leaders saw growing difficulty in procuring materials in sufficient quantities on acceptable terms. There was the added incentive that the highest profits in resource use are associated with extractive operations. By 1971, investments in the resource field had reached approximately US$1100m, nearly one-third of the country's total direct foreign investment. Investment in copper extraction had actually begun in the 1950s, in the Philippines, Latin America and Canada.

However, most of the investments represented only a minority interest in the projects concerned, and in 1970 they accounted for only 6 per cent of Japan's copper imports. The more dynamic investment policy which began in the late 1960s gave Japan a major interest in two large copper deposits, one in Zaire and one in Malaysia. That her interest has not declined is demonstrated by Sumitomo's activity in the Frieda River area of Papua New Guinea. Nevertheless, the Japanese can expect tough competition from the United States and other major capitalist powers, who will not easily surrender the advantages they gain by controlling extraction at its source (Yoshino, 1974: 252-8).

Japan's economy remains highly export-dependent and, despite the reorganization envisaged in 1972, this situation is not likely to alter significantly in the foreseeable future. While, during the boom period, the growth rate of Japan's exports exceeded the rate of growth of its GNP, the dependence of key industries on exports was even more salient. 'In particular, although manufacturing produces about 31 per cent of Japan's GNP, it accounts for more than 90 per cent of Japan's exports. In the case of iron and steel, exports amount to more than one-quarter of total production. If steel embodied in products such as ships and automobiles were included, the proportion would be much higher' (Hollerman, 1974: 177).

To meet the problem posed by import substitution policies of countries within her market sphere, to take advantage of cheap labour resources in some developing countries and to limit further industrial pollution at home, Japan began to invest substantially in manufacturing abroad in the late 1960s. In 1971, this investment reached US$963m or roughly 27 per cent of total foreign investment. Of the total, 35 per cent was invested in Asia, 29 per cent in Latin America, and 23 per cent in North America. The investments designed to overcome import substitution restrictions were in rather small amounts, and at least initially were limited to providing the minimum amount of production facilities needed to satisfy the demands of the host countries. Often only the final process or assembly was undertaken in the local country, the major portion of the product still being made in Japan. A large proportion of this investment was by way of joint ventures with host companies or governments, partly to meet their requirements and partly to minimize political risks.

In the years immediately preceding the crisis, however, it was noticeable that Japanese manufacturing investment abroad was taking on a more coherent pattern, moving towards the transfer of whole industries, and also extending into large capital-intensive and technologically-oriented projects (Yoshino, 1974: 259-68).

Japan's foreign aid programme has always been small, niggardly and expensive for the recipient. Despite the passing of legislation enabling Japan to extend untied official development loans in November 1972, her activity in this sphere has remained small. As Garnaut notes, 'Transfers classed as Overseas Development Assistance (ODA) by the Development Assistance Committee represented only 0.25 per cent of GNP in 1973, well below the international target of 0.7 per cent and the Development Assistance Committee average of 0.3 per cent. Grants comprised only 39.9 per cent of Japanese ODA in 1973, the lowest of all countries except Austria and Portugal and well below the Development Assistance Committee average of 66.7 per cent' (Garnaut, 1975: 5). Despite the revelation of hostility by South-east Asian countries towards Japanese business methods and penetration at the time of Tanaka's visit in January 1974, there is no compelling evidence that Japan will greatly expand her aid programmes on terms that are likely to be acceptable to most Third World countries.

Indeed, Papua New Guinea has already received blunt warning from Japan that aid policy will be tied closely to Japanese business opportunity and the treatment Japanese business receives. In 1976, a Japanese project for establishing a palm oil plantation, smallholder settlement and processing plant at Bialla, in West New Britain province, was cancelled by the Papua New Guinea government on the grounds that the Japanese plant did not measure up to its specifications. Immediately, the Japanese government announced that all aid to Papua New Guinea would be suspended unless the project was reinstated. As of late 1976, the dispute had been submitted to independent arbitration, and no more has been heard on the aid question. It is a timely reminder, however, that the earlier experience of Indonesia, among others, may be repeated in Papua New Guinea.

Japanese industrialists were not slow to recognize the opportunities afforded by Papua New Guinea's resources as the country moved towards independence. For a time, some of them entertained grandiose and unreal plans for integrating the country wholly into Japan's industrial empire. Thus the President of Mitsui Mining and Smelting in 1972 suggested that Japan should acquire a fifty-year 'development mandate' over the whole island (including the Indonesian half) under which, in return for 'developing' the island, Japan would be free to use its raw materials for half a century. Prior to this, the Chairman of Nippon Steel had proposed that Japan buy Papua New Guinea outright (Halliday, 1975: 297). These grotesque proposals, notable not only for their complete disregard of the rights and aspirations of the people of the island, but also for their cavalier attitude towards Australian and Indonesian interests, are exceptional though by no means unique manifestations of Japan's imperialist ambitions. More typical, however, were the business delegations and technical groups which began to descend upon Papua New Guinea and estimate its value and penetrability in the eyes of Japanese big capital. From as early as 1972, these contacts were fortified by political connections established between Japanese businessmen and members of the Papua New Guinea government.

By now Papua New Guinea has come to represent a small but significant pasture in Japan's overall resource farm. Copper, as we have seen, has become the major focus of her interest, and it is from this one product that Papua New Guinea hopes to obtain as much as a third of her budget income by the mid-1980s. But copper, like most of Papua New Guinea's export primary crops, notoriously fluctuates in price, and the experience of 1975, when copper returns to the government fell by more than two-thirds compared with 1974, reveals how drastic an effect such price fluctuations can have on her small, narrow economic base. The greater the country's dependence on copper becomes, of course, the greater will the variations be felt, and the less manageable will copper income averaging policies of the government be. Government revenues and external payments could be hit devastatingly and simultaneously. Japan is not likely to go out of her way to ease Papua New Guinea's difficulties; the country has nothing like the salience in Japan's scheme of things as she has for Australia.

In other areas of Japanese resource interest, timber and fishing, Papua New Guinea is going to earn much less at considerable cost to her own future needs, and she will find it very much harder to ensure even that agreements entered into are observed. Copper mining operates within a confined enclave; it is carried on by very large corporations with a large fixed capital component and a long-term investment interest which inhibits the grosser forms of manipulation and evasion of government controls. Japanese timber and fishing companies, on the other hand, are notorious for their unsavoury practices. They operate in scattered and often remote leases difficult to police; they work in a highly competitive environment which encourages cost-cutting and rip-and-tear methods of extraction; and they count on a very quick turnover of capital. Hence they are apt to resort to a wide variety of evasive techniques to outsmart regulations of the host government, among which bribes to landowners, officials and politicians are common. To date, Japanese companies, alone or in partnership with the Papua New Guinea government, have major timber leases under operation at Gogol near Madang, at Cape Hoskins, Bialla and Open Bay in New Britain, and on New Ireland. Already by 1975, 'there were signs ... that the administration of the [timber] industry [in PNG] was sliding out of effective government control' (Garnaut, 1975: 17).

The Jant operation at Gogol provides a good example of the methods employed by the Japanese companies in this field at that time. The Jant company is substantially controlled by the Honshu Paper Co., a part of the Mitsui empire. It paid a small royalty to landholders and the Papua New Guinea government, but the substantial tax returns which the Papua New

Guinea government had expected from the $A10m operation are never likely to materialize for the simple reason that all sales are made to the Honshu parent at transfer prices which ensure an absence of profit in the subsidiary. Not surprisingly in these circumstances, the Papua New Guinea government has not taken up an option to purchase a 20 per cent equity in the local company. Moreover, Jant seems confident that, despite replanting clauses in its contract, it will be able to evade most of its reafforestation obligations. Japanese company officials openly boasted of the part that bribes had played in securing this satisfactory arrangement so far as they were concerned.*

The Papua New Guinea government is negotiating for the exploitation of other large timber leases in other provinces (*Programmes and Performance*, 1975-76: 113-15). In the meantime, guarded complaints by ministers suggest that similar difficulties are being experienced with the fishing industry, in which Japanese interests are also dominant. The recession has greatly slowed down activity in both these fields, but when activity resumes there is a pronounced risk of deals being made by influential politicians or discrete parts of the Papua New Guinean bureaucracy and Japanese interests outside the formal guidelines set by the central planners in Port Moresby. The risk will be all the greater when provincial government machinery is established, since the investors will have yet another avenue for circumventing the guidelines, despite the constitutional power of the central government to oversee all foreign investment ventures.

On the export side, Japan already contributes substantially to Papua New Guinea's consumption, her share of the latter's imports having grown rapidly to about 17 per cent in 1975. The trend is bound to grow as the demand for cars, trucks, transport and extractive equipment, machinery and processed foods rises. The restricted size of the Papua New Guinea market and its high cost structure by Asian standards will limit Japan's desire to establish branch plants in the country, and

---

*This information is based upon tape recordings of interviews between Jant officials and a foreign journalist.

she is more likely to use her position as major purchaser of Papua New Guinea's crucial exports as a means of securing favourable terms of entry for her manufactured goods.

Developmentally, Japanese economic activity in Papua New Guinea has no more to offer the country than Australian colonial operations or the Australian aid programme. Copper extraction is highly capital-intensive, confined in enclaves, and produces few spread effects. In this respect, it is even more 'external' to the overall economy than the mainstay plantation system of the colonial period. Fishing and timber operations likewise are extremely limited in their general economic effects, generating little in the way of indigenous skills or industrial spin-offs, while producing considerably greater long-term damage to the environment. On the other hand, the obligation upon Papua New Guinea to import increasing quantities of Japanese goods to balance Japan's resource purchases will act as a block to the expansion of an indigenous manufacturing capacity.

The Papua New Guinea government argues, however, that the income from resource industries will be used to promote indigenous business and rural development. There is nothing original in this claim; it has been made by every government which has adopted a similar strategy, but rarely with any major effect. The total relationship with Japan, it is argued here, will be detrimental to Papua New Guinea's diversification and industrial development. The pressure of Japanese imports is only one aspect of this total relationship, which must be viewed in economic, social and political terms.

The whole nature of the dependency relationship affects the politics and attitudes of the host society and government in countless ways, all of them having the effect of consolidating dependency and constraining overall balanced national development. The enclaves and their surrounding infrastructure have first call upon government expenditures, since it is upon them that the country's solvency has been made to depend. These demands become increasingly heavy as physical infrastructure has to be buttressed by the burgeoning costs of meeting the social problems created by enclave development.

Scarce local skills tend to become concentrated in and around the enclaves, starving the remainder of the country of technical manpower which could contribute to diversification and balance. The enclave spawns classes of new rich entrepreneurs in service industries who contribute little to industrial diversification but, through their connections with the multinationals and the host government, exact an inordinate share of public expenditure to satisfy their ambitions for Western amenities and lifestyles, much of which necessarily has to be spent upon high-grade public services and luxury goods imported from the industrialized countries. Finally, the government system itself is penetrated by the values, the interests and the pressures of the great extractive combines; it too takes on an increasingly parasitic role in the society, at the same time assuming the role of 'policeman' in relation to the foreign corporations' workforce, since the state's very dependence upon the income generated by the companies leads the government to think of the multinationals' welfare as coincident with the 'national interest'.

# III
# The class structure

Kenneth Good

# 8
# Introduction: social class in the Third World*

Colonial class formation generally centres around the uneven and differential transformation of pre-capitalist societies into peasantries, working class and bourgeoisie. Our knowledge of the general outlines of such formations has been significantly enlarged by recent studies of peasant societies from several writers, notably Teodor Shanin (1971) and Eric Wolf (1966, 1971). Economic and social inequalities in the Third World arise in a global system which concentrates economic strength and advanced industrialization at the core in the capitalist West, and a backward agriculture and subordinate peasantry on the periphery in Latin America, Africa, Asia and the Pacific. Immanuel Wallerstein (1974: 406) says: 'Industrial activity being disproportionately concentrated in certain parts of the world-economy, industrial wage-workers are to be found principally in certain geographic regions'. Little or no industrialization is indeed characteristic of the Third World, and means that the working class and capitalist bourgeoisie are small in the colonial society.

Abstract models of dominant and dominated classes are inappropriate when global capitalism has penetrated into Third World nations and regions unevenly and with varying intensity. In some instances old systems of production have been left intact, and a resurgence has been encouraged in other activities, for example, traditional artisan work and small-commodity production to satisfy the demands of international tourism for

*This introduction is based on Good (1976a).

97

exotica and the needs of the small wage-earners for relative cheapness (e.g. LeBrun and Gerry, 1975). Some of the old social groupings exist, perhaps in decline, beside new groups and classes rising in the dependent political economy. Rarely are classes clearly defined and demarcated, and there are 'all sorts of what appear to be intermediate groups and strata and even "overlaps"' (Shivji, 1975: 16). The idea of *formation*, and the separation initially of class and class action, of class *in itself* as distinct from class *for itself*, are therefore specially appropriate to the analysis of uneven and ill-seen colonial conditions where key classes are embryonic. These ideas seem present in Robin Cohen (1972: 252) where, in developing an analysis of class for African conditions (but with seemingly wider relevance), he proposes in a simple and sensible formulation 'the notion and manifestations of class *formation* and class *action*' (Cohen's emphasis). He makes a plea for:

> a minimalist definition of class; one that recognises the incomplete and embryonic character of class formation and development on the one hand, but that nonetheless attempts to derive a meaningful frame of reference for explaining a class-based act, on the other. We may thus recognise the relative infrequency and ephemerality of overt class action, but also be careful to acknowledge the existence of such acts and not underestimate their political significance.

Factors such as a divisive 'tribalism' or regionalism and a nakedly repressive state may deny the early realization of class action, and therefore deserve attention. But a premature and perhaps subjective application of the idea of class consciousness ('mere trade union consciousness', 'labour aristocracy', etc.) may, on the other hand, prevent a close examination of the potential for change.

The most thorough-going class action is revolution, and experience of this type of action is now sufficiently widespread to identify the main class relationships involved. In the analyses of Wolf (1971), Alavi (1965), and Cabral (1969), revolutions are made by movements based upon the middle and lower peasantry, and organized and led by elements of new urban classes, principally of the working class and petty bourgeoisie.

In China (Alavi, 1965: 262), the middle peasants were initially the more militant, but the poor peasants were ultimately the most revolutionary. It is clear from direct experience (Cabral, 1969: 49-51) that revolution is a long, complex and arduous process, and that it is idle to romanticize the revolutionary potentialities of the peasantry or ignore the vital leadership role of an educated petty bourgeoisie. Individuals, given the limitations imposed by their formal class positions, choose either to defend a foreign capitalism and domestic exploiters, or to assist the peasantry and working class; it is among the educated middle class that autonomy in this regard is most noticeable.

Revolutions fail more often than they succeed, and experience suggests that the peasantry alone cannot make successful revolutions (Wolf, 1971). A recent illustration is the case of the Land and Freedom Army in Kenya in the 1950s, which forced the British to concede independence but was unable to prevent the rise to power of collaborating rich rural strata or its own political submergence, as a supposedly savage 'Mau Mau', in the independent state (see, for example, Good, 1976b).

If it is inadequate to say that the most wretched are the most revolutionary, it is also false to assume that a small and relatively skilled working class in the Third World is necessarily a privileged 'labour aristocracy' divorced from the unemployed and peasantry and without revolutionary potential. The situation in Kenya in the early 1970s has been considered by Sandbrook (1975: 23-30, 185-91), who concludes that the Kenyan ruling class, with all its relative wealth is in growing contradiction with workers whose wages and living standards are held down: 'Both the words and actions of urban workers reveal their hostility to the consumption-oriented and business-oriented ruling sectors, and their opinion of themselves as relatively impoverished'. Workers were not demarcated from the peasantry, and in unions they constituted 'one of the few organised social classes or class segments'. In the case of Ghana it has been suggested that it is precisely a section of the better-paid and relatively secure manual working class that has proved 'the most radical "mass" force', and that in Ghana and in Nigeria the possession of 'organisational mechanisms for concerted political action' place unionized workers in a position of potential importance in concerted political action by the poor (Jeffries, 1975: 60,70). Thus the term 'labour aristocracy' is misleading in the African situation (Sandbrook and Cohen, 1975: 3).

Most class action stops short well before sustained revolution. If relatively ephemeral movements are to be recognized as possible harbingers of future class action, and the formations which constitute them properly understood and evaluated, an over-emphasis on a coherent 'consciousness' and ideology must be avoided. Even in the case of comparatively educated societies, 'it is fruitless', says Price (1972: 4), 'to look for a systematised and distinct framework of ideology or thought into which working-class attitudes to problems like imperialism can be placed'. Action by workers and peasants necessarily assumes a wide variety of forms (Jeffries, 1975: 69). Finally, in highly repressive colonial situations, the expression of worker discontent must be looked for not in strike action but 'in the nooks and crannies of the day-to-day work situation' (Van Onselen, 1973: 249).

Class formation is central to an understanding of the general position of the Third World and of countries within it, and it is an integral aspect of the process of economic and social change. If it seems likely that the creation of advanced class formations has been the result of violent and disruptive social change (conquest, large-scale land and labour seizures, the imposition of capitalist agriculture and relative industrialization) then where the level of economic activity is low, and social change is slow as in Papua New Guinea, class formation is weak. The existing social classes constitute in both cases the resources for further development or continuing dependency. The processes of class formation and action may be looked upon as key indicators of the changing relations between a country such as Papua New Guinea and the capitalist West. In the simplest terms, certain social categories and classes appear to have a capacity for collaboration with colonialism and foreign capitalism, while others (in the long run at least) do not.

# 9
# The formation of the peasantry

The impact of relatively powerful external forces upon self-contained Melanesian economies had profound but uneven effects on established and slow-changing social relations. The European plantation system dominated a sluggish colonial economy, particularly agricultural production for export, through the first half of this century. The smallholder contribution to total copra exports in 1934-35, for example, was only some 3-4 per cent, and the country's total export earnings reached their pre-war peak of little more than $8m in 1939-40. In the 1950s, however, this situation changed dramatically, and the economy began to surge forward. Total export earnings increased threefold in the fifteen years, 1951-66, and the growth of agricultural exports was almost wholly responsible for this expansion (Shand, 1969: 282-7). Towards the end of the 1960s, three crops — copra, coffee and cocoa — together represented about 80 per cent of the value of total exports. Peasant growers, moreover, had assumed greater significance in copra and cocoa production, while coffee-growing was predominantly an indigenous activity by this time. But the production of rich export crops was highly concentrated geographically. Copra and cocoa were grown mainly on the New Guinea coastal mainland and islands, notably the Gazelle Peninsula, and coffee most intensely over the longest period in the Eastern Highlands. By 1976, the importance of coffee was such that it alone earned K100m, a sum which began to rival that of copper exports; Eastern Highlands' share was K30m. (It has to be remembered that copper slumped in price after the onset of

101

the world economic crisis in 1974, while coffee has enjoyed an exceptional boom owing to crop failures in Brazil; in 1978 coffee prices began to fall.)

## From 'tribesmen' into peasantries

The creation of peasantries out of pre-capitalist (subsistence agricultural) societies is one of the earliest and most important social effects of the expansion of European capitalism into the Third World. Peasants are defined as 'small agricultural producers who, with the help of simple equipment and the labour of their families, produce mainly for their own consumption and for the fulfilment of obligations to the holders of political and economic power' (Shanin, 1971: 240). Capitalist markets and the colonial state represent new economic and political forces within a less dynamic agricultural society, creating obligations — to supply land and labour, pay taxes, etc. — and opportunities to produce for sale in European markets simultaneously. It has been shown that African cultivators in South Africa and in Rhodesia, in their early contacts with an expanding colonial capitalism, responded strongly to the new opportunities for increased agricultural production, and large peasantries quickly came into being (Bundy, 1972; Phimister, 1974).

Change was generally slower in Papua New Guinea, but Vunamami on the Gazelle Peninsula was 'a community of peasant copra producers' by the early 1920s (Salisbury, 1970: 124). But under colonial conditions peasant growers are generally unable to compete with larger capitalist enterprises, where these exist, because they lack capital, technological knowledge and free access to markets and processing facilities, and the colonial authorities act to preserve expatriate advantages. The copra growers of Vunamami, for example, did not establish themselves as independent agents; rather, they became 'a captive labour force' to the plantation economy (Salisbury, 1970: 124).

The transformation of subsistence villagers into peasant farmers is only the first stage in the process of rural social change in colonial situations. The development of capitalist agriculture also engenders deepening inequalities *within* the peasantry. Obligations and opportunities are experienced differentially by individuals and groups within the new peasant communities, partly as a consequence of broad but uneven colonial exploitation. If the alienation of land was only 2 per cent nationally in Papua New Guinea, nevertheless by 1914 the Tolai of the Gazelle had lost some 39 per cent of their fertile land (Rowley, 1965: 116, 118). Land alienation was quick and intense in Goroka in the Eastern Highlands between 1952 and 1954: European planters acquired dozens of agricultural properties, a tenfold increase over the area alienated in the previous three years (Finney, 1973: 45). The impact of these changes on the Gazelle and in Goroka was increased by the fact that both areas either were or were fast becoming densely populated, and was intensified by the tendency to freeze land titles and eliminate the old flexibility of tenure with the planting of perennial tree crops (T.S. Epstein, 1973: 311). Following the introduction of cash cropping, land, the basic resource of peasant society, was becoming scarce, more valuable, and subject to dispute.[1] However, some peasants found in this opportunities for personal enrichment. Selling food to Europeans led to the appearance, in 1910, of 'rich men' within Vunamami society, who drove horses and buggies on the new roads, and built houses with metal roofs (Salisbury, 1970: 242).

The comparative speed of such change, despite the weakness of Australian capitalism, strongly suggests that some Papua New Guinean pre-capitalist societies already possessed *significant inbuilt inequalities*. The pre-European Tolai were 'preoccupied with the accumulation of wealth' and had 'clear-cut concepts' of the ownership of resources, employment, rewards for labour, accumulation and profit (T.S. Epstein, 1968: 28-9), and Eastern Highlanders traditionally have been 'passionately interested in wealth and in prestige associated with wealth' (Finney, 1973: 11). Among societies which used shell money, only wealth represented 'ultimate social advantage and prestige' (T.S. Epstein, 1973: 309), and in some societies, including the Tolai, the use of shell money was highly evolved.

The production and exchange of a range of goods — clay pots, dyes, stone tools, salt — took place within and between certain communities on a significant scale (Hughes, 1975), with consequent interdependence between communities and possibilities for accumulation of wealth by groups and individuals.

The prominent institution of the 'big man' has frequently been interpreted in egalitarian and consensual terms, although the trappings of 'despotism' surrounded powerful leaders in the Highlands at the time of Australian penetration (Salisbury, 1964: 225). The 'big man' not only personified the comparative centralization of political, military, legal and moral authority but, significantly, sometimes also controlled the banking and credit services of the community (T.S. Epstein, 1973). Although these functions served to some extent to distribute wealth within the group, and although the individual leader had no permanent hold on them, the 'big man' possessed the means to amass wealth and mobilize loyal followers; 'the making of the faction', both economically and politically, in a rugged sort of way (Sahlins, 1963: 291).[2] The system tended to combine the values of achievement and competitiveness with the possibility that the 'big man' might attempt to perpetuate his power inter-generationally through inheritance; 'in many societies the heir to a rich man was in a favoured position' (T.S. Epstein, 1973: 308).

The potential for important structural changes was clearly there. The ascribed division of kinship groups into chiefly and non-chiefly ranks, or 'protochiefdoms', as in Sa'a around Buka passage, emerged in several western Melanesian societies (Sahlins, 1963: 294). Hereditary chieftaincies not only developed on the Trobriands and among the Mekeo, as is well known, but there is reason to think that in at least twenty other societies strong hereditary principles were at work (Standish, 1976).[3] Given such preconditions, it is hardly surprising that a *definite social stratification* appeared in certain communities, especially when European activity began to provide a suitable environment. Vicedom's account of the Mbowamb of Mount Hagen at the time of the first European penetration into the region was 'close to that of a class society', with 'three broad

categories ... big men, ordinary men, and men of low status'
(Strathern, 1971: 205, 208); and Oliver (1973: 71) describes pre-
European Bougainville and Buka in these terms:

> At one extreme were those tribal neighbourhoods dominated numerical-
> ly, or in terms of landholding, by one particular matrilineage. In such
> cases the members of the principal matrilineage constituted an
> aristocracy, and their senior member a hereditary chief, to be succeeded
> in time by the eldest son of his eldest sister ... So far had this process
> gone in some coastal tribes, and in the southern part of Buin, that these
> societies reached the point of clear-cut stratification, having been divid-
> ed into two or even three hereditary classes: aristocrats, commoners, and
> intermediaries.

Capitalism and the colonial state established themselves
unevenly upon *the existing hierarchical elements and tendencies* within Papua New Guinea societies. Village leaders were
sometimes encouraged to assist in labour recruitment, for example, and occasionally grew quite wealthy in the process
(Mair, 1970: 193-4). More specifically, initial contacts with the
Tolai saw 'a greater concentration of power in the hands of the
"big man" '. The *luluai* (village head) system was of course
'geared to little more than maintaining the colonial *status quo*'
(A.L. Epstein, 1969: 18, 253); but because *luluais* remained the
representatives of small local communities, 'they continued to
carry out many of the customary responsibilities of "big
men" ' (A.L. Epstein, 1970: 111). European penetration into
Goroka had rather similar effects. Many village boys followed
the patrols of the later 1930s, and patrol officers decided to
pick the most able and educate them as a corps of Pidgin-
speakers who could mediate between the patrols and villagers;
this schooling and informal contacts which ambitious youths
had with patrols were 'crucial elements' in the education of
some of the first Gorokan 'entrepreneurs' (Finney, 1973: 25).
Broadly similar patterns seem to have occurred in the regions
of intense agricultural development. Right up to the time of
the introduction of local government councils into the colonial
political system, on the Gazelle 'the *luluai* continued to display
many of the characteristic attributes of the traditional "big
man" ' (A.L. Epstein, 1970: 111).

There were discontinuities in the development of political institutions and peasant class formation. These were clearest perhaps on the Gazelle, where local government councillors, around the early 1960s, were 'not necessarily the most influential men in their own communities in the traditional sense', and there was 'a noticeable absence of the more educated, English-speaking Tolai' from involvement in council affairs (A.L. Epstein, 1969: 277). It is easy, however, to exaggerate the significance of such changes in the position of different groups and classes within evolving colonial institutions. The general political aim of the new institutions remained constant, as they adapted to a quickening of economic and social development in significant regions. The new local government councils were to provide, in the view of D.M. Fenbury (the early architect of the system) 'evolving formulae which will result in the indigenous inhabitants of the Territory continuing to regard Australia's tutelage as essential to their well being'. Fenbury intended that councils should serve as 'a device for sublimating the energies of native leadership into local channels' and, in order to achieve this, he envisaged that they should appear to fit into village social organizations and build on customary institutions (quoted in Simpson, 1976: 10-14, 28).

Given such calculating, indeed Machiavellian tactics, it is not surprising that the council system was frequently misunderstood[4] and opposed; not only were the more educated Tolai sometimes frustrated, but colonial field officers showed strong suspicion and hostility. Nevertheless, local government performed certain functions fairly clearly. It worked to stifle independent social development in the countryside, specifically those tendencies and movements which might seek serious change in the established system of capitalist agriculture. This was the potential in ideology and strength only of mass peasant movements, such as the seemingly irrational but activist and relatively autonomous cargo-cults. The Paliau movement, for example, was quickly drawn into the specially created Baluan Council,[5] diverted, divided, and stopped (Simpson, 1976). In endeavouring to resist or cast off foreign domination, the millenarian movements of necessity opposed the rapidly evolving big peasant class, the assemblies of 'big men', *tultuls*, catechists, and *bosbois* who represented authority at village level, and who were the 'collaborators' (Gerritsen, 1975: 7-8) in the development of colonial capitalism. The followers of millenarian movements were usually those who had lost out under the highly uneven and unequal pattern of development. The supporters of the Yali movement in Madang in the 1960s, for example, were typically without any kind of post-primary education and, significantly, not engaged in cash-cropping. They were conscious of their deprivation and wished to bring about a redistribution of resources and a completely different way of life. Wanting autonomy from foreign institutions, they frequently did not support councils and councillors; both council and mission therefore opposed Yali (Morauta, 1974: 113-14, 153-6). Councillors in other areas saw cults as threatening their interests, and used their position to denounce the movements (A.L. Epstein, 1969: 273-4; Gerritsen, 1975: 8).

Local government also seems to have strengthened the economic and political position of the bigger farmers directly, whether the individuals concerned were fully aware of this fact or not. While the councils contained independent political development, they encouraged economic activity, not only by establishing aid posts and building primary schools, but also by promoting cash crops. The councils on the Gazelle were active in cocoa production, and this may have contributed to its substantial increase in the area through the second half of the 1950s. Finally, whatever the initial impact of councils on indigenous and earlier colonial institutions, they provided important stepping-stones for many ambitious and better-off peasants to the larger, national institutions. In 1961 representatives of local government councils served as an electoral college to choose the first nationals to sit in the Legislative Council; and in the first House of Assembly elections, in 1964, about two-thirds of successful national candidates had council experience (Simpson, 1976; Brookfield, 1972: 118). For all the complexities and ambiguities of the local government system, it is clear that it operated in the interests of the rising rich peasantry.

It is consistent with the nature of peasant society that much of the long, tortuous process by which class divisions were created within the peasantry took place, literally, deep within the countryside. But of the various groups in rural society, it was the evolving rich peasantry which was in by far the strongest position to speak and to be heard. In a process which can now be seen only hazily, certain general features seem to stand out. Mainly because of the weakness and peripheral position of Australia, Papua New Guinea was only slowly incorporated into world capitalism. The manner in which this was carried on strongly emphasized the production of cash crops for export, and therefore certain other features such as wage labour and particularly the concentration of basic resources — land and labour — in individual hands. New political institutions, such as *luluai* and *tultul*, were also necessary. But the creation of *linkages* between a large number of small-scale, subsistence societies and global capitalism was only possible because certain Papua New Guineans served as *intermediaries* in particular areas. 'Only in two regions — the copra and cocoa growing areas of the Gazelle ... and the coffee growing areas of the Highlands — was there much indication of significant entrepreneurial activity', as Finney (1973: xiv) puts it, within the overall population. This represented almost all the interest shown by Australian capitalism, which also aimed at the preservation of the subsistence economy for the reproduction of cheap labour, and to prevent the emergence of a landless proletariat (see the next chapter). This policy was not, however, inconsistent with the creation of a peasant class, for peasant cash-crop production also required the continuance and support of subsistence farming, which was advanced only in certain regions and which appears now to be moving towards the critical stage of landlessness in certain regions; and subsistence farming depends largely on women while cash-cropping is usually run by men. One of the most outstanding social consequences of the new systems and structures was the rich peasantry, whose appearance has been sketched thus far. Its formation must now be considered in closer detail.

## Formation of the rich peasantry

Samir Amin (1974: 366-7) has identified four conditions under which a 'rural bourgeoisie of modern planters' has come into being quickly in Black Africa. Given the existing limitations of social research in Papua New Guinea,[6] the factors suggested by Amin, with slight variations, may clarify the rise of the rich peasantry.

The first is the existence of a traditional society organized in a sufficiently hierarchical way so that certain strata of the old leadership possess enough social power to appropriate substantial tracts of tribal land. The acquisition of freehold ownership of land is an important further step, or rather series of steps, which will be considered below. In Vunamami, for example, 'the first planters were the heads of the main clans, with pre-eminent claims to land and great involvement in politics, ceremonial, and trading'. With continuing labour shortages for the processing of copra, 'the usufructary rights gradually became securer tenure until, by 1961, the delegation of control to the current (or last) user was virtually complete' (Salisbury, 1970: 123). The old cultural system helped certain leaders to control developmental resources in general, a factor of great importance in societies with but a limited acceptance of the institution of individual land ownership. Among the Tolai in the 1960s there was a trend away from corporate towards individual ownership of such property as trucks, shops, and copra driers (T.S. Epstein, 1968: 70). Labour was of course not the least of such resources, and important men in Goroka were able to employ clansmen as cheap or even unpaid labour in the preparation of their coffee plantations (Finney, 1973: 63, 92-3). In 1974, Sinake Giregire went rather further and built the Gire Coffee Factory in the Asaro Valley with, as it was reported, a lot of unpaid labour (*Post Courier*, 11 September 1974). Individual access to limited capital often worked in similar ways; in the pooling of savings for investment, for example, the resulting enterprises 'were usually under the control of one or two leaders, not the whole group' (Finney, 1973: 77). The ability to mobilize the resources of clansmen and other followers in order to establish private rural enterprises is a

109

general characteristic of the Gorokan peasant leader (Finney, 1973: 101).[7] Both coffee and cattle projects are 'overwhelmingly individual or father-son projects', and there is generally 'an increased tendency towards individualism at the expense of communalism' (Gerritsen, 1975: 38, 12).

Amin's second condition is population density, which should not be so low as to make individual appropriation of land ineffective because of inadequate supplies of wage labour, nor so high as to make it difficult for traditional leaders to appropriate sufficient land. A more flexible and general condition, however, is the availability and suitability to an area of rich crops or products such as cocoa and coffee. The cultivation of these two crops has similarities and both possess the particular advantage that while trees begin to bear after only three to four years they continue to yield for at least twenty-five years. When cocoa first became available as a cash crop among the Tolai, in 1949, its acceptance was soon encouraged in the Vunamami area by Enos Teve, paramount *luluai* and local government council president, and early growers were mostly 'landed and progressive older men'. The growers were active politically in the Vunamami Council, and obtained a loan from the Council to establish a small cocoa fermentary in 1952 (Salisbury, 1970: 135, 140). The establishment of the Tolai Cocoa Project soon followed, and represented 'the first really large-scale enterprise undertaken by Tolai'. At this time, 'participation in economic ventures became more widespread and', simultaneously, 'capital formation more concentrated in the hands of a few' (T.S. Epstein, 1968: 50, 53). The situation when coffee became available to the peasantry in Goroka has been described as follows:

> The Gorokans had land to spare — not all was necessary for subsistence, and only a small proportion had been alienated; they had plenty of manpower, particularly since pacification and steel tools had reduced male labour requirements; and now they had a crop that could easily be planted, tended, harvested, and sold for a considerable profit.

The price was high enough, in fact, 'to stimulate them to grow more and more'. Not long afterwards, it was only 'the bigger growers', with money saved from previous commercial ventures, who were able to invest in the processing equipment necessary for efficient coffee production and other agricultural development (Finney, 1973: 54, 71).

Amin's fourth condition — that the political authority must favour a peasant strategy — has strong relevance to Papua New Guinea. Out of the background of frail Australian capitalism, the Australian colonial state emerged after World War II as an active, interventionist force in agricultural development. This new role coincided with the period of the 'Second Boom' in Australia (see chapter 6 above). The activities of the colonial and also the post-colonial state have recently proved decisive in consolidating the position of the rich peasantry and embryo rural capitalists, through the provision of a wide range of agricultural resources and credit facilities.

The first new moves occurred perhaps on the Gazelle Peninsula where, at the end of the 1940s, the Department of Agriculture, Stock and Fisheries (DASF) encouraged the peasantry to grow cocoa on a large scale. Whereas the Tolai had grown only a few hundred cocoa trees before the war, by 1960 they possessed almost three million. State aid also helped to ensure the production of good quality cocoa through assistance in providing credit for the establishment of the first fermentary (T.S. Epstein, 1968: 49-50). The prime beneficiaries were once more a relatively small section of the Tolai.

The role of the bureaucracy in the expansion of coffee among the peasantry in the Eastern Highlands was perhaps more spectacular. DASF undertook coffee promotion in villages around Aiyura agricultural station as early as 1949, and in 1952 an extension officer was based in Goroka (McKillop, 1976a: 3). Early DASF extension policy 'insisted on individual ownership of coffee plots',[8] and government aid, working usually in conjunction with old hierarchical values and institutions previously referred to, soon concentrated on relatively large-scale production by a few villagers (McKillop, 1975a: 4-5).[9] State agricultural policy in the early 1960s was concerned with the development of individual land tenure, and

111

aimed to produce 'a small class of purposeful elite farmers capable of responding to the opportunities opened up to them' (McKillop, 1975a: 8).

These policies were given added momentum when the Eastern Highlands district was selected for the first cattle projects at about the same time. Not only was cattle ownership also required to be on an individual basis, but official policy was to restrict projects to areas judged to have the greatest potential. The initial costs involved in cattle production exerted further selectivity among potential farmers; a first venture demanded the possession of a relatively large area of grazing land and a sizeable sum of money (some $400-$600 to establish four heifers). The capital resources that were available to certain peasant farmers were indicated by the fact that in 1964 villagers deposited $5740 with extension staff at Goroka for the purchase of cattle, a sum which by 1965 had grown to a total of $22 600. The requirements of the new commercial activity brought new consequences in their train. A fencing boom developed, encouraged by the work of land demarcation committees, and something approaching a 'land grab' resulted (McKillop, 1975a: 6, 9 and 1976a: 6). For a time, DASF extension effort was concentrated on determining land boundaries and supervising the erection of cattle fences in certain areas. Between 1967 and 1970, the area fenced for cattle in Numuyargobo increased from 71 to 1445 hectares, and in the Kainantu area some 6700 hectares were enclosed by 1975. This was not all.

> A parallel development was the emergence of pressure from DASF officials to obtain leasehold blocks for favoured proteges. Some fifteen such individuals have been assisted in obtaining, developing and stocking leasehold blocks in the Eastern Highlands ranging from 64 to 372 hectares.

The result was the restriction of cattle grazing to 'those with sufficient resources in land and capital to establish big projects in the order of 40-350 hectares' (McKillop, 1976a: 8-9).

Agricultural credit from the Papua New Guinea Development Bank, following its establishment in 1967, stressed the policy of 'lending to the man'; those who were well placed to obtain loans included big coffee-growers, local politicians and trusty, long-term government employees. Prosperous capitalist farming required access both to government-controlled agricultural resources and credit facilities, and these were highly concentrated. A farmer applicant with the potential to enclose as large an area as possible for cattle was given preference by the state, and then provided with the capital for such enclosure. Success in the various fields of capitalist agriculture in the Eastern Highlands was inter-related and cumulative. Ultimately 'those who benefited most from the coffee industry were generally those who were able to obtain large Development Bank loans for cattle and fencing materials'; on the other hand, Bank officials concede that loan applications for less than $500 are too costly to administer (McKillop, 1975a: 11-14 and 1976a: 11). The importance of the credit made available to certain peasant farmers in the Eastern Highlands is suggested by the fact that, from 1970-75, 179 cattle loans worth a total of $516 000 went to the region. The social effects of the individual credit system were also important; those who obtained loans were able to cut the obligations they had incurred to clansmen who had contributed capital and labour to their undertakings in their formative stages (McKillop, 1975a: 13 and 1976a: 11).

The inequalities which are resulting from peasant capitalism have only been partially identified, but their basic forms can nevertheless be discerned. In Rapitok on the Gazelle, in 1959, 'a clear-cut economic stratification' existed. Between 'elders' (who managed landed property and the operation of shops, copra driers, and trucks), 'middle-farmers' and 'single-men householders' there was 'a marked economic differentiation'. The economic differentiation between elders and middle-farmers in both migrant and non-migrant categories, was not 'attributable to age', but may of course have stemmed indirectly from old social privileges (T.S. Epstein, 1968: 63-4, 82). In addition, near the end of the 1960s the Gazelle Peninsula was 'experiencing some degree of land shortage' (Shand, 1969: 307), and by 1970, a 'substantial number' of Tolai were landless in the sense of having no claim to land as of matrilineal right (A.L. Epstein, 1970: 108).

In the Eastern Highlands the dominance of the rich peasantry is painfully obvious. Whereas in Goroka in the late 1960s the average coffee holding contained about 450 trees, the plantations of ten selected leading farmers averaged about 9000; in an area where per capita income was then around $25 per annum, the gross income (including rural trading activities) of these leaders averaged more than $4500 annually with several gaining well over $10 000 from coffee and other ventures (Finney, 1973: 85). The comparatively bad position of the majority of coffee growers in all districts was suggested by a survey in 1973, which showed that the average farmer had only 879 trees, on a holding of 0.2 hectares, from which an actual return (after expenses) of only $10-$15 could then be expected (McKillop, 1975b: 2). Certain Gorokan leaders, however, had become extremely rich. Sinake Giregire, for example, had gained individual ownership over about 75 acres of land, and owned some 24 000 coffee trees by the late 1960s, and Akunai Rovelie had obtained undisputed title to 25 acres and owned 18 000 trees. The rural capitalism of Hari Gotoha and Soso Subi, built mainly on trucking and food selling, and developing out of their coffee growing, together represented a value of some $100 000, around the same time (Finney, 1973: 84-107, 110-12). By 1976 Hari Gotoha had gone on to become involved in the ownership of four helicopters which operated out of Goroka under the name of Pacific Helicopters. Such men represent the appearance of rural capitalists. This category places in strongest relief the relative poverty of the mass of the peasantry in the key development areas.

## Class action by the rich peasantry

Capitalist development in Papua New Guinea is so rudimentary and pre-capitalist tedencies so strong, that class and even party politics are relatively embryonic; the Australian colonial state purposefully aimed to prevent their appearance.[10] It remains true, however, that 'it is only possible to constitute and even delimit classes ... by considering them in the historical

114

perspective of class struggle' (Poulantzas, 1973: 49). When this is considered, as well as it can be in Papua New Guinea the rich peasantry is 'increasingly self-confident', 'assertive', and 'active' (Gerritsen, 1975: 6).

The rich peasantry is active politically at local and national levels. Various farmers' and marketing organizations have been formed with the aim of gaining more resources and assistance from the state. The initial formation of such groups is often the result of the extension of important state aid and in their later survival they are something similarly dependent. When the Lowa Marketing Co-op in the Eastern Highlands faced competition from the government-owned marketing agency in 1975, the Minister for Primary Industries, Boyamo Sali, told a meeting of its directors: 'I am prepared to close the Government Fresh Food Market if the leaders here see it as a way to revive the Co-operative' (*Post-Courier*, 5 February 1976). He had earlier noted that the former Minister for Agriculture, Sir John Guise, had issued instructions restricting the activities of the Government market in Goroka in favour of Lowa (*Post-Courier*, 20 January 1976).[11] While such groups may ostensibly function in the interests of the whole rural community, their real position is different. The Lowa Marketing group, in its heyday, comprised a 'self-conscious, exclusive, big-peasant elite, seeking to arrange the production and marketing of a certain agricultural commodity in a manner serving its own interests' in competition with similar groups (Gerritsen, 1975: 10). In the Eastern Highlands generally, 'powerful interest groups with restricted membership have emerged which have taken policy stands directly opposed to the interests of the majority of village people. Two of the issues ... have been the attempts to ban the sale of coffee cherry and claims for land tenure conversion' (McKillop, 1975b: 3). There are some similarities with class conflict and rich peasant domination of coffee co-operatives in Kenya (Lamb, 1974).

These local actions have dovetailed closely with those of the rich peasantry in local government and in national politics. A number of leading Gorokans showed a high degree of involvement in local government councils and the House of Assembly at the end of the 1960s (Finney, 1973: 115-21) and, following the national elections of 1972, some 30 of 99 MHAs appeared to be of the rich peasant or rural capitalist class (Hegarty, 1972). Thereafter all Eastern Highlands MHAs, for example, '[had] little difficulty in obtaining credit for their projects' (McKillop, 1975a: 16). It is still true that 'House of Assembly elections are, in effect, contests between rival business leaders' as Finney (1973: 119) puts it. The introduction of provincial government in 1976 holds out prospects that the rich peasantry will be able to enhance its political and economic power in relation both to other rural classes and the national government. East New Britain and the Eastern Highlands were among the first few such bodies to be inaugurated. Given the stronghold that the 'big man' and ethnicity has in the rural areas, and the absence of strong competition in most provinces from urban educated groups, the odds must favour the rich peasantry in the struggle for control of this new tier of power and privilege.

The rich peasantry has shown a consciousness of its position and a readiness to act in relation to the key resources of land and labour. The demand for the demarcation of land has been strongest in areas of high population density where cash-crop production has been intensive (Howlett, 1973a: 123; Bredmeyer, 1975: 273); on the Gazelle, for example, the demarcation committees 'functioned well and were keenly valued by the land-owners' (Bredmeyer, 1975: 273). Moves towards increased individual control over land have occurred in the Eastern and Western Highlands, as already suggested above. The requirements of cattle production demanded the fencing of large areas of land, and this was followed by the leasing of substantial tracts to selected individuals; in addition a significant amount of land has been sold at high prices (see note 1) in an informal but nonetheless relatively conclusive manner.

Thus there are strong pressures for individual ownership of land in key areas. It is significant that prominent Eastern Highlanders have recently proposed changing existing laws which give traditional owners the right to stop the sale of land; as James Yanepa, Premier of the interim provincial government said, they 'hinder the more active people who wish to be involved in business' (*Post-Courier*, 9 November 1976).[12] Similarly, a report on the East New Britain Province has stressed the problems of land availability in the region and suggested more stringent action to release unused and unimproved land for sale (*Post-Courier*, 19 April 1977). These proposals are themselves a reflection of the underlying transformation where, in the words of a former consultant on land matters to the Papua New Guinea government, 'in many places villages are themselves modifying the traditional distribution of rights, usually for the purposes of gaining more secure tenure for cash cropping, and for certain rights of succession for their children' (letter to the editor from Alan Ward, *Post-Courier*, 22 February 1977). It would seem as difficult to reverse this movement to individual land ownership (assuming for a moment that the national government wished to do so) as it is relatively easy for the rich peasantry to continue to profit most from it.

The position of the rich peasantry in relation to rural workers is unclear but strongly suggestive. Both Akunai and Sinake, as employers of labour, have appeared before rural wages boards to argue against increases in rural wages (Gerritsen, 1975: 46). The latter, when leader of the Country Party, declared that high workers' wages and conditions were deterring investment, and that rural development was impossible unless the government gave active encouragement to foreign and national businesses (*Post-Courier*, 12 March 1976).[13] There is much evidence to suggest that existing conditions for rural workers are bad and that breaches of rural minimum wages laws are not infrequent (see chapter 10 below). For example, only the most successful farmers around Madang employed labourers on their coconut and cocoa plantations at the end of the 1960s, and they paid them very low wages; several received 'only $36 p.a. plus access to land for gardens and occasional extra gifts' (Morauta, 1974: 55). The problem becomes more acute as national growers and nationally-owned plantations become considerable employers of labour. For example, the Bena Development Corporation of the Eastern

Highlands (in which the local MHA, Akepa Miakwe, is an influential figure) employs a labour force of about 200 people, rising to 1200 at the height of the coffee season (*Post-Courier*, 29 March 1977).

## The dependency of the rich peasantry

The entrepreneurial and innovative qualities of the rich peasant have been celebrated in many writings on Third World economics and sociology, but in point of fact in most cases — Papua New Guinea included — these characteristics are present, if at all, only to a very limited extent.

This rich peasantry and rural bourgeoisie appears as the quintessential product of colonial agricultural capitalism, of the system of raw materials exports which is the basis of Papua New Guinea's dependency. The class has not merely benefited passively from the system, but has actively collaborated in its establishment. The widely observed but rather misunderstood fact that the big peasantry invests in trading activities, not in manufacturing industry (for example, T. S. Epstein, 1968: 52), underlines its position within a dependent economy. Unlike the mass of the peasantry, however, this class does comparatively well out of agricultural capitalism precisely through the exploitation of its fellow countrymen. Its so-called innovations represent its services to world capitalism, its own profits, and Papua New Guinea's continuing dependency. National industrialization is beyond the capacity of such a class, but to the class itself a dependent situation is acceptable so long as its pre-eminent position in its domain is not threatened.

The negative attitudes of the Highlands rich peasantry towards self-government and independence are well known (e.g. Finney: 161-2). Few Tolai sought independence in 1968, and even men who were more critical of the colonial status quo, such as Epineri Titumur and Oscar Tammur, limited their campaign to calls for greater autonomy and political education (A. L. Epstein, 1970: 113-16). Significantly, some Madang councillors in 1969 regarded 'the withdrawal of Australian support as synonymous with acute poverty and anarchy'

118

(Morauta, 1974: 91). The latter view seems a fairly explicit recognition both of conflicting interests with the poorer peasantry and external dependency. The rich peasantry seems heavily committed against internal social and economic change. Large European coffee interests in Goroka, beginning around 1962, promoted certain rising rich peasants like Sinake in order to strengthen the opposition against any moves to alter the large plantation system (Finney, 1973: 167-9). The former leader of the Country Party has been the only indigenous voting member on the Highlands Commodity Exchange,[14] and he has extended explicit support to colonial agricultural interests: 'Plantations, which have been criticised', he has said, 'have done a lot of hard work. I do not want Papuans and New Guineans to oppose the planters' (quoted by Woolford, 1973: 60).

It has been suggested that land-population ratios place strict limits on cash crop expansion in the Highlands, and that therefore rich peasantry faces the prospect of 'terminal development' (Howlett, 1973b; Gerritsen, 1975). It is true that the amount of arable land is relatively small, perhaps only 12 per cent nationally (Barnett, 1976), and that the population is growing at a rate of around 3 per cent. But this does not necessitate arrested development for the bigger producers of coffee and cocoa. They are continually seeking ways to separate smaller producers from their land, as has already been indicated — to reduce them to labourers or push them into the urban areas — in order to continue their rise to greater wealth and power. So-called terminal development is consistent with the whole trajectory of colonial and neocolonial agricultural capitalism, which results not in the impoverishment of rural society *in toto*, but in deepening differentiation within the peasantry; there is no necessary end-stage to this process. The intensive production of coffee in the Eastern Highlands has brought riches to the few and 'frustration and disillusionment' to the majority (McKillop, 1976: 4). And inequalities and frustrations will increase much further, since in the Highlands some evidence suggests that the average age of coffee growers is increasing, perhaps because of a lack of access to land and other vital resources (statement by government official at UPNG seminar, 6 April 1977). The position of the rich peasantry is embedded in the system of cash-crop exports; it is, simultaneously, the productive class and leading 'traditional' social element within Papua New Guinea, and the class which stands in the way of independent development in the countryside.

The introduction of coffee production into the Chimbu, has 'not effected any structural transformation ... [it] has had the effect of partially integrating the Chimbu economy into the national economy in the role of deprived periphery. The traditional system has been in some measure impoverished' (Brookfield, 1972: 127-8). Increasing dependency in the Highlands as a whole is terribly clear. The windfall of high coffee prices today means that villagers are less willing and able to cultivate food and obliged to spend more on goods imported from abroad: in the words of Barry Holloway, then Speaker of the House of Assembly, in October 1976: 'the people in most Highlands areas have more than doubled their purchases of such items as beer, tinned fish, rice and frozen meats in the past three months'. Consequently, some 30 per cent of Highlands' children are malnourished and, in national terms (again in Holloway's words), 'the amount of money going out of PNG on luxury and replaceable food items is reaching a peak far more beyond the point of necessity than ever before' (*Post-Courier*, 20 October 1976).[15] The country's expenditure on imported foodstuffs rose from $8m in 1954 to some $23m in 1966, in which year it represented almost 50 per cent of total export income (Shand, 1969: 287); in 1973 however, food to the value of some $48m was imported (Handbook for Industrialists, 1975: A2.4).[16] All these weaknesses stem from the increasing concentration upon cash-crop production for export. They are, in human terms, the responsibility not only of the metropolitan bourgeoisie in, say, Sydney, Tokyo and New York but, more directly, of the newly rich peasantry within the country.

Inchoate, unorganized action against rich peasants is already evident in the Highlands (e.g., Gerritsen, 1975: 21), often expressed in clan warfare. Clan fighting in the Kup area of the

Chimbu has been interpreted as protest against social tensions which have grown up under colonialism (Kerpi, 1974: 1), and in Enga it is significant that there 'is little fighting outside land pressured areas' (Harris, 1976: 8). However, such situations remain open to manipulation and distortion. Unrest over land and related issues in the Chimbu, for example, is associated with leadership competition both within and between socio-political groups (Standish, 1973 and 1976), but when it appears as so-called tribal fighting it is suppressed by the state. The existence of widespread hostility to the rich peasantry is also suggested by the frequent calls from Highland leaders for the introduction of curfews and generally stiffer penalties against law-breakers, in the big fences and dogs which today guard the houses of 'business leaders', and by the introduction of the Sorcery Prevention Bill into the Assembly by an Eastern Highlands wealthy peasant in 1974. But the underlying tensions and hostilities are tending to become more overt and specific. Coffee stealing occurs in the Eastern Highlands with increasing frequency. In the words of the manager of the Asaro Estates, 'villagers walk on to coffee plantations in broad daylight and steal the coffee and then sell it on the road'. Akepa Miakwe too has voiced the concern of the large growers, and interim Premier James Yanepa firmly declared that 'the answer to all these problems is that the police must be tougher and the penalties must be higher' (*Post-Courier*, 27 April 1977: 1). Clearly no end is in sight to this underground war.[17]

The rich peasantry depend on external sources for their prosperity and their protection. The new, active element in this relationship is the post-colonial state, especially the educated petty bourgeoisie within it. Whether the independent state will continue to extend wide-ranging support to the rich peasantry is a crucial issue. No prosecution of a national 'businessman' for infringements of minimum wages legislation has occurred yet, and the state has refrained from entering (or voluntarily withdrawn from) certain activities in favour of rural producers and traders.[18] At the same time, the educated petty bourgeoisie have much the greater understanding of the outside world and strategic control, and some rich peasants are aware of their

121

relative weakness.[19] The new administrative bourgeoisie has a limited but real freedom to choose national policy, and the situation within the country is sufficiently critical to require new initiatives. Strategies such as an all-out exploitation of minerals and water resources, or efforts to achieve self-sufficiency in food, are open to the educated petty bourgeoisie and are under discussion. The former Minister for Primary Industry, Boyamo Sali, has referred to 'a tendency during the recent years for some people to play down the importance of agriculture in the overall development of the country' (*Post-Courier*, 7 October 1976), and the former Governor-General, Sir John Guise, has repeatedly called for top priority to be given to agriculture, with 'self-sufficiency in food' as the 'basic aim'; as Minister for Agriculture he had advocated drastic action to replace food imports (*Post-Courier*, 20 October 1975; 22 July 1975). Future uncertainties therefore face the rich peasantry, though much remains on their side. Moves to increase food production could be to the advantage of the richest peasantry if costly, mechanized processes were chosen for the production of such commodities as poultry, sugar, rice, and beef; on past and present experience, this may occur (McKillop, 1975a: 17). But their fundamental strength is simply their dominant and integrated position within village society and agricultural capitalism.

# 10
# The formation of the working class

## Kenneth Good and Peter Fitzpatrick*

The formation of the working class in Papua New Guinea is at present at a preliminary and indeed critical stage. The basic reasons are to be found in the longevity of the indentured system of labour and the weight of agricultural capitalism in the country. This encouraged the growth of a fragmented, unskilled, impermanent and largely rural work force, and when more permanent, skilled and urban categories began to emerge with the developments of the 1960s, specific new controls were already to hand to contain the class politically. Despite this some relatively strong unions have appeared in the main centres and some notable action has taken place there. However the absence of industrialization and concentration on enclave projects are likely to restrict the further development of the working class, and the unions face the hostility of the rich peasantry and the veiled but growing opposition of the state.

### Indentured labour: the first system of control

The indentured system has been basic to the supply and growth of wage labour in Papua New Guinea. It was used to help tie Papua New Guinean societies into the colonial economy in such a way as to ensure and maintain a supply of cheap labour.

---

*Part of this chapter is based upon Peter Fitzpatrick, ' "Really Rather Like Slavery": Law and Labour in the Colonial Economy of Papua New Guinea', in E.L.Wheelwright and Ken Buckley (eds), *Essays in the Political Economy of Australian Capitalism*, vol 3. Sydney: Australia and New Zealand Book Company, 1978.

It was inherited from Germany in New Guinea and from Britain in Papua; Australia did not make any basic changes in the legal structure or the operations of the system, but it initially modified its workings in the interests of the planters (Salisbury, 1970: 40; Legge, 1956: 156-7). There were three main aspects to the system of indentured labour. Firstly, it recognized that the colonized people had to be forced to work for the colonizers; Papua New Guineans usually preferred village life to work on plantations or at mining sites. Secondly, 'the gesture at justice' (Rowley, 1971: 66) comprised measures that purported to protect the worker and to assure his welfare. In the well-known terms of the Covenant of the League of Nations, 'the well-being and development of such peoples form a sacred trust of civilization'. Labour laws in Papua and in New Guinea made provision for such things as maximum hours of work, minimum wages, health, diet and accommodation standards. The laws also provided for the protection of workers against fraud and cruelty on the part of employers and labour recruiters, and required the repatriation of the worker after some three or four years in employment. Limitations were sometimes imposed to prevent over-recruiting of workers from particular areas. Thirdly, there was the conscious relegation of the Papua New Guinean worker to the position of unskilled labourer almost in perpetuity. Lieutenant-Governor Murray said, in 1912, that Australia would 'succeed in our solution to the native problem, by preserving the Papuan and raising him eventually to the highest civilization of which he is capable'; the civilizing influence would be provided, not by schools, but through work on the 'plantation and the mining field' (quoted in Jinks et al, 1973: 118).

The labour force on plantations in German New Guinea grew from 869 in 1890 to 17 529 in 1914 with labour being drawn from a very wide area. The number of indentured labourers rose in the inter-war years, generally in production of copra for export; between 1923 and 1940 the indentured labour force rose some 60 per cent to reach a peak of 41 899 workers in 1938. Within the period, however, there was a big increase in the work force 1932-37, due to the development of the

Bulolo gold fields. The breakdown of the labour force on an average over the years 1937-40 showed some 5 per cent employed in the colonial administration, 10 per cent in domestic service, 17 per cent variously in shipping, commerce or industry, 18 per cent in mining, and 50 per cent on plantations (quoted in Curtain, 1977: 1-2 and Table 1). In Papua the work force, reflecting the region's lower levels of development, was consistently far smaller. A total of some 9700 labourers were under indenture in the relatively prosperous mid-1920s, only some 6000 in the mid-1930s and still less than 10 000 in the years preceding World War II (quoted in Mair, 1970: 176).[1]

Within the indentured system, breaches of the labour laws by employers were in fact flagrant, widespread and usually uncorrected; in the early days of Australian rule, labour-related atrocities were common (Nelson, 1976: 146-52, 214-17; Willis, 1974: 70-1). The system was such that the use or threat of violence represented 'the basic labour incentive' (Rowley, 1958: 115), sometimes rubbed in by the fact that the death rate among labourers in the early period, especially on the goldfields, was frequently extremely high (mainly due to inadequate dietary standards).[2] Oppressive practices have continued. Breaches of the minimum wage provisions have in recent times been common in the Highlands and in rural areas generally (Brookfield, 1961: 306; Isaac Report, 1970: 24).[3] Officially recorded complaints by workers that could warrant prosecution run into hundreds and sometimes thousands each year, but prosecutions of employers are few.[4]

The plantation itself (and to a lesser extent the mine) was a 'total institution' — a 'small state' — with the employer as ruler (Beckford, 1972: 19). The worker was dependent on the employer for the basics of life, and only participated in the wider economy through the employer and his trade store; this position was emphasized in laws which said that while indentured the worker could not enter into any other contract apart from his contract of employment. The indentured labourer was subject to a range of criminal penalties and it was for some time an offence for a worker 'to create or foster a bad influence among his fellow workers'. As Lieutenant-Governor

Murray of Papua said (1931: 9), to this extent the system was 'really rather like slavery'.

The practice of the system is vividly reflected in the colonized people's response to it. Usually they chose not to sign on again after a period under indenture and, on the available figures, at least 4 per cent of the indentured workforce 'deserted' each year.[5] Desertion is particularly significant, for there were many pressures on the labourer to stay: as well as the standard criminal sanctions against desertion, the deserter stood to lose his deferred pay, and the half of his wages accumulated by the employer for payment on expiry of the indenture; he would usually find himself in a strange and hostile area and, even if he got home, he could be in trouble with the village leader who perhaps had helped to recruit him in the first place. And there would still be the economic pressure of the 'native tax' forcing him to return or to find work elsewhere.

## Maintaining backwardness and the labour supply

In the perspective of dependency theories, the advance of the capitalist economy 'partly derives from the extraction of cheap factors of production from the ['traditional' sector] thereby maintaining its backwardness' (Bernstein and Pitt, 1974: 516). More particularly, colonialism of the variety experienced in Papua New Guinea involves 'using the economic basis characteristic of lineage society to establish the conditions of transition to capitalism' (Dupré and Rey, 1973: 147). But the transition is ambiguous for, as Bettelheim (1972: 298) puts it, 'the main tendency is not to dissolution of the non-capitalist modes of production but to their *conservation-dissolution*'. Indeed capitalism has 'imparted a certain solidity' to 'traditional' society (Banaji, 1973: 395). Meillassoux (1972: 102) sees the supply of labour as the reason for conserving pre-capitalist society, and this emphasis accords with part of the reality in Papua New Guinea: 'The agricultural self-sustaining communities' form 'an organic component of capitalist production', performing the 'functions of social security' that capitalism avoids in the colonial situation. The worker's wage

126

is enough for his sustenance while working, and for family tax, and there is sometimes a small savings component to encourage further recruits; village society continues to support the worker's family and the worker himself when he is not under indenture, and in other ways bears the costs of maintaining the supply of labour.

The introduction of time-saving technologies in the period of initial trade and later under colonialism, as well as the reduction in warfare, helped the village to accommodate to the absence of men under indenture (Lawrence, 1964: 228). Indenture built itself upon the conservation of so-called traditional society. Although restrictions on recruiting were not always enforced, the repatriation laws were closely administered — in fact employers constantly complained about them. The tendency of workers not to sign on for a further period, combined with the application of these conservation-oriented laws, had the effect of pushing the 'labour frontier' further and further back (Brookfield with Hart, 1971: 264). Other important aspects of the labour laws can be explained in terms of conservation[6] and it is in this light that the basis for the Australian ideology of 'sacred trust' becomes clearer.

Australian colonialism in Papua New Guinea was able to build on and solidify particular aspects of pre-capitalist society that helped in supplying labour. This was done through using existing patterns of authority in Papua New Guinean societies. Labour recruiters used village leaders to put pressure on young men to sign on; for this purpose a bonus was paid, and some leaders became wealthy in the process (Rowley, 1958: 124-5; Mair, 1970: 193-4). Village authority also lent itself to the maintenance of the labour contract for, as already noted, the returning deserter could incur the displeasure of the *luluai* or other leader who had helped to recruit him. This factor further explains the worker's dependence and isolation and why he served out his contract. Other measures helped maintain both the labour supply and relative socio-economic backwardness. Taxation created a need for cash and forced people into wage labour. Before World War II, Australian colonialism (in contrast to that of Germany) discouraged cash-crop production and processing among New Guineans, and thus restricted an alternative source of money to pay the tax — cash-cropping was of course greatly preferred to indentured labour. Similar considerations lay behind the provision for a time of a legal maximum wage (ten shillings a month) in New Guinea, since a higher wage would have enabled more people to pay the tax and decreased the pressure on them to seek wage labour.

Expropriation of land was in general also strictly controlled, with the aim of preserving pre-capitalist society as a supplier of labour. For the towns, a detailed system of laws dealing with curfews, migration, vagrancy, residence location, and recreation was used to restrict severely the extent to which Papua New Guineans could stay and associate together in towns (e.g. Jackson et al, 1976). The repatriation of workers was thereby facilitated, village society maintained, and the formation of a working class inhibited. All these policies were grounded in Australia's weak position in Papua New Guinea, a weakness which was aggravated by the ever-receding labour frontier and the wide dispersion of the capitalist economy (Brookfield, 1972: 51-2).

Given the many barriers against class formation and action, the Rabaul strike of 1929 was a significant event. This was a 'peaceful and purposeful' strike (Gammage, 1975: 23) of almost all New Guinean workers in the town (including the police) and so effectively organized that no white resident knew of it until it happened. Since the Australian colonialist, with some accuracy, perceived his position as weak and precarious,[7] the response to the strike was fearful and furious (Gammage, 1975: 25-8). The *Rabaul Times* declared that 'the alarming thing is that the matter was well organized' (quoted in Woolford, 1974: 15).[8]

The system of wage labour and other key aspects of the colonial political economy were designed to counter organization by the colonized people outside the 'traditional' context and independent of colonialism. The specific aims in preserving pre-capitalist societies included preventing detribalization and the creation of a landless proletariat.[9] The adaptation of the main political structures was closely related to the development

128

of the colonial capitalist economy. For most of the colonial period, development was limited to plantations and mining and this in itself made the formation of a permanent and skilled wage-labour force of any size impossible; and colonialism stood ready to suppress (but did not prevent) all attempts towards class action from within the indentured system.

## The emergence of 'free' labour and the quasi-indentured system

To be an effective means of containment and control, the indentured system had to cover all or almost all employees. But the state did allow some very limited exceptions — for employment near the worker's home or for short periods of employment. Through these exceptions a non-indentured or 'free' labour force emerged, and the exceptions themselves were progressively widened. With Australia's increasing economic intervention from the 1950s onwards, the indentured system could no longer meet the demand for labour (Radi, 1971: 132).[10] It was also inconsistent with investment in more diversified economic activities which required a more permanent and skilled work force. The non-indentured work force grew fairly rapidly and by around 1950 a 'free' labour force had emerged which, as the *Review of Native Labour Legislation* said, was 'forced to rely on the European for existence' (quoted in Gregory, 1975: 2). This dovetailed neatly with the partial abolition of the indentured system at the end of 1950.[11]

However, the formation of the working class remained a slow and gradual process, for at this stage some 33 per cent of the total work force was still under indenture (*Cochrane Report*, 1970: 33), and the abolition of indenture and its replacement by the 'agreement system' amounted to little more than a change in name. While most of the penal provisions were repealed, the basic structures remained (especially repatriation provisions), and to a considerable extent (at least initially) the system 'survived by bluff' (Rowley, 1965: 106).[12] Officials would act as if the penal provisions still existed; and the worker, not having heard otherwise, would usually fall into line. Alternative sanctions were then introduced, where the employer could apply to have 'damages' paid out of the worker's deferred pay for such offences as being absent from work for more than seven days and 'exerting a bad influence on his fellow workers'.

The formal abolition of the indentured system was accompanied by the opening of the Highlands Labour Scheme, thereby offsetting any dangers to the colonial political economy from changes in the composition of the work force. The Highlands Labour Scheme was a massive recruiting operation run by the state; while its formal start was not until the end of 1951, it began on a trial basis two years earlier (Collins, 1974: 1-24). By the time the old-style indentured system was abolished in 1950, 14 per cent of the 'agreement' work force was being supplied through the Highlands Labour Scheme; by 1965 the proportion had grown to more than half (*Cochrane Report*, 1970: 33).

The 'free' or non-indentured labour force increased from 33 927 in 1950 to 41 746 in 1960 and reached 93 771 in 1968. Labour laws were changed in 1958 in order to broaden the exceptions under which employment could be entered into outside indenture. The number of indentured workers peaked in 1960 and thereafter gradually declined (*Cochrane Report*, 1970: 33). On 28 March 1963 all restrictions on entering into employment outside the indentured system were abolished. On the same day, new methods of controlling labour came into effect — the trade union and industrial relations legislation.

## The modern controls: trade union and industrial relations legislation

The first Papua New Guinean trade union was an organization of workers based in Port Moresby and founded in 1960; it emerged out of an ethnic welfare association set up in 1958. Both bodies had political as well as economic aims and to a limited extent they asserted both. Paul Hasluck, the Australian Minister for Territories, was quick to provide assistance for the union in pressing its economic claims (Kiki, 1968: 97-9, and

1970: 616). As a result the union was instrumental in obtaining in 1960 a doubling of the minimum wage in certain urban areas. In the same year a union based in Madang was formed, also out of an earlier ethnic and welfare association (Stevenson, 1968: 14). Soon after, unions were organized in Lae and Rabaul, and in the next few years several more appeared in other urban areas.

Of the first two unions the colonial administration said that 'special attention is being given to such organisations to ensure that they are founded on sound principles and develop along constructive lines ...' (*New Guinea Report*, 1960-61: 118). Until these organizations appeared, official ideology had declared that the time was not ripe for trade unions because workers would be unable to organize them, and state 'protection' of the worker would have to continue (*New Guinea Report*, 1958-59: 101). On 15 August 1961, however, Hasluck announced a major change in colonial policy. He said that 'new labour measures' would be introduced which would be particularly concerned with an emerging group of 'urban workers'. The changes explicitly anticipated the accelerated capitalist development of the 1960s.[13] Hasluck instanced co-operatives and local government councils as indicating that Papua New Guineans could rely upon colonial officials 'to give impartial and disinterested counsel and guidance to those wishing to form a trade union, and to arrange for the training on accepted lines of their union officers'.[14] He described the measures themselves as being 'the minimum necessary' and as leaving 'as much room as possible' for Papua New Guineans to work things out in their own way (*Parliamentary Debates*, House of Representatives, 15 August 1961: 11-15). Dr John Gunther, the Deputy Administrator, in introducing the new measures to the colonial legislature, added directly that registration as an 'industrial organisation' would be compulsory because of the 'relatively greater degree of supervision and perhaps assistance' trade unions would need and because without this compulsion there would be 'a strong likelihood' of unions being used 'for purposes which were basically non-industrial, perhaps subversive' (*Legislative Council Debates*, 1961: 220-32).

The new industrial legislation provided the state with wide-ranging controls over trade union organization and action. Affiliation with political parties was obliquely but effectively prohibited, expenditure for political purposes was forbidden, and strikes by organized workers were prohibited in effect, if not in clear terms.[15] The industrial organizations law makes it an offence for any person to manage or act for an unregistered union. The Registrar of Industrial Organizations has wide powers of supervision and control over registered unions, and in their internal ordering trade unions are subjected to a system of complex and detailed legal rules.

The actual operation of the legislation followed and refined its general orientation. Under the guise of the new policy 'to facilitate the growth of industrial organisations' (*New Guinea Report*, 1960-61: 109), colonial officials became closely involved in the affairs of trade unions, sometimes going to great lengths to sustain trade union organization. The colonial state clearly intended that trade unions would integrate organized workers into a controlled system of 'industrial relations'. A former head of the Department of Labour has said that the colonial administration could not wait for unions to develop 'entirely from below' because opposing political views could otherwise gain a foothold, and another former head has said that his aim was to create 'tame-cat' unions (Worsley, 1966: 41, 60-1; Paterson, 1969: 28; and personal communication). Observers find the system introduced in the early 1960s restrictive and repressive; the legislation and its application existed to smother and hinder working class organization and, more especially, action (Martin, 1969: 159-61; Seddon, 1975: 103). The colonial trade union and industrial relations laws continue to apply within an independent Papua New Guinea and there appears to be no substantial move afoot to liberalize them.[16]

## Position of the working class today within underdeveloped capitalism

The enumerated wage- and salary-earning indigenous work force has been in decline, despite an overall population growth rate of some 3 per cent, since it reached a peak of 124 585 in 1970 (representing some 5 per cent of total population). The comparable figure in 1971 was 124 143, in 1972 it was 120 014, in 1973 it was 118 482, and in 1974, 118 523, showing no change over the previous year (this constituted some 4.5 per cent of total population). The rural work force also declined, from 49 510 in 1970, to 33 003 in 1973, and 35 325 in 1974, while in manufacturing only slight growth was detectable with a work force of 9179 in 1970, 9568 in 1971, 10 121 in 1972, 9438 in 1973, and 10 497 in 1974 (*Labour Information Bulletin*, 14 February 1976).[17]

The situation by the late 1960s, of a labour force which was heavily dominated numerically by unskilled workers (Martin, 1969: 137), appears to have changed very little. There is an 'almost total absence of handicraft workers and small-scale traders, shopkeepers, and service-repair establishments that provide such a large volume of employment, especially urban, in many other countries' (World Bank, 1976: 19). The 'agreement' or quasi-indentured system still lingers on, although most of the repressive controls regulating migration to and residence and association in towns were abolished in the 1960s. And this is a work force of which a significant and growing number are salaried personnel — senior bureaucrats, managers, teachers and others. The problems represented by the dearth of skilled manual workers are compounded by the formation of an educated petty bourgeoisie, and opportunities exist for this new social category to exercise political domination over the unskilled manual working class.

The working class is also seriously handicapped by specific features of underdevelopment. There is, for example, 'little evidence of a national labour market, except to Port Moresby', and a large part of the work force has 'no total dependence on wage income' (Wright, Garnaut, and Curtain, 1975: 2). It is also a highly dispersed work force. The major concentrations of indigenous wage and salaried workers, in 1972, were as follows: Eastern Highlands 7.2 per cent; Bougainville 8.2 per cent; East New Britain 12.1 per cent; Lae 5.4 per cent; and Port Moresby 15.9 per cent (*Summary of Statistics*, 1973-74:

52-3). Even where workers are gathered in some numbers they tend not to be concentrated in their actual work place. The widely scattered islands of wage labour represented by some 1000 plantations have been referred to already; in addition, of the 4529 urban and rural establishments in Papua New Guinea, as of 30 June 1973, only 214, or less than 5 per cent of all establishments, contained more than 100 employees, and more than 50 per cent of all working places had only one to ten workers. Communications among the work force are still further reduced by the complete absence of railways and the poverty of the road system — no road links exist between the two main towns, Port Moresby and Lae, where some 50 per cent of all urban workers are located. The working class of the main centres, furthermore, is not only separate but different from the work force nationally, because 'the urban populations of Papua New Guinea are very dependent on wage income' (Wright *et al*, 1975: 2).

Finally, the weak position of the working class in Papua New Guinea is directly attributable to the types of foreign investment attracted to the country. Between 1969 and 1974 more than 75 per cent of total overseas investment was in mining and quarrying. Most of this was accounted for by Bougainville Copper developments, yet the mine today employs less than 4 per cent of the total wage- and salary-earning work force. In addition, the wholesale and retail trades, restaurants, hotels, finance, insurance and real estate attracted more foreign investment than manufacturing. The attractiveness of these non-industrial categories is clear from the fact that in 1973 more than 51 per cent of total taxable income accrued to companies in the finance, property and commerce sectors. Of the total companies (other than finance companies) registered in Papua New Guinea in 1974, 63.4 per cent of the foreign companies and 74.7 per cent of the local companies claimed commerce as their primary activity. Agriculture was dominant for only 2.6 per cent and 13.6 per cent respectively, and industry for 11.4 and 10.0 per cent (*Summary of Statistics*, 1973-74: 36, 126 and 165).

The overall situation is thus of a working class that is small numerically, weak in skills, and dispersed in a number of regional and urban locations. Serious barriers to class formation and action clearly exist.

## Trade union organization

An assessment of the trade unions in Papua New Guinea must not only take into account the weakness of the working class but also the absence of party organization and the dominance of the state within the political economy — it is the *relative strengths* and *potentialities* of the unions which are important.

Total union membership almost quadrupled between 1963 and 1967 (Martin, 1969: 142); there was a 'striking increase' from 17 900 to 32 300 between December 1969 and June 1972, mainly based upon the resurgence of the Port Moresby and Lae unions (Clunies Ross & Langmore, 1973: 169) and, during a period when the total work force was in decline, trade union membership rose to 40 220 in June 1974 (*Labour Information Bulletin No. 9*, n.d.: Table 3.1). Unionization, therefore, had grown from some 13 per cent of the total work force in 1967 to some 30 per cent in 1974. These gross gains, however, disguised many significant weaknesses. Individual unions commonly experienced massive fluctuations in membership; the Lae Miscellaneous Workers Union, for example, recorded 300 members in 1971, 30 in 1972, 2347 in 1973, and 440 a year later; and, with the exception of the Public Service Association and the Teachers and Police Associations, no union has been able to maintain a membership in excess of 1000 (Lepani, 1976b: Table 1). Beset by financial difficulties, with ethnic splits, part-time committee members and thus ineffective organizations, many unions exist merely in name (personal communication from employee of Department of Labour, 29 October 1976). There is still a shortage of experienced union leaders (Martin, 1969: 138); the government's establishment of the Bureau of Industrial Organizations in March 1972, as an element detached from the Department of Labour, has done something to correct this — along the established welfare line.

The main unions of state and semi-state employees — the

135

# Registered industrial organizations

| Organizations | Registration | 1970 | 1971 | 1972 | 1973 | 1974 |
|---|---|---|---|---|---|---|
| Lae Miscellaneous Workers Union | 28-8-63 | 300 | 300 | 30 | 2347 | 440 |
| Madang District Workers Association | 27-8-63 | 207 | 207 | 207 | 130 | 130 |
| Rabaul Workers Association | 27-8-63 | 408 | 408 | 408 | 49 | 350 |
| Public Service Association of PNG | 17-1-64 | 13114 | 16851 | 16351 | 16851 | 15885 |
| East Sepik District Workers Association (formerly Wewak Workers Association) | 26-3-64 | 55 | 55 | — | 300 | 188 |
| Port Moresby Miscellaneous Workers Union | 22-5-64 | 769 | 769 | — | 277 | 1081 |
| Timber Industry Workers Association of Wau-Bulolo | 12-6-64 | 118 | Dissolved (see Wau-Bulolo Association) | | | |
| Goroka Workers Association | 25-8-64 | 204 | — | — | 63 | 130 |
| New Ireland District Workers Association | 16-11-64 | 211 | 211 | 211 | 187 | 187 |
| Northern District Workers Association | 19-2-65 | 66 | 66 | — | 123 | 123 |
| Police Association of Papua New Guinea | 19-2-65 | 2830 | 2830 | 2830 | 2656 | 2656 |
| Western Highlands District Workers Association | 10-5-65 | 95 | 20 | 20 | 22 | 20 |
| Milne Bay District Workers Association | 18-6-65 | 290 | 290 | — | 330 | 200 |
| Local Teachers Association | 5-1-66 | 32 | Defunct | | | |
| Bank Officials Association of PNG | 16-6-67 | 187 | — | — | 205 | 205 |
| Staff Association of the University of PNG | 29-9-67 | 234 | 234 | — | 142 | 150 |
| Manus District Workers Association | 10-10-67 | 314 | — | — | 134 | 134 |
| Staff Association of The PNG Institute of Higher Technical Education | 4-1-68 | 105 | 105 | — | 52 | — |
| Abau District Workers Association | 4-3-68 | 80 | 80 | — | 163 | 350 |
| Western District Workers Association | 25-10-68 | 71 | — | — | 84 | — |
| Bougainville Catholic Teachers Association | 18-11-68 | 299 | 299 | 299 | 299 | 299 |
| Central District Building & Construction Industry Workers Union | 29-1-69 | 800 | 800 | 800 | 800 | 800 |
| Central District Waterside Workers Union | 28-1-69 | 479 | 479 | 479 | 175 | 175 |
| Senior Police Officers Guild | 10-2-69 | 30 | 30 | 35 | 39 | 49 |
| West Sepik District Workers Union | 4-7-69 | 199 | 199 | — | 110 | 209 |

# Registered industrial organizations (cont'd)

| Organizations | Registration | 1970 | 1971 | 1972 | 1973 | 1974 |
|---|---|---|---|---|---|---|
| Airline Employees Association of PNG | 4-11-69 | 38 | 388 | 388 | 38 | 160 |
| Bougainville Mining Workers Union | 12-12-69 | 171 | 228 | 228 | 800 | 800 |
| Gulf District Workers Association | 13-7-70 | 155 | — | 20 | 20 | 25 |
| Bougainville Construction & General Workers Union | 21-8-70 | 428 | — | — | 172 | 151 |
| Air Traffic Services Officers Association | 7-10-70 | 20 | 40 | 40 | 143 | 89 |
| Port Moresby Clerical Workers & Shop Assist. Union | 10-11-70 | 200 | 200 | 800 | 46 | 56 |
| Local Government Offices Association | 19-1-71 | — | 33 | Defunct | | |
| Lombrom Naval Civilian Workers Association | 19-1-71 | — | 120 | 175 | 140 | 160 |
| Kainantu Workers Association | 26-3-71 | — | 29 | 21 | 55 | 55 |
| Papua New Guinea Teachers Association | 1-4-71 | — | 5000 | 5000 | 8000 | 9869 |
| Airline Hostesses' Association of PNG | 18-5-71 | — | 31 | Defunct | | |
| Merchant Service Officers Association of PNG | 24-9-71 | — | 31 | — | 200 | 150 |
| Central District Transport Drivers & Workers Union | 30-3-71 | — | 24 | 24 | 42 | 42 |
| Papua New Guinea Nurses Association | 12-12-72 | — | — | 20 | 148 | 148 |
| Lae Stevedoring Union | 12-12-72 | — | — | 658 | 658 | 657 |
| Papua New Guinea Seamens Union | 12-12-72 | — | — | 28 | 28 | 28 |
| Madang Waterside Workers Union | 12-12-72 | — | — | 47 | 94 | 94 |
| Wau-Bulolo Workers Union | 27-12-72 | — | — | 472 | 472 | 472 |
| Port Moresby Council of Trade Unions* | 31-5-73 | — | — | — | 4 | 5 |
| Papua New Guinea Air Pilots Association | 8-8-73 | — | — | — | 100 | 100 |
| Chimbu District Workers Association | 4-1-74 | — | — | — | — | 21 |
| National Broadcasting Commission Staff Association | 24-1-74 | — | — | — | — | 100 |
| West New Britain Workers Union | 24-1-74 | — | — | — | — | 50 |
| Menoi Workers Association | 13-5-74 | — | — | — | — | 20 |
| Morobe District Rural Workers Union | 26-7-74 | — | — | — | — | 59 |
| Ukarumpa Workers Association | 11-7-74 | — | — | — | — | 50 |
| Aircraft Engineers Association of PNG | 15-10-74 | — | — | — | — | 25 |
| | | 22 509 | 30 357 | 29 591 | 36 698 | 37 147 |

*The number of registered unions which are members are of the Council

Source: Lepani, 1976

Public Service Association (PSA), Teachers Association (TA), and the Police Association — are notably free of the disabilities that plague the unions of manual workers. The Police Association, registered in 1965, has maintained a membership in excess of two and a half thousand; the Teachers Association, registered in 1971, has grown dramatically from 5000 members to 9860 over four years, and the PSA represented 15 885 members in 1974 (Lepani, 1976). The PSA, in the early 1960s, was 'the only articulate and well-organized association', and by the middle of the decade it had a majority of Papua New Guineans (Ballard, 1972: 12). It had the potential to become 'obviously the most powerful union in PNG' (Langmore, 1973: 169), and now contains approximately 40 per cent of the country's total union membership. The methods by which the Teachers Association has grown are suggestive of the good resources and close contact with the state which all these public service unions command.[18] But the bureaucracy is also in a good position to influence the policies of such unions, and through them (given their majority — some 70 per cent in 1974 — of total trade union membership) over the wider movement as well.

'Craft' or specialist unions have not developed except in Port Moresby, where building and construction workers, transport workers, clerks and shop assistants, waterside workers, and miscellaneous workers each have their separate organization as well as being linked together through a federation, the Port Moresby Council of Trade Unions. Of these five, the waterside workers are the best organized, although their membership has declined from 479 in 1970-72, to 175 subsequently. They possess an experienced secretary and organizer (Reg McAlister, who is also secretary of the Council of Trade Unions), and a nearly homogeneous membership recruited mainly from the Gulf and Western Provinces of Papua. The Port Moresby Council is in turn affiliated with the Papua New Guinean Trade Union Congress, based in Lae; this national federation is beset with financial problems, mirroring the tenuous existence of many of the manual unions affiliated with it.[19] There are only few exceptions (the Bougainville Mining Workers Union is one perhaps) to the general condition of weakness among the unions in the 'private sector'.

The situation among rural workers in primary production is worse still, despite the fact, as already noted, that they constituted in 1973 some 28 per cent of the total enumerated work force. Dispersed widely over the country, with the most limited commitment to wage labour, and with an almost total lack of communications between the various 'islands of labour', the organization of rural workers only began in 1973. Despite the encouragement of the then Minister of Labour, Commerce and Industry, Gavera Rea, and the (then) Director of the Bureau of Industrial Organizations, Charles Lepani (*Post-Courier*, 13 February and 21 March 1974), very few rural unions exist and fewer have reached a membership over a hundred.[20]

The dominance of the state — through industrial legislation, its disposable resources, its position as largest employer — within the trade union movement is paralleled and extended by the leadership position of the educated, salaried elements within the unions — both the weak manual unions and the strong public service associations. While it is true that, for example, Sir Maori Kiki, Minister for Defence, Foreign Relations and Trade, 1975-77, and Gavera Rea (both of whom are Papuans) made a large contribution to the manual unions of Port Moresby, their accession to ministerial position meant that 'trade unionists have gained political power' (Langmore, 1973: 158) only in the narrowest, individualistic sense.

Defining the boundary between the working class and the educated petty bourgeoisie is complex and in some cases critically important;[21] but what really seems to have happened in Papua New Guinea (and to be happening still) is that the better educated have profited from the organizational strengths of the unions, and their easily attained leadership positions within organizations of significant social diversity (as in the regional or area workers associations, and in the PSA which represents both manual and salaried workers), to mobilize ethnic support and move upwards to a position in the state which is in structural terms that of the petty bourgeoisie. Gavera Rea resigned as secretary of the Port Moresby Council of Trade Unions when he became a Minister, but Sir Maori Kiki remained as president of the Council. It is noteworthy that many of the early union leaders became high state officials following self-government (see Langmore, 1973; and Lepani, 1976), but the statement that 'unions have a considerable amount of sympathy and influence in the Government' (World Bank, 1976: Annex 6, 4), is only partly true as will be seen below. It is just as likely that the rise of educated union leaders into government has increased the already great influence of the state over the unions and widened the power base of the educated petty bourgeoisie in government.

## Working class action

Action by workers, both organized and unorganized, urban and rural, has taken a variety of forms in Papua New Guinea, and at times involved large numbers of people. Wages have been the key issue, and big gains were made, particularly by urban workers, in the early 1970s. Stevedores in Port Moresby have been particularly successful; the PSA has not always acted in the interests of higher-paid bureaucrats alone; and the action and reaction over the Bougainville Copper strike of May 1975 constituted an important event in the country's trade union history. These will be considered separately below.

In highly oppressive situations like that of the indentured labour system, it is not enough to concentrate upon 'the relative absence of overt industrial action aimed at securing improvements through readily identifiable organizations with articulate leadership' (van Onselen, 1973: 239).[22] The 1929 Rabaul strike, already referred to, was significant because of the level of organization briefly achieved by the workers. But this was preceded by strike action at Sudest and Woodlark and then at Samarai, and the full record of worker action for higher pay and similar matters may well be much longer and more consistent than is suggested by these better-known events (e.g. Nelson, 1976: 23, 58). Desertions and go-slows also occurred frequently over long periods, and given the big barriers which workers faced — very heavy penalties, distance from home, the tax obligation, etc. — they should be seen as a form of combination, a reflex action to the system, and an indication of worker consciousness (van Onselen, 1973). The widespread cargo-cult activities may at times have deserved a similar interpretation. They are inchoate but meaningful forms of class action by workers in the early stages of the development of agricultural and mining capitalism. In Papua New Guinea such conditions and actions persisted until well after World War II.

Given more rapid development, it is not surprising that strikes increased and that they occurred with greatest intensity where economic activity was concentrated, in Port Moresby. While work stoppages nationally over the period from 1959-68 were both 'more frequent and more severe', the national capital, in late 1965, experienced a 'strike wave', during which membership in the then Port Moresby Workers Association rose at the rate of 150 or more a week (Martin, 1969: 164-5). In the early 1970s, stevedores in all centres were among 'the most active unionists', and building and construction workers were also particularly inclined to strike (Langmore, 1973: 169-71). In 1972, some 16 per cent of all trade unionists were involved in some kind of industrial dispute, and in the following year Port Moresby waterside workers took action which tied up 36 ships in the harbour for five days — perhaps the country's largest strike to that time (World Bank, 1976: Annex 6, 4).

In April 1976, the waterside workers repeated their action over a period of a week, disrupting commercial activity in the capital and beyond. Given other trade union action and government reaction at the time, it is notable that the then Minister for Labour, Commerce and Industry, Gavera Rea, only intervened openly on the fifth day of the Moresby dock strike to refer the dispute to an arbitration tribunal (*Post-Courier*, 7 April 1976: 1), and that, at the end of the year, the waterside workers' secretary, Reg McAlister, was able to refer to the great improvement in wages and conditions of service — including six months long-service leave after 15 years with the same company — won by members of the union (personal communication from Esekia Warvi, October 1976). Among the factors contributing to the success of this action were the unity and organization of the union, the strategic position of the Port Moresby docks in the economy and, not least, the important ethnic and other links between the Minister and the members of the union; they were fellow-Papuans, and the Minister's present educated petty bourgeois position owed much to the union movement. The capital experienced another large-scale strike on 22 October 1976, when the Port Moresby Council of Trade Unions effectively closed most of the retail outlets in the town for a 24-hour period, in protest against the recently announced wage freeze.

The Bougainville copper mine at Panguna represents a new and most important sector in the country's economy, or rather in the international economy as it impinges on Papua New Guinea, and it has already in its short period of operation begun to generate significant new trends in workers' action. In May 1975 Papua New Guinea's most militant strike occurred at the mine, and while its direct causes remain unclear (not having been discussed at all in the public media) both immediate and underlying factors seem to have played their part: on the one hand, the issue of alterations in differentials for skill, and on the other the remoteness of the expatriate management from the workers and, more generally, the alien nature of the enterprise within agricultural communities on the island (confidential personal communication by officer of the Bureau of Industrial Organization, May 1975).[23]

The workers' action lasted for hardly two days, but even on the first day the heavy use of police was resorted to and, shortly after, white women and children were dramatically evacuated and there were mass arrests of workers. Official statements thereafter showed no sympathy for the workers whatsoever. The Police Minister, Pita Lus, said after his return from the island that the entire incident had been disgraceful; and the Police Commissioner, Pius Kerepia, said that he felt 'deeply ashamed' of his countrymen, and he hoped 'all Papua New Guineans would learn a lesson from such stupidity' (*Post-Courier*, 19 May 1975: 1). The Chief Minister, Michael Somare, was 'shocked' by the violence and damage, and placed the blame squarely on union leaders. He would not accept their claim that the police action had made the riot worse, and said that the police had a duty to maintain law and order. Somare appeared to want to ram the message home to all workers, pledging government action to prevent industrially-inspired violence of the type which led to the riots (Office of Information newsletter, 21 May 1975). When six Bougainville Mining Workers Union officials appeared before the Supreme Court in Port Moresby on 23 May, the charges against them included the following: 'that they behaved in a threatening manner and made statements to an assembly intended to pro-mote ill-will or envy between different classes' (*Post-Courier*, 26 May 1975: 3).

The Bougainville Mining Workers Union has not been set back by the severe experiences of May 1975; indeed, perhaps the opposite. Their organization towards the end of the follow-ing year was described as strong, and they had gained a heightened appreciation of their strategic position (confidential personal communication from official of Department of Labour, 29 October 1976). A week-long seminar at Arawa, culminating in a number of radical proposals, was arranged by the union in September.[24] Statements made by certain guests and delegates further indicated that the Mining Workers Union was militant. Tony Ila, President of the Papua New Guinea Trade Union Congress (and member of the House of Assembly), said that the Congress would have to look again at the Mining Workers Union's application to join it in view of the union's declared interest in affiliation with the Communist-organized World Federation of Trade Unions. Following a statement by an Australian union delegate, Pat Clancy (who was first refused and then granted a visa by the Somare government), that capitalist countries were not the only source of help for developing countries, Ila also said he could not totally agree to what he termed socialist involvement in Papua New Guinea (*Post-Courier*, 16 September 1976: 3). Finally, the remarks of the newly appointed premier of the North Solomons Province, Dr Alexis Sarei, were in close agreement with the views of Somare of May 1975, when he, as was

143

reported, warned the delegates against striking and other forms of protest of a trivial nature as being against the common interest (*Post-Courier*, 14 September 1976: 4). The Bougainville Mining Workers Union seems, temporarily at least, to be exceptional in its organization and ideology among trade unions in Papua New Guinea.

What it does not have, of course, is the membership and resources of the PSA, a union which also holds an important position within the political economy. The actions of the PSA, given the close structural links between the association and the state and the petty bourgeois nature of part of its membership, are, not surprisingly, somewhat ambivalent. Its development through the 1960s as an umbrella organization of national public servants may well have stifled some potential leaders in that it absorbed people who otherwise would have joined manual unions and devoted their energies to strengthening these bodies (Deech, 1976: 16). But the PSA also helped other unions get started in the 1960s and early 1970s, and it advocated flat-rate across-the-board wage increases — the same for both cleaners and senior bureaucrats, say — at official hearings in 1972.

In relation to wider social and political issues, however, the PSA follows a moderate line firmly within the established system. It has condemned the plantation economy in Papua New Guinea, but has done little or nothing to improve the position of plantation workers (Deech, 1976: 13). It opposed the government's Public Order Bill in 1976, but so did the parliamentary opposition, students, and others in real fear of the limitations on freedom of expression and association which the legislation contained (*Post-Courier*, 10 August 1976: 1). According to the former General Secretary, Jacob Lemeki, the PSA had become critical of the Pangu Party in the Somare coalition government because it 'gives us very little support', but he merely concluded that public servants would be wise not to vote along party lines in future: 'Our best bet is to vote for individual members who can give us support in Parliament' (*Post-Courier*, 17 June 1976: 9).[25]

Because of the government's wage-freeze policy, introduced

under the impact of the world recession, the PSA by 1976 had become more concerned with its own members and their loss of real income, and less interested in wider association with other unions. In November 1975, it forced the government to submit the issue of wage indexation to arbitration, by threatening to go on strike, despite the fact that public servants do not have that legal right. Overall, however, PSA displays a petty bourgeois-bureaucratic (rather than a working class) consciousness; both the manual and the salaried workers it represents have a strong common interest in the preservation and expansion of the bureaucracy they work in, and the educated, salaried elements dominate the manual workers inside the union. Although its concerns, especially on wages, may at times include manual trade unions, the strong tendency is for the PSA to reflect the outlook of the educated petty bourgeoisie which controls the state.

As already suggested, there have been very good reasons for workers in Papua New Guinea to be strongly concerned with wages and conditions of employment, and not only in colonial times either. Urban minimum wages 'remained low and constant' throughout the 1960s (Langmore, 1976: 1). Thereafter, however, wages grew rapidly, increasing from K8 for the minimum weekly wage in Port Moresby in 1971 to K25.80 in 1975 (Langmore, 1976: 6), as a result of successful trade union pressure under the exceptionally favourable conditions of the transfer of political power. But, because of the country's high rate of inflation (the consumer price index rose 63 per cent between 1971 and December 1975), the increase in real wages was less than the nominal advance. The weekly minimum for plantation workers rose by 114 per cent in five years from some K4.50 in 1971 to K9.62 in January 1976, but by only some 30 per cent in real terms; and the Port Moresby urban minimum wage increased by 240 per cent nominally and by some 100 per cent in real terms (Langmore, 1976: 5).[26]

By 1976, the period of successful union action for wage increases had ended, and in the words of the World Bank, the government has 'begun to take a stronger stand against union pressure for higher wages'. Examples of the new government attitude are the hard line it took during arbitration of the wage indexation dispute in that year (the government refusing to index against the cost of living more than a small proportion of its wages bill), and the government's proposed reorganization of the country's wage-setting machinery to give greater control over the process to the state. Such opposition to union demands is in close accord with the proposal of the World Bank itself, that 'it is particularly important that the [Papua New Guinea] government remain firm in its determination to contain salary increases' (World Bank, 1976: Annex 6, 3). The state-owned Bank of Papua New Guinea has also warned against further increasing the urban minimum wage (*Post-Courier*, 17 March 1976: 1).

Given inflation, and the fact that cost of living increases apply only to a portion of total salaries, 'the people who have lost the most are those at the higher end of scales: about a third of all government workers have experienced a fairly substantial erosion of real income, with the greatest losses being experienced among senior officers whose nominal salaries have increased only 5 per cent in the past three years [till 1976] when living costs rose 46 per cent' (World Bank, 1976: 55). At the same time, occupational or skill differentials have been reduced in both public and private sectors; the ratio of the maximum pay for public officials to minimum urban earnings dropped from 12.3 to 1 in 1972, to about 6 to 1 in 1976 (World Bank, 1976: Annex 6, 3). Put another way, the minimum weekly wage of a qualified tradesman rose by 63 per cent between 1971 and 1976, while that of a public service chief of division (clerk class eleven) increased by only 31 per cent during the same period (Langmore, 1976: 5). Thus there were significant egalitarian tendencies at work within the wages structure which seemed to favour the urban manual worker at the expense of the petty bourgeois bureaucrat, but the levelling out effect was diminished by the lowering of real wages — 'anyone earning over K2,000 has experienced a decline in real income' (World Bank, 1976: Annex 6, 3).

The General Secretary of the PSA, Jacob Lemeki, told the Minimum Wages Board in April 1976 that his union's past wage claims had been restrained and reasonable, and that the PSA had done everything to limit the dispute over indexation (*Post-Courier*, 23 April 1976: 1).[27] The urban manual unions showed a far less compliant attitude on the wages issue. Some 3000 manual workers demonstrated in Port Moresby, on Saturday 10 July 1976, against the decision of the Minimum Wages Board to freeze urban wages until March 1977. The three main public service unions (PSA, Teachers and Police) did not participate in the action, although the industrial advocate of the PSA, Paul Arnold, took part and was a leading speaker. Demonstrations were also held in Madang and Daru, and a similar action, involving perhaps a thousand workers, occurred in Lae (*Post-Courier*, 12 July 1976: 1).

But the workers who have been the greatest losers are not in the towns at all but in the countryside. Urban/rural wage inequalities have been 'sharply increased' (Langmore, 1976: 5), with the urban/rural differential growing from 1.5 to 1 in 1971, to 2.4 to 1 in 1975 (World Bank, 1976: Annex 6, 3). Given the past subordination of unskilled rural workers in Papua New Guinea, and their near-total absence of organization even today, this outcome is not surprising, and any indication of a readiness for action is all the more notable for this reason. The strike among unorganized timber workers employed by the Japanese-controlled Jant Company at Gogol in the Madang Province over two or three days in late 1976 was a significant small event. The action was over claims for improvements in wages and conditions, but was also grounded in deep community dissatisfaction with the foreign-owned timber company: the destruction of the forest and bush and the food resources within them, and the low royalties accruing to the villagers (in comparison with the earnings to the company in Japan) for the loss of important resources. The strike was resolved without any concession to the workers other than agreement with their claims over company messing facilities (confidential personal communication from an officer of the Forests Division, 26 October 1976). But in the longer term, the interaction between unorganized rural workers and villagers over an issue of deep importance to the community may prove significant for the future of Jant and perhaps other foreign timber projects in the country as well.

To sum up, an assessment of working class action in Papua New Guinea must bear two things in mind: that the new class has been formed out of a long and debilitating experience (more than half a century) of subordination as an impermanent, unskilled and fragmented rural work force; and, since the early 1960s, of tight legal constraints upon trade union organization and action. Despite these heavy limitations, certain relatively strong trade unions have appeared among manual workers in the two largest towns, among wage and salary workers in the bureaucracy, and at the Bougainville Copper mine; rural workers, with almost no resources to turn to, are still largely unorganized. Action has been most sustained over issues of wages and conditions and, while big advances have been made, the unions are now facing opposition from the state to further increases.

The present situation is therefore one of potential confrontation between state and unions on a basic issue, but the direction and impact of working class action is reduced by the structural weaknesses of the working class and by the absence of political ideology within the unions. It is not by chance, but for important systemic reasons, that only the Bougainville Mining Workers Union appears interested in developing policies of wide socio-political action, and only the workers on the Port Moresby docks have experience of prolonged industrial action. The unions will not find themselves in a strong position in any situation of sustained conflict with the state.

## The working class and structural change

For the achievement of long-term structural change and Papua New Guinea's escape from dependency, the organized working class is of fundamental importance. But because of the low level of capitalist development, this process would necessarily involve collaboration with other classes. The educated petty bourgeoisie, given its small size nationally and the rapid localization of the bureaucracy, has so far been attracted upwards, sometimes on the steps of the unions, into the state; but

148

members of this important social category *could* in the future act as committed political organizers for trade unions. The mass of the peasantry, on the other hand, are those whose relationship to the means of production is most like that of the working class, and there are indications that 'a very high proportion of the urban population maintains close contact, both through visits and the transmission of goods and money, with their home villages', and that the volume of gifts which moves between the towns and villages is 'significant' (Wright *et al*, 1975: 2-3).

But these personal contacts are perhaps of smaller significance than urban/rural structural difference and the opposition of the rich peasantry. Urban/rural income inequalities have increased in recent years, as noted above. Planters and other capitalists have resisted an increase in rural wages — for example, in March 1976 the Planters' Association of New Guinea opposed any change in basic rural wages regardless of the indexation base (*Post-Courier*, 18 March 1976: 4). Sinake Giregire, archetypal rich peasant of the Eastern Highlands, blamed poor economic conditions in the rural areas on the high wages and good living conditions enjoyed by 'the ten per cent living in the towns on regular incomes', contrasted these conditions with 'the remaining ninety per cent of the people, self-employed in the villages, rely[ing] on primary industry for their small income', and opposed all wage increases to boot (see the previous chapter, and *Post-Courier*, 12 March 1976: 3). Despite the fact that real wages have been declining at the same time as the returns to rich peasant coffee producers have shot up, Giregire's kind of argument may strike a chord in the countryside and weaken the ties between urban workers and villagers, given the absence of rural trade unions and working class ideology in general.

The capacity of the working class for radical change is reduced in other ways. The Central District Waterside Workers Union, despite its record of militancy, is inclined to favour foreign investment, particularly as it provides further employment; consistent with its attitude to big companies and the union's achievements to-date, it says that 'you have to have

149

them to squeeze them' (personal communication from Uwe Lilje, 28 October 1976). Some unions have also established a limited but direct involvement in petty capitalist activities. The Central District Waterside Workers have bought shares to the value of K1000 in a new Port Moresby taxi company, Red and Yellow Taxis, and the President of the union, Daniel Hairoi, is one of the directors of the company (*Workers News*, May 1976). The Lae Miscellaneous Workers Union is also involved in taxi ownership and operation, and the PSA is selling office space in its new and very impressive headquarters building adjacent to the government office at Waigani (financed, incidentally, through loans negotiated by the business arm of the dominant party in government, Pangu).

Present development strategies favour neither the growth of the working class nor an increase in working class radicalism. Not only is there a negligible manufacturing industry, but in the view of the World Bank the present attention being given to specific industrial possibilities by the government 'seems rather weak' (World Bank, 1976: 36). The government relies heavily on the enclave pattern of development, with copper at Ok Tedi and timber at Vanimo considered as important projects for the future. The corollary of this general strategy is the importation of skilled personnel and capital from abroad, with a consequent stagnation of the local working class and the possible further incorporation of its leadership.

Whether the state will, as it were, force the unions to be far more active in encouraging the organization or rural workers is perhaps the relevant question. Opposition to the trade unions from the rich peasantry and elements of the petty bourgeoisie in government is intermittent but nonetheless real. The House of Assembly, in the latter half of 1975, defeated a bill requiring employers to deduct union fees from employees' wages — the crucial check-off system. The Director of the Bureau of Industrial Organizations, Frank Igo, described the rejection as a 'betrayal of the Papua New Guinean workers', and a Southern Highlands parliamentarian, Ron Neville, expressed anti-union ideology with some clarity when he said: 'Many workers are illiterate and would not understand why money was being deducted from their pay and where it would go' (Deech, 1976: 15). One must admit that this view, like that of Sinake Giregire above, is likely to be persuasive, especially when it is voiced by the rich peasant leader in the village.

What some unions have in their favour at the present stage of capitalist development in Papua New Guinea is, as already noted, a greater degree of organizational strength than political parties and other non-state bodies. But this limited advantage is most unlikely to be realized without the collaboration of a part of the rural population, and this in turn would be difficult to attain against the social and economic strengths of the rich peasantry in the countryside and the power of the state. The basic problem for the working class is the development of union organization in the countryside.

# 11
# A note on the formation of the educated petty bourgeoisie

The educated petty bourgeoisie was formed much more recently and rapidly than other urban and rural classes and its members have little or no control over the means of production at present. By acquiring Western education and collaborating with the colonial state they have risen to fulfil most of the functions of controllers of the independent state. They are skilled and urban, but most are drawn from coastal or island groups. They are far more knowledgeable about the outside world than are the more productive rich peasantry; they are at the same time less well-integrated into the old rural societies.

## The weakness and lateness of colonial education

The educational expert on the Permanent Mandates Commission of the League of Nations said, at the last meeting of that body, that 'she knew of no territory under mandate in which education progressed so slowly' (Mair, 1970: 225). In the 1930s there was no policy of co-operation between the state and the missions in indigenous education, and very little money was provided. Provision for education lapsed 'almost completely' during World War II, and post-war education was slower to develop than either public health or indigenous agriculture for export (Mair, 1970: 225-6). The rich peasantry was therefore earlier formed and is better integrated into the political economy than the petty bourgeoisie.

The years from 1945 to 1955 were, in the words of the

Australian Minister for Territories 1951-63, years of 'poor achievement so far as education was concerned' (Hasluck, 1976: 99). Although the missions provided little or no real education,[1] in 1951 there were in round figures over 100 000 pupils in mission schools and only about 3000 in schools conducted by the state. Australia obviously should have rectified this, but what Hasluck actually decided was to support mission schools financially and to concentrate first on setting up more primary schools. He rejected any suggestion of creating an indigenous élite. In April 1956, there were just fifty-six 'native scholarship holders' at secondary schools in Australia, but very few even of them were able to get beyond the Junior or Intermediate examination (Hasluck, 1976: 86-7, 221). The result of long years of neglect (and Hasluck's antipathy for an elite) was that the adult generation of the early 1960s, when Australian colonialism was 'engrossed' with questions about the higher training of its bureaucrats (Hasluck, 1976: 386), represented a shallow pool from which to draw the future state leaders. Fewer than 1 per cent of adults had had a full primary and less than a hundred persons a complete secondary education (Mair, 1970: 227). No Papua New Guinean attended an Australian University before 1960, and the first graduate, in agricultural science, obtained a degree in 1964 (Hastings, 1973: 121).[2]

## The rapid rise of bureaucratic power-holders

Because the existing educational system was totally inadequate for decolonization, a whole range of new training institutions mushroomed into existence through the mid-1960s. Teaching began at the Administrative College at Waigani in 1963, Lae Technical College was upgraded to a higher technical college in 1966, the University of Papua New Guinea started in the same year, and in the following year the Goroka Teachers College opened. What was a small pool for the colonial state was also a fine opportunity for well-placed nationals within it. In Sir Maori Kiki's view:

Most of us had felt unhappy about many things we saw in Papua New Guinea, but it was only at Administrative College that we began to see the practical means of doing something about it. Most important of all, the Bully Beef Club[3] developed a kind of group feeling among us. We came from all parts of the country but felt we had a common cause. Indeed, many of the members of the Bully Beef Club have stuck together during all the recent developments (Kiki, 1968: 149).

For Michael Somare also, the matriculation course at the Administrative College in the mid-1960s was 'one of the most important [years] in my life. It was then that I met many like-minded men who are still my friends today. Together we began to plan the future of our country' (Somare, 1975: 45).

An event of central importance in the formation of the new social category at this time was the introduction of the dual wage system[4] in the bureaucracy in 1964, which established separate salary scales for expatriates and Papua New Guineans. The embryonic class was given greater cohesion through its concerted opposition to this decision, and its links with the bureaucracy were strengthened. For Kiki it was 'the biggest political blunder the Australian government [had] ever made in the territory' (Kiki, 1968: 144), and for Somare 'there was probably no other single issue that made Papua New Guineans more aware of the injustices of colonialism' (Somare, 1975: 43). Separate wages provided an issue over which 'all the politically conscious people' in Papua New Guinea might unite (Kiki, 1968: 149), and it reinforced the tendency towards elitism among them as well. Their resentment and what followed from it stemmed from the fact that some Papua New Guinean civil servants 'had always hoped for a standard of living commensurate with that of the expatriate Australian' (Hastings, 1973: 98).

Western education conferred distinction upon the fortunate minority; in Somare's words: 'There were very few educated Papua New Guineans then. Only a few of us could see and understand what was actually happening ...' (Somare, 1975: 44). Consciousness of superior abilities[5] was particularly strong in comparison with the uneducated 'big men' and perhaps big peasants in the first House of Assembly, 1964-68:

Most of the elected members had very little education and found it difficult to cope with the very complicated parliamentary procedure. They were the traditional 'big men' in their villages. They had council experience or mission training and spoke only Pidgin ... The role they played was that of messenger between the government and the people — rather like the old *tultuls* and *luluais* in the past. Most were ill prepared to deal with any specific issues and rarely played an effective part in debate (Somare, 1975: 46).

While it is true to say that the formation of the Pangu Party in 1967 was an important event in the emergence of an indigenous élite (Hudson and Daven, 1971: 163), the most notable consequence was not to strengthen the nationalist movement; little or no sustained political action outside the state resulted. As Kiki (1968: 148) has said, 'The idea of a political party came very slowly to me and to most of my colleagues'; and subsequently parties served not as a vehicle for the mobilization of the working class and peasantry but simply as further stepping-stones to high office in the state, as Hegarty and Mortimer show below. The tacit collaboration between rising petty bourgeoisie and the changing colonial regime proceeded with remarkable smoothness, although the gains for this administrative élite have stopped well short of economic power.

## The absence of a national bourgeoisie

As the rich peasantry is characterized by its control over export-orientated agricultural resources, so the petty bourgeoisie's basic resources are Western education and administrative position. But it has tried to get at least a limited entry into the economy, through such ploys as tax holidays for indigenous businessmen and the creation of business wings of political parties, as well as joint ventures with foreign capitalists, and the creation of small trading activities like those around the Bougainville copper mine. The Development Bank also continues to play an important role in establishing and financing the small entrepreneur. Quite comprehensive assistance may be offered, as this text indicates:

> Where considerable management and technical assistance is necessary the Bank's Projects Department has set up the business, trained the entrepreneur in management and commercial techniques, and closely supervised the business. Over this period ... the Bank ... takes the business risk. When the manager's experience has increased to the point where he can take control, the business is handed over to him and the Bank's equity is converted to a loan to the new owner (Development Bank, *Annual Report and Financial Statements*, 1973-74: 7).

At that time the Bank had established in this helpful way such enterprises as an artifact dealer, a joinery, car hire firm, footwear factory, customs agent, a cleaning and a painting contractor, and a printing company. The total capital of businesses set up under this scheme was, however, only some $700 000 and they employed only 160 workers (*ibid.*, 7), testifying to the characteristically small-scale nature of most of these activities. Other indigenous entrepreneurs are quite dependent upon large foreign capital; the small firms which cluster around Bougainville Copper are there in order to satisfy the needs of the mine and must of necessity close when operations cease at the mine (Makis Uming, 1976). Finally, in the view of a Bank official in 1971, aspiring entrepreneurs would probably only win assistance if they had superior and in some cases tertiary education[6] (this policy clearly does *not* apply in the extension of state aid to the rich peasantry in the countryside). By manipulating state power and adapting policies the petty bourgeoisie opens the way to the acquisition of business opportunities and interests for itself.

## Division and agreement within the embryonic class

The differences within the educated petty bourgeoisie are mainly of an ethnic or regional and to a lesser extent of an institutional kind. Because of uneven and weak colonial development and unequal access to education, most of the senior posts in the national bureaucracy have gone to New Guinea islanders and to Papuans, and Highlanders are under-represented (Ballard, 1976a: 9).[7] These differences are sharpened by a certain degree of ethnic or regional consciousness in Papua and the Highlands and on Bougainville as well. While the in-

156

fluences behind these movements are complex, on the analogy of African experience it is possible that aggressive regionalism and ethnicity act as a cover for conflict within the petty bourgeoisie (e.g. Good, 1975). In the case of the Papua Besena movement specifically, the ambitions of a disgruntled section of the educated élite are quite evidently at work (McKillop, 1976a).

The new class-to-be is dispersed in a growing variety of institutional locations; not only the national bureaucracy, but also schools, colleges and the two universities, parliament, regional organizations such as the New Guinea Development Corporation on the Gazelle, and the burgeoning provincial governments and their executives. If differences of political and economic interest seem likely to grow in the future, what is most noticable to date is the similarity of world view even among relatively disparate elements of the petty bourgeoisie. Somare and Kiki and the leadership of Pangu did not press for early independence; nor did the supposedly radical student group, the Niugini Black Power, until 1971; in its submission to the United Nations visiting mission in March of that year, Black Power, with Leo Hannett as a leading figure, called for an 'all black' House of Assembly, and for 'self government by 1972', but not for independence (Hannett, 1972: 47).[8] In the same way, Leo Hannett on Bougainville (the North Solomons province) and Josephine Abaijah of Papua Besena later stand as firm as Somare and Julius Chan in support of the exploitation of mineral resources by foreign capital; Hannett, in August 1975, offered generous support for the Bougainville Copper Mine (*Post Courier*, 1 September, 1975: 4),[9] and Abaijah said in February 1974 that Papua Besena wholeheartedly supported the exploitation of Ok Tedi copper by Kennecott (Daro, 1976: 12). Of John Kaputin of the New Guinea Development Corporation and the Mataungan Association, it has been said that he 'presents a picture of immense contradictions and inconsistency', and the writer speculated 'whether Kaputin's greatest weakness lies in his inability to extract himself totally from the system he dislikes so much'; the same commentator added with thoughtful accuracy that such contradictions are 'understood and tolerated in a country such as ours' (Anis, 1974: 273-4). What applies to such sometimes dissident petty bourgeois figures is even more true of the category as a whole, and of the political process in which they operate. The remarkable stability of bureaucratic organisation during decolonization is itself indicative of the absence of ideological differences and of the overriding importance of bureaucracy to the new petty bourgeoisie: 'the constitutional settlement and localisation of the public service effectively took priority over radical political and administrative reform' (Ballard, 1975: 10).

## The parasitic group

The educated petty bourgeoisie clearly plays a far smaller role in production in the country than either the working class or the peasantries. It acts as if the control of the state for administrative purposes was an end in itself; despite early promises to the contrary, the number of public servants in an already over-bureaucratized system grew by 20 per cent between September 1972 and 1976 (Ballard, 1976a: 15). There appears to exist but the weakest impulse towards independent capitalist development, despite the increase in economic power it could bring to the petty bourgeoisie. The possession of political power highlights its neocolonialist outlook and dependency upon inherited economic structures and relationships; no other class or social category, including the rich peasantry, has any similar access to state power, so government policies and administrative practices precisely reflect the horizons of the petty bourgeoisie. Their control of education and political power means that the leading elements of this class could choose other policies if they so wished; not however through the rhetoric and individualism displayed by a number of petty bourgeois leaders to date, but through active and long-term collaboration with other social classes. There are at present no signs of such changes; instead the socio-economic structures of dependent capitalism are conserved through the momentum of established institutions and the weakness of the power-holders.

# 12
# Conclusion: class in Papua New Guinea

The tacit alliance between the rich peasantry, educated petty bourgeoisie and metropolitan capitalist bourgeoisie is perhaps the most outstanding social characteristic of Papua New Guinea in the 1970s. This alliance, represents the ruling classes of Papua New Guinea. Each profits economically and politically from the system of export commodity production which lies at the heart of dependency in the country. There are other signs of the low level of capitalist development, for example, the notable absence of a national bourgeoisie interested in challenging and exposing the given system, the absence of political parties as vehicles for class action, and the existence instead of an array of small, semi-popular and supposedly non-political organizations (cooperatives, savings and loans societies, the new 'developmental' corporations, etc.) and the 'neutral', largely localized, 'developmental' state itself. No over-zealous use of coercive police powers — exceptions are Panguna in May 1975 and to a lesser but continuing extent Highlands tribal fighting — have disrupted these circumstances. The so-called traditional leader, *bisnis* man, and educated élite have generally retained the prestige which tradition and education accord them. Some tensions of a regional kind exist (and others may arise over development strategies) between the components of the ruling class but they have not yet damaged the overall alliance.

The relatively strong organization of some urban trade unions is therefore important, but it is unsupported at present by real links with rural workers and poorer peasantries in the countryside. What has been said of an African working class seems to apply to Papua New Guinea; 'workers have generally failed to make their own struggles relevant to the vast masses outside the urban areas, and have failed to sustain a radical political alternative once the dust has settled on their immediate grievances' (Sandbrook and Cohen, 1975: 316). And the large public service unions are closely associated with the interests of the state and its educated petty bourgeois controllers.

But it is important too that action, interrupted and isolated, by rural workers occurs; and that large-scale, inchoate class action by poorer peasants in the Highlands appears to be growing. Further concentration on cash-crop production promises to widen rural inequalities and encourage the continuance of 'rascal' and criminal behaviour. If increased use of police power is in fact resorted to, greater hostility towards the property owners whom the police protect may well result.

Few truly dynamic influences are now at work within the class structures of Papua New Guinea. No radical educated petty bourgeoisie or educated working class has emerged, ready to join urban manual workers and villagers on an organized and continuing basis. But given the maintenance of low-level, dependent capitalism (with few new jobs available in the bureaucracy, and skills being imported from abroad), this could change in the future. The average level of education among the unemployed is rising, and it is estimated that by 1984 about 30 000 Form 4 (Grade 10) school leavers will be unable to find skilled employment within the country (Castley, 1977: 10-11). This development is dramatically different from the situation which applied in the 1960s and 1970s, and represents a potential threat to the rather fragile stability of the post-colonial socio-political arrangements. The threat could be contained by cutting back on educational opportunities and by a greater resort to force, but at the cost of widening frustrations and disillusionment. And it could also bring more radical influence to bear on the urban trade union movement, and help to provide vital direction to the present circle of crime and punishment in the countryside.

# IV
# The political forms
# of dependency

# 13
# The colonial state: paternalism and mystification

Rex Mortimer

*We went to New Guinea solely and simply to serve our own ends, and this fact should never be forgotten in dealing with the natives of that country.*

Sir William MacGregor, 1912

Preceding chapters have already demonstrated the centrality of the state in shaping Papua New Guinea's colonial economy and society. Precisely because the colony is an extension of the metropolitan power of Australia, integrated into its subordinate and exploited status through the Australian politico-bureaucratic apparatus, the state (in the form of a body of full-time officials) assumes a directing role of unusual force. It would have been impossible to delineate the structure and growth of the colonial economy, or the development of classes within it, without reference to state initiative and intervention. The provision and regulation of cheap land and cheap labour — those twin pillars upon which the colonial economy rested — together constituted the most important and consuming tasks of the administration, as we have already seen.

In this chapter, then, we start from what has gone before, and look at other (ancillary but vital) functions of the state, related less directly to the management of the economy but nevertheless essential to it: those ideological, political and social functions which served to bind the system together, provide it with a rationale satisfying to the colonizers, and imbue it with coherence and order.

Just as the classical bourgeois state is democratic in form, so the classical colonial state is absolutist. All power stems from the governor and administrator, acting upon instructions from his metropolitan superiors. Within the colony itself, neither the white community nor the colonized is endowed with formal political rights. As Ruth First has depicted it in Africa, so in Papua New Guinea the colonial state is 'military in conception and organization ... The chain of authority from the top downwards was untouched by any principle of representation or consultation' (First, 1970: 30). This pure form, of course, seldom obtains throughout the colonial era: in some instances, settlers win substantive political rights for themselves, and even oust metropolitan interests entirely, as in South Africa or Rhodesia; in others, forms of indirect rule give selected groups among the colonized limited but not wholly insignificant powers; and, in the final stages of colonialism, there is generally a movement towards a representative system of some kind.

For our purposes, however, the absolutist model suffices for most of the period we are surveying, since in Papua New Guinea neither white residents nor indigenes were ever given representative powers until the closing years of the colonial era, although the former achieved advisory rights in the 1920s and the latter forty years later. The analogy with a military organization can be misleading, however, if it suggests that the colonial bureaucracy was a monolith uninfluenced by extraneous forces or internal divisions. The success of the colonial enterprise rested upon active collaboration between officials, business interests and missionaries, and passive acceptance at least from the colonized. The first necessitated avenues of communication and negotiation, and the second was at least made easier where such avenues were provided.

In fact, in Papua New Guinea, as in other colonial situations, there were intimate connections between officials and the rest of the white community; the very caste-like conditions of colonial life ensured this. Relations between them were not always smooth, and business interests in particular, impatient at times with the protective attitude towards the colonized which reflected the longer and broader view of administrators and the metropolis, resorted to their own power resources —

press organs, lobbies in the metropolis — to assert their interests. In some areas, such as race relations, liquor policy, income tax and access to copra driers in New Guinea, they were generally successful in overcoming administration views. Overall, however, when the conflicts and differences among administrators, planters and men of commerce are examined, what is most striking is that they all operated within a consensus about fundamentals, and that their differences never erupted into major confrontations. In this respect, Papua New Guinea resembled East Africa rather than southern Africa (cf. Brett, 1973: 39-40). In both cases, business groups in the colony never gained the size or organizational independence to stimulate real confrontation. In addition, in the Papua New Guinea case, Australia was near enough to remain the preferred homeland of most white residents in the colony, and the habit of bureaucratic dominance spilled over from the metropolis.

The colonized for the most part presented even fewer problems of control for officials, for reasons which we shall elaborate shortly. Consultation with them was seldom practised seriously, nor were they considered as having the capacity to make reasoned proposals about their own place in the colonial scheme of things. Nevertheless, it would be wrong to imagine that the colonized Papua New Guineans lacked all influence in administrative decision-making. Sometimes they did so merely by entering fields where colonial policy was not fixed, thereby creating situations which the policy-makers reacted to rather than determined; the zestful entry of the Highlanders into cash crop farming is a case in point. In other cases, shrewd and resourceful Papua New Guineans found means of trading on their loyalty to the administration, usually at the expense of a rival clan or their own villagers. Finally, passive and active opposition to administration policies did sometimes win concessions from the officials. But the crucial limitation upon any indigenous influence or pressure was that it should not disturb white dominance, and in this respect the Australian power enjoyed an extraordinary degree of immunity until very late in the colonial twilight.

The salience of the colonial state in the enterprise has led some writers to magnify its image out of all proportion. Thus John Saul, in writing of Tanzania in particular and Africa more generally, has argued that the state was overdeveloped in relation to the economic base because, as an alien institution, it had to exert control over all classes in colonial society, in contrast to the case in the bourgeois state proper, where the state directly represents one or more classes in the society (Saul, 1974). These propositions do not stand up to analysis. In the first place, as Leys argues, there is no evidence that the colonial state is generally larger, in relation to the economic base, than it is in Western countries (Leys, 1976); in Papua New Guinea, certainly, the administration was exceedingly small until after World War II, and its extravagant mushrooming after that owed more to the bureaucratic mode of inducing and regulating greatly expanded economic activity than it did to problems of social control as such.

Behind this proposition of Saul's lie two misleading implications about colonial control. One is that the administration needs and seeks close, tight supervision of the whole colonial society. Surely Brett is closer to the mark for both Africa and Papua New Guinea, when he stresses that 'pre-colonial formations ... were required to change in favour of new demands only up to the point required for the purposes of the colonial political economy but no further than that ... maintenance of [the traditional social] order, in some attenuated form, was fundamental to a system which did not have the desire or resources to modernize the whole of its new domain in any basic way' (Brett, 1973: 19-20). This appears to fit the Papua New Guinean case precisely, and loose and intermittent official control over great parts of the country for most of the colonial period was not only more feasible, but it also served, as we have seen in Part I, to maintain a reserve of cheap labour for the more dynamic zones.

Similarly, it is mistaken to imagine that such control as the colonial system did require was dependent upon the presence of hordes of officials. Control is imposed or induced by a great variety of means and instruments, and in a society such as

Papua New Guinea's, where history and geography conspired to inhibit co-ordinated human action on any large scale, they were not needed in great quantities. The missionaries and planters were agents of control as much as officials. Axes and tinned food and aeroplanes performed the same role as guns. And control came from within the conquered population as well as from outside it; it was facilitated by clans whose land claims were upheld, chiefs and 'big men' whose authority was entrenched, ambitious men enrolled as police boys and headmen, mission converts devoutly rendering up to God and Caesar. The fact that these men were allotted but lowly roles in the Australian order should not blind us to the fact that they enabled the colonial ship to float upon steady seas with a small crew.

Ultimately, control is achieved by higher technology and organization, and only when the conquered gain access to these, and learn to use them in ways adapted to their own conditions, do the colonizers face real problems of control demanding the deployment of large numbers of officials and troops. In Papua New Guinea, the threshold of that stage was only being approached when the colonial power decided to abandon direct rule.

In what follows, we seek to indicate the major ways in which control — in the widest sense of that term — was established and maintained by the Australian administration in such a manner as to ensure the most peaceful and orderly conduct of the colonial system. We shall be concerned not only with the measures, policies and ideas used to develop conformity to metropolitan interests and norms among the Papua New Guinea population, but also with those advanced to confirm the colonizers themselves in their assurance of embarking upon a noble and responsible enterprise, because their belief in themselves and their project was as important in ensuring its success as the inculcation of dependency among the colonized.

## Colonial control before World War II

Colonial officials in Papua New Guinea did not enter upon their tasks with empty heads. Just as their cabin trunks were filled with commodities strange to their new-found surroundings and a source of wonderment and awe to their subjects, so was their intellectual and emotional baggage packed with notions and behavioural patterns characteristic of the late imperial age. Their common stock of assumptions included a collective belief in the pre-eminence of the white race and the universal validity of the techniques and institutions which had created that superiority; a confidence that 'backward' peoples were not capable of governing themselves in the complex conditions set by the modern world; and an assurance that the interests of 'responsible' colonizers were in no fundamental way incompatible with those of their subjects, but rather formed the decisive element in a beneficially reciprocal relationship out of which the 'native' would in the long run derive the benefits of civilization (cf. Brett, 1973: 41).

In Australia's case, however, there were somewhat special historical conditions which initially threw some doubt upon her fitness to perform her civilizing role properly. Australian treatment of her own Aborigines had been, and continued to be, exceptionally brutal, while the country's situation on the rim of Asia had bred in all classes in Australian society anti-coloured prejudices of a particularly crude and virulent kind (McQueen, 1970b). British officials who had the original task of planting the flag on Papuan soil were not unmindful of the sorry Australian record towards the Aborigines, and it contributed to the reluctance of Her Majesty's government to add what it considered to be a very marginal piece of real estate to the already overstretched domain of the Empire (Jinks et al, 1973: 33).

In the event, fears of Australian brutality proved largely groundless. The landlust which had triggered the savage despoliation of the Aborigine had been sated, the victim himself had been despatched to the almost invisible margins of society, and Australian capitalism had entered upon a stage of more orderly development. The blackbirding phase in the south-west Pacific islands likewise was coming to a demeaning and guilt-stricken end. The more 'progressive' — which is to say rational and long-term — principles of colonial rule characteristic of industrial capitalism were percolating through to Australian political leaders and officials. There was no call for Australia to rape Papua New Guinea as she had the Aborigine: home resources were more than available sources of capital could cope with. Political considerations were prominent in prompting the Australian colonies to have Papua annexed, and by their very nature these demanded that the colonizers take the long view; they primarily sought protection from foreign domination of the land mass and sea lanes to their near north, and a buffer against their fears of Asian expansionism. The net effect of these influences and constraints was to ensure that colonial practice in Papua New Guinea conformed broadly to the pattern of colonial administration elsewhere in the same period.

The initial stage of colonial 'civilizing missions', naturally enough, consists of establishing contact with the local inhabitants and obtaining from them at least nominal allegiance to white authority. In Papua New Guinea this proved to be a long and arduous process, bedevilled by the country's formidable geographical and linguistic obstacles and the shortage of administration resources. Initially, contact was pursued with more vigour than restraint, so that Sir William MacGregor, an early British Administrator of Papua, was moved to admit that 'as a simple matter of fact the administration had to subdue by force almost every district now under control' (Jinks *et al*, 1973: 61). German methods in New Guinea were no better and were more extensively employed, as befitted a greater and more purposeful power than Australia. (Rowley, 1958: 115-16, 192-4). Later contacts, however, proved less costly to the inhabitants; no doubt word of the painful results of resistance spread from village to village, dampening martial ardour, while on the other hand the colonizers — especially when Australian parsimony placed severe limits on their capacity — gained greater skill in approaching and 'pacifying' villagers. Hubert Murray, Australian Lieutenant-Governor of Papua from 1908 to 1940, and the epitome of the paternalistic official, expounded the philosophy behind 'peaceful penetration', as he did on so many aspects of Australian colonial policy. The 'scientific method' of contact, as he called it, was to be preferred to the punitive expedition for two reasons: the latter 'is an abandonment of our principle of individual responsibility, and an adoption of the savage's crude idea of tribal vengeance, which we consider to be a lapse into barbarism and a sin against civilization'; it was, moreover, 'inconsistent with the peaceful association which is the end that we have in view' (Murray, 1931: 6). Here, as in so many passages from Murray, we are struck by the ambivalent strains in administrative paternalism. Humanitarian considerations and the exaltation of individualism merge into an assault upon the cultural norms of the colonized; at the same time, bureaucratic realism about establishing order and its economic benefits is not forgotten. The policy was a substantial success, partly because of the administration's generally strict controls on non-administrative contacts with local populations before official order was established. A native constabulary, officered by whites, was formed to maintain the *pax Australiana*.

For the majority of Papua New Guineans, administrative control remained a slight and intermittent affair throughout the greater period of colonial rule. Officialdom was unable to do more, a weakness for which it compensated in some measure by encouraging and assisting missionaries to perform *their* civilizing role. Whatever their motives, and their other concerns, the missions performed very similar functions to those carried out by the administration in lightly controlled areas — they inculcated respect for Western order, receptivity to the white man's domination and his values, worship of the work ethic, and attention to hygiene.

Once control was established, it was rarely challenged directly and openly until the late 1960s; even the celebrated strike and demonstration in Rabaul in 1929 revealed, for all the fears of the expatriate community, that even the most dynamic Papua New Guinean community of the time still lacked the leadership, the coherence, and the wider social experience to carry through its protest. The lightness of the Australian presence helps explain the comparatively few instances of forceful resistance, as does the isolated and small-scale character of Papua New Guinean societies. It would not be surprising, too, if the enormous technological gulf between the parties had not overawed the Papua New Guinean to the point of near-paralysis; the emergence of the cargo cults in fact suggests something of the kind in the way they sought to negate the white man's control over industrial artefacts and claim them for their own. The documentation of resistance has naturally concentrated upon these cults, since they offer the clearest insight into the forms taken by Papua New Guinean disenchantment prior to the rise of the modern nationalist movement. At the same time, it is as well to appreciate the fact, recorded in many a *kiap's* fieldnotes, that for most Papua New Guineans who found the white man's burden too onerous, the simplest and, for a long time, most effective form of protest was just to run off into the bush until the demanding intruder had made his departure.

In dealing with those drawn closely into the colonial orbit, the official was armed with a social theory justifying to himself and them the respective roles of white master and black servant. Essentially, the theory rested on one blanket assertion: the native could not improve himself, and therefore it was the responsibility of the white master to uplift him by hard work so as to ensure not only his improvement, but indeed his very survival. To some hard-nosed colonials, the colonized were congenitally lazy and incapable; to a more enlightened few, work was a necessary surrogate for the clan fighting and ceremonial which colonial rule had outlawed or undermined, as well as a means for equipping the indigenous people for adaptation to the modern world. Once again, Hubert Murray has stated the sophisticated view eloquently: '... if we wish the Papuans to survive we must encourage them to work and endeavour to change them from a non-industrial to an industrial people ... we have taken away his old ideas of war and bloodshed, and it is our duty to put a new ideal in their place — to substitute the activity of labour for that of fighting, and to transform the tribe of disappointed warriors into a race of more or less industrious workmen' (Murray, 1912: 362-3).

The limits of Australian colonial enlightenment are only too apparent from Murray's vision: the colonized were to be ennobled by work, but work of the most ignoble kind in the colonizers' own world view; in other words, work that they were not prepared to do. For the most part, work for Europeans was given the greatest emphasis, on the grounds that mere association with the white man would prove beneficial to the native or that the Papua New Guinean could not be relied upon to undertake even the simplest tasks without constant supervision (Hunt, 1905: 5-7, 28; Jinks *et al*, 1973: 93-4). But where, as in Papua, white settlement and investment proved inadequate to meet metropolitan pressures for financial self-sufficiency, the alternative of forcing Papuans to work their own plantations was incorporated into the notion of development. Thus Murray, earlier a strong proponent of European-run enterprise, responded to Papua's economic stagnation in 1920 with a new-found rationale for compulsory cash crop planting by Papuans. Labour in the service of the white man, he now argued, was only a beginning in industrial training;

> if the whole race can hope for nothing better than to be, till the end of time, hewers of wood and drawers of water for European settlers, I do not think they will have much cause to be grateful to the democracy of Australia. It is probable that modern industrialism will offer but little attraction to the Papuan, and we should therefore try to discover a form of civilization which may appeal to him more readily; and this, I think, we shall find in a life based upon the cultivation of the soil for the benefit of himself and others.

Murray then went on to justify his policy also by reference to the lack of incentive for European capitalist development in Papua (Murray, 1920: 32-6).

Clearly, Murray was envisaging some kind of peasant-type development in Papua by 1920. In the event, his village planting programme was not a success (Oram, 1976: 28), and it was not until the opening up of the Highlands to large-scale coffee production in the 1950s that a peasant-based strategy began to be realized on a substantial scale.

On the whole issue of work relations between white and black, Rowley has drily and aptly commented, 'The argument that the villager should either work in his village to make copra for sale, or go out to work for wages, was of course very good for business', and the achievement of the administration's aim of financial self-sufficiency. 'This conditioned governments to accept arguments about the 'educational' value of going to work, of engaging in trade, or giving up village lands for use of Europeans' (Rowley, 1972: 92).

So long as the administration was able to confine Papua New Guineans to menial tasks, its rationalizations of their incapacity remained securely moored within the colonizers' own small world. Various features of colonial policy helped to put off the moment of truth, but by far the most important until well into the 1960s was the refusal to educate Papua New Guineans beyond the most elementary levels. Until the 1960s, even this token education programme was almost entirely left to the missions, with minimal financial support from the administration.

One critical observer of Australian education policies — or lack of them — noted in 1943 that only 300 Papua New Guineans were then enrolled in elementary schools and 75 in recently established technical schools; he also drew attention to the fact that Government spending on education had actually shrunk from £A18 000 in 1923 to £A5000 in 1937. Acknowledging the administration's financial stringencies only to dismiss them as an inadequate justification for this situation, he went close to the heart of the matter:

> ... an education along European lines is virtually useless to the New Guinea native. There is, in short, no place for an educated native in modern New Guinea. A few may become teachers, and every year a dozen or so from the technical school get positions demanding some slight skill. But there are no clerical positions, and only a few of the most menial government jobs are open to natives — educated or not ...

> There is one more factor in the situation which must be noted, ie., the definite hostility of Europeans toward the native being given any education at all. One inevitably receives the impression that the Government's policy, notwithstanding its limited budget, is shaped on the do-nothing model in response to the attitude of the non-official population. The exploiting class has a very real fear that intellectual training will make the native less amenable to labor (Reed, 1943: 187-90).

173

Allied to educational deprivation, and in fact an essential complement to it, was a policy of keeping Papua New Guineans insulated from all contact with the outside world, an aim pursued with such success that until recently there were few communities on earth so ignorant of the affairs of men other than their own. Geography conspired to aid the Australian purpose, but it was reinforced by every means at the administration's disposal. The extreme parochialism of Papua New Guinea's present leaders and educated groups, their imitation of the attitudes and prejudices of Australian provincials, and their simplistic notions of international affairs, can all be traced back to this miserable and benighted policy.

Even so, some light could not fail to penetrate this bleak and dismal Australian fog, even in the 1930s. Murray, who condemned the grosser forms of racism prevalent in the colony, but who nevertheless shared the view that the Papuan was inherently inferior in mental and psychological makeup to the European (Jinks *et al*, 1973: 135), was honest enough to confront the dilemma when he could no longer ignore it. In 1937, Father Louis Vangeke, a Papuan, returned from Madagascar to Port Moresby a fully ordained priest. Reflecting on this totally unprecedented event, Murray felt constrained to reiterate his belief that 'Europeans as a whole have an innate superiority over Papuans', but immediately conceded that 'if a Papuan can qualify for the priesthood, there is no reason to suppose that another Papuan could not qualify for medicine or law'.

This was a shattering admission, since at one blow it destroyed the whole mythology sustaining the monopoly of status and power which Murray and the entire Australian administration had reserved for the European. Murray could not cope with the implications. Instead he declared himself opposed to the 'creation of a Papuan intelligentsia', pointing out the danger of an 'intellectual proletariat' emerging. But why should the training of Papuan professionals necessarily lead to their becoming unemployed or confined to submissive roles? The answer, alas, had to be spelled out: it might be all right for the French or the British to train professionals and officials in their colonies, 'but with us in Papua anything of the kind would be impossible'! The most that Murray could foreshadow was that some day in the dim distant future 'we may be able to hand over petty acts of administration and trivial cases to Papuans themselves to deal with' (something, note, that the Germans in New Guinea had done thirty years earlier), but essentially Murray favoured 'the diffusion of an elementary education, with a knowledge of English, over as wide an area as possible' (Jinks et al, 1973: 135-6). In this sentence, Murray anticipated by almost twenty years the concept of 'uniform development' which Paul Hasluck, Australian Minister for Territories, was to make the cornerstone of his autocratic policies in the 1950s and early 1960s with the same objective of blocking Papua New Guinean development towards control of its own affairs.

## Post-war development

After World War II, a great transformation began in Papua New Guinea. The Australian government, for so long content to allow its sleepy colony to exist on what private business interest and missions could accomplish, suddenly awoke not only to the strategic importance which the Japanese invasion had so dramatically confirmed, but also to the economic opportunities afforded by a regenerated world capitalist economy. Australia was itself transformed in the course of the war, emerging more highly industrialized and richer from the conflict, and some of its new-founded dynamism was injected into Papua New Guinea. Expensive programmes in the fields of transport, health, primary schooling and agriculture began to take shape. Grants-in-aid to the colony (now for the first time administered as one unit) rose dramatically from $A4m in 1947 to $A96m in 1969-70. The horde of officials which Saul erroneously equates with an earlier stage of colonialism descended upon the colony in earnest, to orchestrate the expansive chorus and, not so incidentally, to redirect much of the financial largesse back home in the form of salary savings and other emoluments.

175

Some commentators have argued that the Australian post-war effort in Papua New Guinea can be attributed basically to the reforming, anti-imperialistic benevolence of the Chifley Labor government in office from 1945 to 1949 (see Langmore, 1972: 4). In fact, however, Labor's aims were anything but anti-imperialistic. In 1943 the Cabinet, then headed by John Curtin, had initiated a campaign to extend Australia's imperial domain over the whole of the South-west Pacific including Dutch New Guinea, and continued by various means to pursue this expansionist aim until firmly put in its place by the United States and Britain in the final stages of the war (George, 1974). Reluctantly compelled to confine its new-found ebullience to Papua New Guinea, Australia embarked on a rapid growth strategy there.

A more general interpretation of this new phase in colonial development has been offered by several writers. Speaking of Melanesia as a whole, one authority has referred to 'changes in the ethos of the metropolitan Powers' characterized by 'a new awareness of the rights of colonial peoples and a new concern over their underdeveloped condition' (Brookfield, 1972: 96). As an explanatory framework, passages of this kind are unhelpful. Not only do they leave us to seek the causes of major socio-economic changes in the free-floating minds or souls of metropolitan leaders and publics, but they make no effort to relate processes taking place in Melanesia to similar evolutions elsewhere in the colonial world.

The two most palpable facts about the immediate post-war situation are, firstly, that the aggrandizement of American wealth and power, rapid economic recovery in Europe and Japan, and a far smaller but regionally significant accession of industrial and financial strength by colonial powers such as South Africa and Australia, quickly began to transform the world economy; and secondly, that the outbreak of national and socialist revolutions and movements, particularly in Asia, posed a major new threat to the dominance of the imperialist powers everywhere. The combined effect of these developments, so far as the colonies were concerned, was to awaken the metropolitan powers to the necessity of expanding their

176

investments and government programmes so as to realize their potential as raw materials suppliers and consolidate the economic and political position of the colonizers for as long as possible. In some cases, as in India, devolution was regarded as an immediate necessity; in most, however, the strategy was directed towards the maintenance of direct colonial rule until the most favourable arrangements for a transfer of power to nationals could be created.

Australia's programme in Papua New Guinea, then, was no exception to the general trend of colonial practice in the postwar period, although for various reasons — Papua New Guinea's proximity to and defence significance for Australia, and its peculiar situation as a single small colony of a relatively large and rich country — it came to receive an exceptionally high proportion of its income from the metropolis.

Enlarged welfare programmes and greater indigenous participation in the economy necessarily formed part of the imperial design, but they were subordinate to the central aims of consolidating colonial power and exacting greater profit from it. Papua New Guineans were not to be elevated to be masters of their own fate, but rather to be given a more prominent place in a larger economic domain consistent with their status as dependents and servitors.

The stimulation of European-dominated enterprise remained firmly in the centre of Australian programmes. Once they themselves had perceived and seized the opportunities, Papua New Guineans were encouraged to enter cash crop production as peasant proprietors, but this development dovetailed with the interest of the metropolis in expanding colonial production and it posed no significant challenge to Australian economic and social domination. The Highlands peasants remained dependent upon their Australian mentors both for the viability of their farms and for the expression of their political aspirations, as later events were to confirm (see part III above).

The real limitations upon Australian developmental programmes, as they affected Papua New Guineans, were in those spheres where the advancement of the indigene could only take place at the cost of the colonizer and threaten the whole edifice of white domination and Papua New Guinean subordination. The record here, right up to the closing stages of the colonial era, is one of determined resistance by Australia to changes which challenged the entrenched social framework of the colonial order. Education above primary levels remained restricted to a handful until well into the 1960s; provision for skilled training in crafts and industrial occupations was almost nonexistent. The closed preserve of the public service was opened up only slowly, reluctantly, and at the lowest possible levels. Contact with the outside world was kept to an absolute minimum. Attempts by Papua New Guineans to develop autonomous movements for their own advancement were generally hindered and repressed, the ubiquitous label of 'cargo cult' being used assiduously to disparage these efforts.

Finally, the blockage of all avenues of political participation, until external pressures made it no longer tenable, testified to Australia's intention to remain in direct control of the colony for as long as possible, and to prevent any Papua New Guineans from escaping the web of dependency. What Clifford Geertz has said of the East Indies under late Dutch rule is equally apposite for Papua New Guinea under Australian rule right up until the mid-1960s: they were intent upon bringing their products, but not their people, into the modern world (Geertz, 1963). The dominance of Australian interests in Australian thinking does not need to rest on assertion or induction: in one of its earliest post-war policy statements, the administration had linked its expanding activity directly to the promotion of metropolitan economic interests and financial self-sufficiency (Jinks *et al*, 1973: 335). In 1952 Paul Hasluck was still insisting that 'the opening of the riches of New Guinea to the world will be as a result largely of white direction and endeavour' (Hasluck, 1952: 226-7).

In all these respects, Australian colonial rule was essentially no different from its counterparts across the globe. Colonial practice differed in style and emphasis from place to place, but everywhere the basic objectives were the same. If Australian bars upon higher education, outside contact, and employment in other than menial tasks were severe by comparison with, say, British policy in Africa, this may have had something to do with the greater provincial prejudice and insecurity of Australian colonialists. The main point, however, is that the specific conditions of the colonial situation allowed this provincialism to ride unchecked for such a long period of time. Australians could carry features of the colonial system to an extreme because there was nothing to prevent them doing so — no opposition of any consequence in Australia itself; no nationalist challenge in Papua New Guinea until a very late date; and no serious international scrutiny until the 1960s.

## Paternalism: palliative or rationalization?

Paternalism represented the other side of the coin whose head was stamped with a white *kiap* rampant and a fuzzy-wuzzy angel couchant. It was the colonialists' reply to charges of self-interest and denial of opportunity to the colonized; it was also their own sincere defence of their role in the colony. If it is accepted that the native is not capable of playing any other than a subservient role in the colony, then the most that the colonizer can do is to ensure that he is made as comfortable in that role as possible.

Protection and welfare were the administrative slogans of paternalism. Under the heading of protection, local inhabitants of the colony were prohibited from being supplied with or possessing firearms, liquor, drugs, and the like; from being removed from their own home districts without administration permit; from dealing in land; and from forming associations for any purpose not approved by the administration. Undoubtedly, many of these provisions did prevent Papua New Guineans from being unmercifully despoiled by the more unscrupulous expatriate element. For this very reason, trading and plantation interests sometimes came into conflict with an officialdom which they regarded as unduly benevolent. In the long run, however, the more percipient business interests recognized that governmental paternalism had in fact assisted rather than hindered capitalist interests in the colony. Thus one of Murray's most intransigent critics in the 1920s had the wit

179

to recognize later that 'through its safeguarding of the natives [the administration] had prepared the way for industrial and commercial development' (Jinks *et al*, 1973: 147). Indeed, by curbing unbridled exploitation and social dislocation, particularly at a time when the economic benefits would have been marginal, Murray and his counterparts in the Mandated Territory had done just that. In this light, protection represented as much a mark of prudent farming of resources as of nurture of the subject population.

Welfare too had its dual aspects. Public health was the sphere in which administration efforts were most concerted and most effective, but even here the impact was highly uneven and it is impossible to disentangle the elements of indigenous welfare and colonial self-interest represented in the programmes. From the outset in both Papua and New Guinea, medical treatment and prophylaxis were directed first towards the protection of Europeans and secondly towards the preservation of the work capacity of their labourers, but it could not easily be confined to those groups either administratively, in human terms, or for prophylactic purposes. Consequently, health measures were gradually extended to those parts of the country where there was a European presence or a labour recruiting zone, but only slowly and primitively to regions beyond the Europeans' interest (Jinks *et al*, 1973: 198-200; Hastings, 1973: 62). The areas which today exhibit the most acute disadvantages in public health provision are the Highlands provinces and the East and West Sepik provinces, precisely the last labour frontiers in the country (National Public Expenditure Plan 1978: 48). Besides being hampered by over-centralization, a too-rigid insistence on professional qualifications and a lack of integrated planning, administration programmes in this field as in all others were necessarily limited by the failure to educate Papua New Guineans or to repose any but the most menial responsibility in them. One prewar attempt to train Papuan medical assistants in Sydney came to grief after three years largely because the colonizers feared that 'Papuan lads, while in Sydney, may be brought into contact with undesirable elements, and especially with low-class white women; and that this may affect the good relations between the races, which is so jealously guarded in Papua' (Jinks *et al*, 1973: 134). In other words, the scheme threatened the precious fabric of white superiority, with its underlying sexual taboos. These restrictions remained in effect until the last decade of colonial rule.

Ultimately, the ambivalent motives and effects of welfare and protection have to be measured against the unambiguous reality of discrimination, which was omnipresent, categorical and dehumanizing. The administration may not have been the most virulent force in imposing discrimination — informal social attitudes and practices in this area were of cardinal importance — but it did establish a code legitimizing discriminatory practices and setting precedents for more avid white supremacists. As we have seen, even the most enlightened Australian paternalists such as Hubert Murray shared the common stock of racial prejudices and stereotypes, and official policies gave them specific form. These regulations covered a wide range of behaviour, ranging from the clothing Papua New Guineans might wear to the hours at which they were permitted to be abroad in the towns. They were forbidden to beat drums or dance in towns and villages after 9 p.m. Insulting or threatening Europeans, or behaving in a disrespectful manner towards them, or begging from them, were all offences (Jinks *et al*, 1973: 149-50). Movement into urban areas was strictly controlled. Residential areas, public transport, cinemas, hotels and bathing beaches were either segregated or placed out of bounds to Papua New Guineans (Oram, 1976: 101, 139). While conditions in Papua and the Mandated Territory differed in no essential respects, because of the presence of a larger white population and greater Western economic activity in the latter, relations there were regarded as being more strictly controlled and 'the native employment ordinances were extraordinarily detailed' (Jinks *et al*, 1973: 286). The first regulations issued under the Native Administration Ordinance in the Mandated Territory in 1924 provide an all-too-vivid specimen of the degrading demands made upon the subject population by white officials (Jinks *et al*, 1973: 260-3). Taboos on sexual relations between black men and white women were held with an intensity bordering on hysteria by large numbers of whites in the colony. The whole sorry story of the unreasoning panic and blind prejudice which culminated in the passing of the White Women's Protection Act (*sic*) in Papua in 1929 exemplified the racialist sickness rampant in the colony (Inglis, 1974).

After World War II, it was recognized by some officials that the expansion of the economy demanded some improvement in race relations. As the first postwar Administrator (Colonel J.K. Murray) stated, in a period of rapidly growing economic activity 'race-prejudice constitutes an irrational barrier to the full development of the country's resources, and is in the long run an enemy of the economic interests of all' (Jinks *et al*, 1973: 336). But old habits and prejudices die hard, and the formal apparatus of discrimination alone took many more years to dismantle. Even so, it proved much easier to sweep away the laws than to eradicate the attitudes implanted within their shade among white and black alike. The Papua New Guinean has had a long and difficult struggle to assert his dignity and competence after so humiliating an experience of tutelage and suppression.

## Towards 'independence'

Political rights for Papua New Guineans, it need hardly be stressed, found no place in this colonial scheme of things. A people who were regarded as incapable of fending for themselves except in a subsistence setting were hardly to be seen as having the potential to participate in their own governance, whereas the Australian administration was only too ready to provide the wise guidance and leadership which they lacked. Until the 1960s, Papua New Guineans were confined to having their wishes and aspirations interpreted for them either directly by Australian *kiaps* (patrol officers) or indirectly by Papuan constables and New Guinean *luluais* and *tultuls* appointed by the administration and empowered solely to carry out administration decisions delegated to them. Under Sir Hubert Murray, it is true, Papua had been introduced to a system of village councils, but these had no decision-making powers and were limited to making representations to administration officers (Oram, 1976: 48-51).

It is not without significance, in view of Australia's repeated emphasis upon its vital defence and security interests in Papua New Guinea, that the only indigenous group which was given skilled training as a matter of policy, and — after World War II — gradually introduced to sophisticated techniques, indoctrination and technical training in Australia, positions of some responsibility, and a lifestyle infinitely superior to that enjoyed by any other class of Papua New Guineans, was the defence force personnel. Although dependent still on Australian logistics and other services, by the time of independence the indigenous officers of this force were indisputably the best-trained Papua New Guineans for the jobs they were to have.

In 1952, Hasluck did contemplate, very much in the style of an abstract intellectual exercise, the possibility of Papua New Guineans taking some part in running their own enterprises and government 'very gradually, over a number of generations', but even this distant prospect was cast within a scenario in which white settlers would become a permanent part of the country and enjoy an equal political voice in its affairs (Hasluck, 1952: 226-7). Four years later, Hasluck was still inclined to place self-government for Papuan New Guineans in 'the distant future' (Hasluck, 1956a; 28-9). In a Canberra lecture in 1956, he proposed a programme of political representation which would begin at the lowest and most circumscribed level, under close supervision, and extend by slow degrees to the eventual creation of a national legislative council, not wholly elective, and operating within a partnership with Australians which would 'be free, close and permanent' (Hasluck, 1956b: 15-16).

In fact, even as the size of the public service grew from almost nothing in 1946 to near twelve thousand in 1960 and over twenty thousand in 1969 (Oram, 1973: 6), the site of effective decision-making became still more remote from the Papua New Guinean. Hasluck insisted on the centralization of all power in Canberra, to which even routine proposals had to be submitted as a matter of course (Oram, 1976: 211). In order to prohibit still more effectively any exercise of initiative in the field, or any comparison with colonial administration elsewhere, he placed a ban upon Australian officials going overseas to study developments in their field (Oram, 1973: 5). Despite the grotesque effects of such a policy in a country whose diversity and communications problems cried out for highly decentralized administration integrated at the district level (Parker, 1966: 188), the Hasluck system, with its plethora of departments, agencies and boards in Port Moresby waiting upon Canberra's word, was not formally dismantled until 1970 (Oram, 1976: 211).

The year 1960 is usually taken as the time when the Australian government first came to appreciate and provide for the fact that the 'free, close and permanent' association which it envisaged with Papua New Guinea might not be attainable. A number of simultaneous pressures came to bear upon Canberra, shaking its confidence in the long-term nature of its colonial role and setting the stage for changes which for the first time contemplated real indigenous entry into the closed preserves of power. At the Commonwealth Prime Ministers' Conference in 1960, when for the first time Asian and African leaders outnumbered white, Australian Prime Minister Menzies clearly had an experience which seriously unnerved him. Speaking at a Press conference in Sydney immediately upon his return, Menzies said:

> Whereas at one time many of us might have thought that it was better to go slowly in granting independence so that all the conditions existed for a wise exercise of self-government, I think the prevailing school of thought to-day is that if in doubt you should go sooner, not later. I belong to that school of thought myself now, though I didn't once. But I have seen enough in recent years to satisfy me that even though some independences may have been premature, where they have been a little premature, they have at least been achieved with goodwill. And when people have to wait too long for independence, then they achieve it with illwill, and that perhaps is the difference between the British colonial policy of this century and that of some other countries. Question: Would you apply that view to [Papua] New Guinea, sir? Prime Minister: I would apply that to any country (Jinks *et al*, 1973: 373).

Naturally enough, Menzies' statement, coming out of a clear sky, produced a furore among an unprepared Cabinet, business community, Papua New Guinean administration and white society. Menzies himself soon backtracked on his statement, emphasizing that self-government could not come to the colony before the ground had been fully prepared economically by external investment, and that 'a friendly New Guinea is essential to Australia'. But external pressures on Australia to modify its stand continued to mount. Over the border in West New Guinea, the Dutch had carried through a crash programme of political education and training in the 1950s and early 1960s which made the rationale behind Australia's attitudes look as thin as it in fact was. Of far greater significance in deflating Australia's confidence, however, was the campaign unleashed by Indonesia in 1961 to 'liberate' West New Guinea (West Irian) by force, which was successful the following year in persuading the United States, over Dutch and Australian opposition, to accede to the transfer of control to Indonesia. Australia was now faced with a militant anti-colonial power on its doorstep, and one regarded by defence planners in Canberra at the time as a distinct security threat. The Dutch had tried, too late, to pre-empt Indonesian pressures by rapid progress towards self-government in West New Guinea; could Australia do less in the eastern half of the island if it was to withstand a possible Indonesian anti-colonial challenge cast in terms bound to appeal to the Afro-Asian bloc at the UN?

At this point, more moderate UN opinion began to write warnings and prescriptions on Australia's wall. Following shortly upon the General Assembly Resolution of 1960 condemning colonialism, the Foot Mission in 1962 called for much faster progress to keep up with world trends, making a particular issue of the need for a long-range economic plan, a system of higher education, and a more representative legislature in the colony. Hasluck's initial reaction was to sit upon Australia's legal rights as the governing power (Jinks *et al*, 1973: 380-6), but gradually the logic of the metropole's position obliged it to make grudging progress in the directions indicated by the UN Mission.

Nevertheless, steps towards real political participation by Papua New Guineans came very slowly. Until 1968, when the first mainly elected but little more than advisory Legislative Assembly was installed, the only bodies which were chosen by anything resembling democratic processes were the local government councils inaugurated in the early 1950s. However, a recent study of their origins provides strong evidence that they were designed to divert Papua New Guinean aspirations towards political participation into such routine and well-supervised activities as the provision of roads, bridges and latrines (Simpson, 1976).

Until very late in the day, 'partnership' between the colonial power and its subjects remained firmly under the paternalistic mantle. Planter-politicians took 'big men' and councillors under their wing to make good trusties of them; colonial officials carefully selected earnest and devoted public servants to train as their aides; but every spark of independence in Papua New Guinean thinking was treated with suspicion and disfavour, as the biographies of Maori Kiki and Somare illustrate.

The final episode in the story of political devolution will be reserved for a subsequent chapter. We may conclude our survey of the control concepts of the colonial state by referring back to our starting point — namely, that the primary objective of administration policy was to establish dependency in all its forms. There is no doubt that, on these terms, the colonial state in Papua New Guinea was conspicuously successful. As Oram notes, 'the psychological effect of smothering paternalism ... led to a passivity and an attitude of dependence in the face of external challenges which were to leave the villagers defenceless against rapid social change in the future' (Oram, 1976: 61-2). The notion that Papua New Guineans were incapable of standing on their own, that they required constant tutelage from their colonial masters, had penetrated the consciousness of the colonized only too effectively in a context where the gulf between the techniques, organizational power, education and self-consciousness of the parties was already great. Papua New Guinea nationalism never succeeded in pre-independence days in surmounting the obstacle posed by this internalized ideology, which remains one of the most powerful chains of dependency in independent Papua New Guinea.

# 14
# The political parties
David Hegarty

Papua New Guinea's political independence, attained in September 1975, was not the product of stuggle. There had been no nationalist movement and little clamour for an end to colonial rule. Political parties, which elsewhere in the Third World formed the vanguard of the independence movement, emerged late in the colonial period of Papua New Guinea and played only a limited role in the process of constitutional change. It was not until the late 1960s that domestic pressure for political autonomy in the form of the Pangu Party and two anti-colonial movements, the Mataungan Association and Napidakoe Navitu in East New Britain and Bougainville provinces respectively, began to mount. Although these pressures certainly influenced the mid-1970 change in Australian policy on decolonization, they were more than outweighed by the structures and feelings of dependency throughout the country. Most initiatives towards political independence were taken, in fact, by the metropolitan power: Independence was largely the result of negotiation between an Australian government increasingly anxious to devolve power to what it regarded as an acceptably compliant regime, and a political élite increasingly willing to assume it.

The political parties which developed in the late 1960s and early 1970s and which survived into the post-colonial period — the Pangu, United, People's Progress and National parties — have remained weak and undeveloped, both ideologically and organizationally. Despite their often elaborate constitutions, all (with the exception of Pangu perhaps) are essentially

187

parliamentary factions: and despite their often detailed policies and programmes, all are pragmatic in outlook, none having elaborated a coherent programme of social change. The extra-parliamentary wings of these parties (when they exist) have had little control over their parliamentarians and have usually functioned intermittently as electoral machines. The political parties have not mobilized the people, but rather given coherence to the political élite and provided mechanisms through which that élite gains access to, manipulates and retains political power. Developments in party politics since self-government in 1973 — the convergence of party policies, the increasing importance of their leaders, the sloughing off by Pangu of any radical elements, the acquisition of business interests, and the adoption of patronage as an electoral strategy — indicate the role that parties have played in the consolidation of Papu New Guinea's neo-colonial condition.

The late emergence of political parties in Papua New Guinea is closely related to the absence of a nationalist movement. The development of nationalism was inhibited by a number of factors. Firstly, the country has no common history of statehood; its people are fragmented into hundreds of often mutually antipathetic ethnic groupings, there is no single common language and the various regions have experienced different colonial rulers. Ethnic fragmentation and topographical diversity have hindered communications, and suspicion between ethnic groups prevented wider political association until recent times.

Secondly, the nature of Australian colonial rule has militated against the appearance of a nationalist movement: in style heavily authoritarian (see preceding chapter) and thoroughly paternalistic; in substance highly restrictive of autonomous political activity, and non-participatory. Successive generations of colonial administrators (and Ministers), imbued with the basic colonial assumptions of 'native inferiority', contented themselves with the translation of essentially political problems into technical administrative ones,[1] and attempted the ultimately impossible task of denying politics in the affairs of the colony. When representative institutions were introduced at the local level they were intended merely as another arm of the Administration and in some areas were introduced with the deliberate intention of harnessing indigenous political activity. Any sign of political activity was discouraged; cargo cults were interpreted as a deliberate threat to colonial authority and were suppressed; and even consultation with the people about the introduction of these institutions was minimal, for fear of awakening 'ideas' and 'false hopes' among the people (Jinks in Biskup *et al*, 1968). When the largely popularly elected legislature, the House of Assembly, was introduced in 1964 it was not intended by the Administration that it be a source or focus of *political* activity, but only an arena in which representatives could bring their constituents' problems to the benign Administration; it was regarded essentially as an appendage to the executive. As Dr John Gunther remarked, the House of Assembly was not intended to be a parliament in the usual sense of the term, but more a debating chamber (Gunther, 1963). When the first political party which appeared to have significant indigenous inspiration — the New Guinea United National Party — met in 1965, it was carefully watched by special branch police (Wolfers, 1970: 445).

The third and perhaps most important factor inhibiting the development of a nationalist movement was the absence of a sufficiently large and independent class or group to sustain one. Colonial economic and education policies had not produced, until the 1960s, significant social differentiation. In 1966, one year before Pangu — the first viable political party — was formed, the educated élite was miniscule (see part III above). Self-employed business and professional men were few and those with some secondary education were usually employed either in the public service or as mission school teachers. In rural Papua New Guinea the Administration's policy of cultivating a rich peasant class had by the mid-1960s only recently got under way, and as yet the class was insufficiently large and strong to form the basis of any organized political body. The small size of the élite then ensured easy co-optation and the dependence of the élite on the government for its income ensured a cautious approach to political change.

The absence of a nationalist movement, however, did not signify the absence of an anti-colonial sentiment in many parts of the country. Resistance to colonial intrusion took many forms, from violent opposition to passive obstruction, and patrol reports in particular indicate that this resistance was much more widespread than had previously been believed. But the opposition to central government dominance, to stifled autonomy, and to the economic dominance of foreigners found outward expression only in the more advanced regions. None of it was linked up at the national level, and consequently those parties which eventually emerged were generally loose collections of individuals, and conservative in character.

A further factor which inhibited party development was the sheer difficulty of establishing a mass-based party within Papua New Guinea's political communities. To establish party officials and branches with any authority within a small-scale political framework, and in opposition to a colonial administration which had generated such a high degree of dependence that it was seen as the 'giver of all things' (Somare, 1970: 490) was not easy. It was not an impossible task, as Voutas demonstrated in the Morobe District in the 1960s (Voutas, 1970; Hegarty & Samana, 1976), but, with the transfer of power coming so soon after parties had developed, the incentive to mobilize disappeared. As the new political élite acquired a material interest in the continuation of the colonial institutions and economy, mobilization became, in its eyes, unnecessary.

## The formation of Pangu Party

The political party which is the best known (outside Papua New Guinea) and which has survived longest is the Pangu Party. Pangu was formed in 1967 by a group of young public servants who at various times had studied together at the Administrative College and by some more 'progressive' MHA's, 'progressive' in the sense that they had organized a study group of parliamentarians in an attempt to reduce the dominance of the Administration over the legislature. Together they constituted, in Wolfers's phrase, 'Papua New Guinea's organizational and educational elite' (Wolfers, 1970: 448). Pangu's policy centred around the themes of 'home rule leading to eventual independence'; unity between the two parts of the country; localization of the public service; and 'economic development' — a policy which remained largely undefined except for a stress on the involvement of Papua New Guineans in the economy. These policies certainly were nationalist in design and were by far the most radical so far proposed by any group in the country's colonial history, but because of the immediate backlash which the party's formation provoked, Pangu rarely publicized its home rule platform.[2]

In the second House of Assembly (1968-1971), Pangu had the support of ten of the eighty-four MHA's and consequently had few victories. Immediately the House sat, Michael Somare, who had succeeded Paul Lapun as Parliamentary leader, declared Pangu's intention to become the 'loyal opposition'. Somare also declared himself in favour of 'gradual' as opposed to 'radical' change (Melbourne *Age*, 10 June 1968). Outside parliament, Pangu established an organization of varying strength in the country. In the Morobe District, for example, Tony Voutas attempted to establish a mass base for Pangu by extending his personal 'Toni' machine from the electorate of Kaindi to the whole District (Voutas, 1970). By the time of the 1972 elections he had established branches in most sub-districts, trained twelve cadres or *komiti* to act as his Pangu agents, and disseminated *Pangu Nius*, party T-shirts, badges and other symbols throughout the district. The branches were based on separate ethnic communities and used the central branch in Lae as the pivot. Few if any of the branches became self-sufficient and active without Voutas' initiative (although some *komiti* manipulated them for their own purposes) but they did succeed in spreading the name of Pangu throughout the district. The fruits of organization of this type were seen in 1972, when Pangu won eight of the nine seats in Morobe.

In Port Moresby, Albert Maori Kiki, who became full-time secretary of the party after his parliamentary defeat in Kikori in 1968, doubled as an active trade union organizer, recruiting unionists and Pangu members at the same time. Although the Port Moresby branch never officially met, Pangu picked up considerable support from public servants who were at this stage running into increasing promotion difficulties in competition with expatriate officers. In Lae, both Voutas and Tony Ila personally linked a section of the trade union movement to Pangu. In Madang and other major centres, Pangu branches had been established, attracting a range of members from Administration personnel to local artisans. Sometimes the Public Service Association representative in a town would also serve as the Pangu organizer. In the East Sepik, Michael Somare and Pita Lus both had large personal followings. It is difficult to estimate Pangu's membership, but at the height of the 1972 campaign an estimate of 3000-4000 appeared reasonable. The sources of Pangu's finances at that time were membership dues (20 cents each); a levy on Pangu MHAs' salaries, donations from liberal whites, and the occasional contribution from a far-sighted businessman. Bougainville Copper Company Limited's contribution of $3000 to each of the three major parties on the eve of the election enabled Pangu to finance its campaign.

Pangu's policy in the 1972 elections consisted essentially of catch-all slogans with, by this time, a definite emphasis on self-government (but still not on independence). Pangu's ten-point programme included calls for unity; improved quality of life in both rural and urban areas; higher pay for workers; secondary education for all; the return of alienated land to the people; and greater involvement in businesses by Papua New Guineans and easier access to government credit and business training.

In the 1972 elections, about twenty of the party's endorsed candidates were successful and at least four more parliamentarians joined the party immediately after. Insofar as one can generalize about the social and occupational backgrounds of these members, most had been attached to the public service either as clerks or teachers, some had had experience as clerks or supervisors in private enterprise, and a few were private entrepreneurs.[3] Consequently they were generally better educated than other MHAs and many had had previous experience with such modern political organizations as trade unions and voluntary associations.

Despite its reputation Pangu was never a radical party. It had shown its willingness to play the intended parliamentary role by declaring itself the 'loyal opposition' in 1968, and Somare made little secret of the fact that state power was Pangu's major ambition (Somare, 1970: 490). Pangu, like the other parties, had not developed a radical critique of colonialism or of colonial economic policy; it simply wanted an end to colonial rule. Most of its leaders felt keenly the indignities heaped upon them under colonialism and some, like Kiki, had taken risks by leaving secure employment to undertake the tasks of party organization, but their nationalism always appeared muted by an enormous reserve of goodwill for their colonizers (and a naive but strong belief in a multi-racial society).

## Party alignments in 1972

In April 1972, with no party emerging as the clear winner, the approximate numbers in the 100-member House were: United Party (UP) 44; Pangu 24; People's Progress Party (PPP) 10; National Party (NP) 7; Mataungan Association (MA) 3; and Independents 12. Despite Pangu's minority position, the party leadership fairly quickly won the support of the smaller parties and sufficient Independents to form a coalition. Within this disparate governing coalition, the PPP is the archetypal parliamentary faction. Formed in 1970 as an offshoot of the Independent Members' group (see below), the PPP maintained remarkable cohesion throughout the latter part of the second House and during the third. In the 1972 elections the PPP recruited about ten MHAs who had, broadly speaking, a small trader-entrepreneur, petty bourgeois background, and this was reflected in the PPP's early policy statements on the protection of private ownership, the encouragement of foreign investment, and 'the advancement of free enterprise through individual participation'. The solidarity of this faction has been

193

reinforced by regular executive meetings and small social functions. In 1972 the PPP had no electoral organization beyond its immediate leadership. It offered endorsement to a small number of candidates who campaigned largely as individuals and only rarely identified their party affiliation.

The National Party began as a one-man party with Thomas Kavali, the MHA for Jimi, its sole parliamentary representative. During the 1972 campaign, however, the NP was solidly supported by young educated Highlanders and, as the negotiations for a coalition government proceeded, it managed to pull together seven MHAs and bargain its way into the government. Although it is difficult to generalize about the background of NP members, its two leading figures, Kavali and Iambakey Okuk, were non-traditional leaders who had acquired some higher education and technical skills. The general orientation of the NP was similar to that of Pangu; it desired a more rapid move towards constitutional autonomy than did fellow-Highlanders in the United Party, and it too was keen for more business opportunities to be opened up to Papua New Guineans.

The three Mataungan Association members (two ex-teachers and one business manager) initially saw themselves as being to the left of Pangu, being more radical in their demands for autonomy (both regional and national), popular participation and economic nationalism. They supported the coalition but were generally suspicious of the bureaucratic background of Pangu leaders.

Despite its unexpected relegation to the Opposition benches, the United Party settled down to the role. The UP had been formed in 1970 largely in an effort to prevent a rapid transition to independence and to destroy Pangu. It came into being in the wake of the visit to Papua New Guinea of the (then) Australian Prime Minister, John Gorton, and the changes he announced both in increased internal responsibility and in state personnel which effectively speeded up the transfer of power in the colony. Both expatriate and indigenous leaders of the Independent Members Group (IMG) — a loose alliance of conservative and dependent politicians who considered their interests best served by the continuation of the colonial regime — realized the inevitability of independence and determined to minimize the extent and speed of those changes. At a meeting of IMG politicians (excluding some influential expatriates), Highlands councillors and 'big men' in November 1970 in Minj, it was decided to form a party called Compass. Early in 1971 (with the expatriates again united behind the common cause) the party's name was changed to the United Party. The UP was thus an alliance of expatriate businessmen-politicians who still supported the partnership concept, in politics if not in business, and most Highlands politicians who saw their regional interest (and no doubt their own private interest) as being best protected by continued colonial rule. There were also a few non-Highlands politicians (e.g., M. Toliman, T. Lokoloko), whose collaboration with the colonial power in the past had placed them in the UP camp. Almost all the indigenous UP members were men of some means, usually of rural wealth. In 1972 only one classified himself as a subsistence farmer. About one half classified themselves as farmer/planter/trader; the other half as former government officials of some kind (e.g. interpreters, clerks).

UP policy in 1972 was a blend of conservatism and dependence. It emphasized the attainment of (unspecified) levels of economic development in the less developed districts (including the Highlands districts) before serious moves were made to decolonize; the encouragement of foreign investment to facilitate economic growth; and law and order. The UP organization was designed specifically with the 1972 elections in view. The executive of the party was divided between largely expatriate business interests based in Goroka and expatriate business interests in Port Moresby. There was considerable squabbling between the two over campaign tactics and the choice of organizers and candidates. Attempts were made to establish branches throughout the Highlands and for a short time a Party newspaper, *Poroman* (earlier *UP News*) appeared, but the UP was ultimately more successful in recruiting winning candidates than in mobilizing the people. An organization established at Goroka Teachers College by Anton Parao (who became UP secretary in 1971), known as the 'Four Brothers', heightened an anti-coastal feeling among the very small Highlands educated élite and provided support for the UP's campaign.

Thus by 1972 there were some substantial differences between parties in terms of the social and occupational background of their members, regional bases of support (for the two largest parties at least), and policy, particularly over the question of self-government and independence. Common to the parties were their rudimentary levels of organization and ideological poverty of their policies.

## The interval of policy dispute

In the period from April 1972 until self-government in December 1973, the basic conflicts between the coalition partners and the UP opposition concerned the timing of constitutional changes; the speed of public service localization; the government's approach to a new lands policy, especially on expropriation of plantations; and the adoption of the 'Eight Point Plan' as a strategy for economic development. For both sides in Parliament it was a period of consolidation. Loveday (1976) has demonstrated how, in the first two years of the third House, both government and opposition maintained voting cohesion. The government began to make tentative pushes toward new policies, and numerous committees and commissions of inquiry were established on a wide range of issues. Pangu seemed to be heading for a more radical phase in its development. In 1973 it adopted the Faber Report on alternative development strategies out of which grew the Eight Point Plan; it accelerated the rate of localization by reducing the number of expatriates employed in the public service by 15 per cent per year; it established an all-party constitutional planning committee with the intention of producing a home-grown constitution; it established an inquiry into land matters and hired consultants strongly committed to a reversal of the colonial policy on registration of individual titles; and it attempted to hasten the progress of rural development by creating extra-bureaucratic bodies such as the Village Development Task Force.

The Pangu executive was taken over by a group of young university graduates (including Moi Avei, Meg Taylor, Rabbie Namaliu, Mark Opa) who in 1974 forced a Cabinet reshuffle which reduced the PPP's dominance of the economic port-folios and gave more economic power (for example, over foreign investment controls) to Pangu ministers. In mid-1973, Mataungan spokesman John Kaputin joined the Cabinet as Minister for Justice. He entered his ministry with the avowed intention of destroying the colonial legal structure (Kaputin, 1975a).

This new radicalism was inspired in part by the influx of new MHAs to the parliamentary party and by the recruitment of young nationals both as ministerial assistants and party ex-ecutive members. It was also inspired in part by ideas introduc-ed into the country by the Faber team, and by Ivan Illich, René Dumont, and Lloyd Best who spoke at the 1972 Waigani Seminar held at the University of Papua New Guinea in May. Some of the credit is due also to the energies of Tony Voutas, former MHA and from mid-1972 Research Officer to the Chief Minister.

But by late 1973 the writing was on the wall for this radical phase. Delegates to a Pangu convention in Port Moresby in November 1973 laboured to produce a party policy which would set the pattern for the run-up to independence. The con-vention was attended by branch secretaries and other officials from many parts of the country, by members of the Mataun-gan Association, the Kabisawali Movement of the Trobriands, and by groups such as the Nemea Landowners Association; but there were few MHAs present and even fewer Ministers. From this point on, relations between the party executive and the parliamentary wing deteriorated. Disputes between the Constitutional Planning Committee (CPC) and the government forced the issue to a head. In mid-1974 the executive was directed to stand loyal to the Chief Minister in his confronta-tion with the more radical CPC over the latter's attempts to confine citizenship virtually to Melanesians and to place severe curbs on foreign investment. The authority of the parliamentary wing (and in particular Somare) over the party triumphed.

Outside the legislature, virtually from the last polling day in the 1972 election, the parties' extra-parliamentary bodies atrophied. Occasionally a branch of one party or another would be declared open, but this was usually a token gesture indicating that the party had found either a contact man in the area or more probably a prospective candidate. Within the House, the solidarity of party support and the cohesion of the government, as reflected in MHAs' voting behaviour, began to break down as the CPC's challenge to the government on some fundamental policy questions proceeded. Although the CPC's final report on a proposed constitution for Papua New Guinea was not by most standards a radical document, it did question the ultimate goals of Papua New Guinean society, the approach to decolonization, the economic nationalism of the government, the power of the executive *vis-à-vis* the legislature, and the proper conduct of national leaders. In a sense the CPC recognized the inadequacy of parties as agents for change and attempted to use the constitutional document instead. Throughout 1974 the government (cabinet) increasingly interpreted the CPC as a challenger to its authority. The government (and particularly Somare) were preoccupied with a smooth transition to independence with as little change as possible in existing institutions. Political independence was its immediate objective, and it was not prepared to join the debate on ideological issues. CPC members, late in 1974, formed a Nationalist Pressure Group (NPG) in an endeavour to steer their constitutional proposals through the House. At its highest point the NPG mustered twenty-eight votes, but since on most issues it was soundly defeated by an across-the-floor vote, the nucleus of an opposition which it promised did not materialize.

At about the same time, a Papua New Guinea Country Party (CP) was formed by Sinake Giregire, a successful Highlands rural capitalist, and Michael Pondros, a Manus politician disillusioned with his treatment as a government backbencher. The CP claimed eighteen members but saw its numbers reduced to eight when leaders of the major parties applied pressure.

The CPC-government dispute had destroyed voting solidarity. There were few changes in party affiliation by MHAs, but there was a greater tendency for cross-voting, so much so that by June 1975 there was a possibility that the government would be toppled. Early in June it appeared that a combination of most sections of the UP, dissident government backbenchers, the NP and the CP could take power. Fr John Momis, Deputy Chairman and effective head of the CPC, was reluctant to lead this combination, however, and hasty deals with some Chimbu politicians by the government were sufficient for it to retain a majority. Throughout the dispute the government had relied increasingly on the support of the UP and particularly that of its leader Tei Abal.

## Independence and pro-capitalist convergence

From 1975, party policies converged. The basic conflict over the timing of independence had been resolved. There was no longer any disagreement over economic policy, the initial enthusiasm of the coalition for the Eight Point Plan — now the 'Eight Aims' — having waned. Rhetoric about 'self-reliance' had become increasingly empty and the constraints on change were being emphasized by decision-makers. Localization of the public service had slowed down, particularly since the most senior levels had already been filled by nationals. All parties were by now totally committed to capitalism. In fact it was the PPP's policy which had emerged as the winner. This convergence of party policy coincided to a large extent with an increase in the private business interests of parliamentarians. Politicians quickly grasped the opportunities available through their relatively privileged access to the resources of the state. Development Bank loans for themselves (and their clientele) were obtained to start and enhance private business individually or in partnership with foreign companies. Most politicians may have commenced their parliamentary careers as men of modest means, but it was a rare politican who had not enhanced his material well-being by independence. The political élite had rapidly acquired a material interest in supporting the neo-colonial economy.

In terms of party structure, this convergence process had several important effects. In Pangu, a core of party stalwarts including Somare, Kiki, Barry Holloway, John Yocklunn, Paul Cowdy — whose prime purpose was to buttress and protect the Prime Minister — became dominant. Critics within the party were eased out or co-opted; the last 'radical', Moi Avei, was outmanoeuvred early in 1975 when, having lost a by-election for Central Province, he resigned as president of the party and was succeeded by Somare himself. Somare's own position within the party and in parliament became extremely powerful. In addition to using his powers of patronage, he and his core supporters monitored many of the business deals undertaken by MPs, storing information for possible use when members needed to be disciplined or mobilized to support him. The government's strong emphasis on wage restraint as an incentive to foreign investment cost Pangu its once-close link with the trade union movement. Tony Ila, perhaps the most powerful unionist in the country, found himself frequently at odds with his colleagues, and there were moves inside Pangu early in 1977 not to re-endorse him as a Pangu candidate, though these eventually came to nothing.

With the advent of the National Party and with independence imminent, the UP lost its previous cohesion and became divided into at least three camps of varying size. The first, led by Tei Abal (and supported by the expatriate members), was pro-government; the second and much smaller faction, led by Anton Parao (whose personal dispute with Abal in the Enga Province reinforced the split) desired more assertive leadership; and the third centred around the Deputy Opposition leader Paul Langro, who was one of the few shadow ministers to perform an effective oppositional role.

The National Party split early in 1976 when, after Somare sacked its two leaders Kavali and Okuk from Cabinet, the remaining NP members refused to leave the coalition. It appeared to have lost all semblance of organization. The PPP, largely through the efforts of Julius Chan, retained its internal cohesion. Chan insisted on the party meeting before each session of parliament; on the party members fraternizing together; and on the Ministers supplying the backbenchers with information. He used his skills in the distribution of resources to ensure that PPP electorates also benefited.

The most significant development in party politics immediately after independence, and one which clearly signalled the orientation of the post-colonial regime, was the formation of 'business arms' for each of the major parties. The rationale of these party business ventures was essentially to provide finance for election campaigns and to meet residual party expenses. Parties realized that in the absence of a mass base, their survival could only be ensured if finance was available for political patronage. The catalyst for these business ventures appears to have come in mid-1975, a period of disinvestment by foreign businesses in the economy, when there arose the prospect of buying out Papua New Guinea Associated Industries, a major automobile importer and distributor which had other subsidiaries, including one marketing air conditioning equipment. The Pangu Party registered its business arm Damai Pty Ltd in August 1975,[4] and together with the UP group, Tarangu Pty Ltd, formed Melanesian Investments and prepared to take over PNG Associated Industries. The combined deal was to be financed largely through tax savings which the company would enjoy as soon as it was registered as a national company.

Opposition to this move came from within Pangu, from other car dealers, and from members of a committee appointed by the government to recommend means to rationalize key imports like motor cars, whose members saw a clear conflict of interest on the part of government. The outcome was that Tarangu retained its interest in the deal and Damai backed off. However, a holding company known as Ginada Investments, which has an overlapping directorship with Damai, has virtually retained Pangu's interest. Damai has undertaken two other roles. Through its subsidiary, Tropical Real Estate, it acquired considerable rental property around Port Moresby. It also established itself as an international finance broker, with an office in Hong Kong, Damai Hong Kong Pty Ltd, and was involved in 1976 in the negotiation of a loan of $1.8m from the Shanghai Banking Corporation for the construction of the new

Public Service Association building in Waigani, from which it gained a considerable commission. One of Damai's objectives, included in its charter, was to obtain support for or oppose ordinances, acts, or regulations or exemptions which its directors deemed to be expedient to the interests of the company.

Tarangu appeared less diversified, although it too invested in real estate in addition to its share in PNG Associated Industries. The PPP was less forward in the development of its business arm, although the party acquired a supermarket in Port Moresby and it was assumed that some finance flows from the private shareholdings of individual members back into party coffers. The management of these businesses and the way in which funds are spent leave considerable room for corruption. Internally and externally, of course, such ventures link the government and the political élite as a whole to the preservation and encouragement of foreign investment.

## Parties and the 1977 elections

The nature of political parties, their use of patronage and their links with business became much more explicit during the campaigning and lobbying which accompanied the general elections of 1977. Party organizations had generally atrophied in the years between elections, and such organization as existed, was dominated by a core of leaders and party officials in Port Moresby. This lack of organization meant that party leaders had to recruit candidates in an ad hoc manner by attempting to choose potential winners with large clans or other local bases of support. Candidates were offered various financial and political inducements to accept party endorsement, and to join the parliamentary party should they be successful. Parties based their appeal to both candidates and voters largely on the personalities of their leaders. The governing coalition parties made some play on the symbolic achievements of the government — the smooth transition to self-government and independence, the introduction of a national currency, and the renaming of such bodies as Air Niugini — while the Opposition pointed to examples of government and ministerial extravagance. But by and large, policy issues (of national significance) were not discussed and played little part in the campaigns.

Parties, however, had a much more significant impact on these elections than they had had in 1972. Of the 879 candidates who stood for the 109 electorates, 295 were endorsed by the three major parties, Pangu, PPP and UP. There were more direct contests between endorsed party candidates than occurred in 1972, and the fear of party attachment had largely dissipated. Party labels were more widely known throughout the country and although the concept of parties had not penetrated to the village level, candidates in particular were aware of their significance both in terms of the financial support they could offer and their linkage role at the national parliamentary level. Disputants in local conflicts occasionally adopted national party labels.

All parties produced detailed platforms for the elections. They were bland documents but reflected the clear convergence of ideology and policy which had become apparent in preceding years. All platforms emphasized rural development programmes; the encouragement of foreign investment to stimulate industry and mineral resource projects; the extension of road and transport infrastructure; increased educational opportunities; and the necessity for law and order for the maintenance of stable government. The differences in party platforms (insofar as they provide a guide to government action) were only minor. Pangu, for example, was slightly more cautious in its approach to foreign investment than was the PPP, calling for investment which 'truly benefits the people'. The PPP was less emphatic about the decentralization of government structures, and in the area of foreign policy it called for active co-operation with members of ASEAN. The UP's platform was little different in substance, but was critical of government spending and the practice of political appointments to the public service. One novel suggestion included in the UP platform was for the introduction of state farms. All parties, however, emphasized the role of the state in encouraging indigenous capitalism.

Party campaign expenditure was much higher in these elections than in the past. Pangu spent in excess of K200 000, financed largely by expatriate business interests and by mortgages on party-owned real estate. After self-government, foreign businessmen quickly realized that Pangu represented little threat to their interests and switched their financial backing away from the UP which they had supported during the 1972 campaign. Both the PPP and UP spent about K100 000 each in their campaigns, although the UP had some difficulty in raising finance. The coalition partners also had the very firm backing of the foreign-owned press.

The elections resulted in the return of Pangu and PPP to government. When counting was finalized Pangu and PPP-endorsed candidates accounted for 48 of the 109 winners and they effectively lobbied for the support of Independents, bringing their total support in the new parliament to 69. Both parties increased their support throughout the country and in particular made inroads into the Highlands region which had previously been a UP stronghold. Astute cultivation of strong candidates in the Southern Highlands Province by Chan and in the Eastern Highlands Province by senior Pangu member Holloway resulted in majority support from those provinces going to the coalition partners. The UP once again formed the Opposition, although this time its numbers were depleted to twenty-seven and its organization was left in considerable disarray. It did, however, have the support in opposition of the Papua Besena group which had seven of its representatives elected to Parliament. Together with six Independents the opposition now numbers forty.

# 15
# The evolution of the post-colonial state

## Rex Mortimer

### Transition to independence

In previous chapters, it has been demonstrated how poorly prepared Papua New Guinea was for an independence which the colonial power conceived and executed with such haste that many doubted its ability to preserve its vital economic and strategic interests. The fact that the transition did proceed with minimal dislocation owed little to Australian forward planning, but a good deal to the durability and penetration of its administrative structures and techniques. Other factors, most of them fortuitous, played their part too, among them Papua New Guinea's favourable external environment, a long run of economic expansion, and the short-term negotiability of her internal conflicts.

As we have seen, nationalist pressures had not constituted a major source of concern for the Australian administration, nor were there settler groups with a sufficiently strong economic or political base to enable them to sabotage proposals for self-government or independence. The emerging nation did not face the kind of difficulties experienced by many Asian and African states in dealing with irredentist claims by their neighbours. Lastly, although regional pressures were already being felt and were to increase in severity, the country was not troubled by the existence of substantial minority groups that had remained effectively beyond the reach of colonial power (such as the Muslims of the Philippines or the Karens of Burma).

The Somare government which took office early in 1972 was generally acepted as having a mandate to govern, although it possessed no clear authority to negotiate independence. The Australian government, having learned from its mishandling of Pangu and the troubles on Bougainville and the Gazelle, decided, against minor resistance from Administration diehards, to work with the elected government and persuade it of the convergence of its interests with those of the metropolis. Consequently, the Somare government acted in many respects as the leadership of a sovereign state from the time of its formation. The Australian administration retained reserve powers of approval for legislation until self-government late in 1973, but was never obliged to use them. It also retained control of foreign affairs and defence until independence, but these areas of policy produced no overt hostility between the parties either.

In fact, despite the earlier conflicts between Pangu leaders and Australian officials, there appeared to be a remarkable degree of harmony and consensus between them during the interregnum, the new government leaning heavily upon the advice of its former masters. The most energetic campaign of the coalition was for the localization of the public service, a reform which the Australians themselves conceded as being long overdue, and which they had anticipated by providing extremely generous severance payments to redundant Australian administration officials out of the annual grant to Papua New Guinea.

Buoyant economic conditions also eased the changeover. Papua New Guinean economic growth rates were very high in the 1960s and early 1970s, exports were expanding and fetching good prices, and the entry of the Bougainville copper mine into full production just as the country passed from self-government to independence provided a major boost to revenues and a ballast of confidence in the country. Australian promises of continued large-scale aid appeared to assure the government of budget support, as well as encouraging its disposition to accommodate Australia's interests.

Inexperience and the narrowness of its parliamentary majority created problems, but the government faced only one major threat, though a potentially disastrous one. Several major regions of the country were sponsoring movements with mass support and demanding extensive concessions from the government. From the outset, the Somare government was compelled to give urgent attention to the crisis on the Gazelle Peninsula, where the Mataungan Association had been in open conflict with the Australian administration and other Tolai factions since attempts had been made to establish a multi-racial council in the late 1960s. During 1972, the Association was demanding the takeover of expatriate plantations, greater business opportunities for Tolais, and substantial control of Gazelle affairs. Pangu had expressed support for Mataungan demands well before the election, and the government moved quickly and successfully to placate them by promises of early action on their demands, the appointment of sympathetic officials in the area, and the selection of a turbulent young Tolai leader, John Kaputin, as Minister for Justice. Within a year, Kaputin and the government had parted ways, but the coalition's handling of Gazelle affairs, aided by continued rifts among the Tolais themselves and the capitalistic spirit of the Mataungan Association, could be accounted one of its most successful ventures in political management.

In the Highlands, the opposition United Party, sedulously encouraged by white planter interests, was spearheading a campaign to delay self-government and independence, many regional leaders believing that the Australian administration would do more to overcome the lag in Highlands services and public service representation than a Papua New Guinean government dominated by 'coastals'. The government went to considerable lengths to reassure Highlanders and overcome their fears, and the demonstration that its policies were by no means radical or militantly nationalist did much to placate UP leader Tei Abal in particular. When self-government passed without a crisis, and the government began clearly to round upon its more radical critics, toleration if not enthusiasm was won from Highlands leaders for the next step of independence.

A more intractable problem was presented by the Papua

Besena movement and its fluent spokesman, Josephine Abai-jah. Claiming to speak for all Papuans, she argued that unity with New Guinea was being forced upon them against their will, and that it would result in the submergence of their interests under the weight of New Guinean numbers. At first, the movement sought to ingratiate itself with Australia to obtain separate independence or at least autonomy, but when it found that both major parties in the metropolis were adamantly opposed to any form of separatism, it adopted a highly critical stance toward the colonial power, threatening an appeal to the International Court of Justice and other steps to safeguard Papuan interests. The Somare government sought to undermine Papua Besena by favouring Papua in development allocations, establishing a Village Development Task Force especially aimed at infiltrating Papua Besena strongholds, and wooing Papuan influentials. In the 1977 elections, however, Papua Besena increased its parliamentary representation from two to six, demonstrating that its strength is far from spent. On the other hand, however, Papua Besena has not been able to justify its claim to speak for all Papuans, nor could it make its bid for separate independence stick. Essentially, its support is concentrated in Port Moresby (where the large influx of New Guinean immigrants provides it with fuel for its agitation among the local Motuan population); in the Central Province as a whole; and among coastal villagers adjacent to that province. These factors are gradually transforming it from a separatist movement into a very effective pressure group for the strong Papuan component of the public service (see below) and local communities in Central Province (Griffin, 1975; McKillop, 1976b).

But by far the biggest regional threat to the government emerged on Bougainville island. Separatism has been a recurring theme on Bougainville for many years, and will very likely continue. Its highest peak to date, however, coincided with the passage to independence. There are many strands to secessionist feeling on Bougainville, including its isolation from the rest of the country, its painful history of European contact and exploitation, its comparative neglect by Australia, and the fact that the major missionary influences upon the island derived from the neighbouring and ethnically related British Solomon Islands. A new factor was injected into the situation by the establishment of the copper mine, which provoked intense conflict over land rights, royalties and compensation in the late 1960s and, by introducing into an agricultural and fishing community a high-technology industry dominated by Europeans and employing labour from other parts of Papua New Guinea besides Bougainville, caused considerable disruption to established ways of life (Mamak and Bedford, 1974). Although Bougainville leaders deny it, it is hard to accept that the prospect of exclusive control over public revenues from the mine had no part in propelling the surge of secessionist activity in 1974-76; revenue demands certainly figured high on the programme of the secessionists. Finally, the specific political disagreements that developed in 1973 between the government and the highly influential Bougainvillean member of parliament, Father John Momis, undoubtedly had a significant effect in promoting secessionism, particularly among young educated islanders (Griffin, 1975).

Bougainville declared a separate independence on 1 September 1975, two weeks before the national date. If this looked like a determined act of unilateralism, subsequent events were to contradict it and indicate that the Bougainvilleans were open to compromise. For a considerable time, the government was clearly divided on how to handle the issue, and lack of clarity, unity and decisiveness on its part seemed likely to destroy any hopes for conciliation. But a majority of Cabinet stood firm against the temptation to resort to force, and in 1976 when conclusive evidence that the secessionists had overwhelming mass support for their stand was available,* negotiations began to be taken seriously and succeeded in resolving the issue, at least for the time being, in July of that year (Conyers, 1976).

Regionalism is, and will remain for the indefinite future, a factor of the greatest importance in Papua New Guinean

---

* A successful boycott of the by-election for the regional seat of Bougainville, held by Fr Momis until his resignation following Bougainville's UDI.

politics, affecting decision-making and politico-bureaucratic alignments in countless ways. It will serve as a cloak for class conflicts, as well as an impediment to the growth of class consciousness. Regional leaders have been among the most vocal critics of the Somare government, both from a conservative standpoint and from a radical or radical-seeming one. Overall, however, there is no sign yet of regional movements coalescing into any concerted ideological opposition to the government, though abortive moves in that direction have been made from time to time. The trajectory of government policies, which have steadily been becoming more conservative and subservient to foreign interests, has in fact not met substantial resistance, and regional leaders have for the most part been pursuing parochial interests only, though sometimes under the cover of more general slogans.

Just how quickly and thoroughly the Somare government abandoned early promises of promoting a break with the colonial past and sponsoring experiments in social change becomes apparent as soon as we focus in more detail upon crucial areas of policy. For the purposes of this study, the most important and revealing fields are those of socio-economic policy and foreign policy.

## Socio-economic policies

On 18 December 1972 the Somare government adopted as its socio-economic philosophy Eight Aims fashioned for it by a consulting team from the University of East Anglia and a group of internal white advisers (Somare, 1975). The aims, obviously inspired by Tanzanian official goals, committed the coalition to a programme of self-reliance, social and regional equality, rural development, accelerated economic opportunity for nationals, decentralization and enlarged rights for women. At that time, many observers believed or feared that the government was about to take off in a socialist direction, and some noticeable jitters were detected among Australian investors already nervous at having to deal with black officials. Within two years, however, the aims had been emasculated, surviving merely as withered slogans and diversionary devices, and the government had decisively committed itself to a strategy of maximizing national income, state revenues and business opportunities through the agency of foreign aid and investment.

From the beginning, commitment to the Eight Aims, while it may have been sincere, was essentially abstract and unreflective. Politicians such as Somare were undoubtedly attracted to the ideas enshrined in the platform, and conscious of the popular ring they had for a society where the overwhelming majority of the people live in villages on low incomes and look to the government for initiatives for renewal and improvement. But, as we have seen, neither Somare nor his colleagues were political radicals or even populists.

It was clear to the distanced observer even in 1974 that little was being done to put teeth into the Eight Aims, and that government activity was limited to general publicity and the enunciation of the vaguest rhetorical slogans. The kind of political education and organization that would have been necessary to enlist a popular campaign for their implementation was never attempted. Nothing systematic was done to uproot the colonial attitudes prevalent in the society, or to arouse the people to the dangers to their dawning independence of neo-colonialism and imperialism. Planning guidelines drawn up by one or two white advisers to give some content to the aims were quietly shelved. Desultory discussions about mobilizing the people for self-reliance petered out; the government relied for its support on 'pork barrel' politics, opportunist political alliances, and the colonial-style administration. In short, nothing was done to develop the crucial political resources without which the social change indicated by the Eight Aims could only remain a chimera. As the government's own Associate Director of the Central Planning Office (later Director) put it early in 1976:

> Such radical changes, however, necessitate the development of a political machinery and mass mobilization.
>
> For Papua New Guinea, then, in the broad sense, the restraints or limits on alternative approaches to development are first of all political.

211

> Although many Papua New Guineans have called for the 'Papua New
> Guinean way' or 'Melanesian Way' as an ideological basis for develop-
> ment planning, there has been a consistent failure to develop this into a
> meaningful social theory. It is merely the hopeful expression that some
> way other than 'western capitalism' and 'communism' exists for coun-
> tries such as Papua New Guinea (Lepani, 1976a: 25).

The path of minimal reliance on the world capitalist system
is a hard one in any circumstances, and only becomes feasible
if a government completely identifies with the interests of the
underprivileged. It must create the ideology, organization and
confidence required to harness the people's energy, skills and
enthusiasm to provide, in simple, co-operative ways, sub-
stitutes for the expensive, bureaucratically-administered projects and services made available selectively by the administration and foreign agencies. Neither Pangu nor any other of
Papua New Guinea's political parties sought to construct a
political movement of this kind; the politics to which they
gravitated was the politics of management, bargaining and
accommodation, political attributes typical of an early neo-
colonialist polity.

It may be argued that the government was so beset with
routine problems of the transition that it was unable to cope
with the task of political mobilization. While it is true that
transitional tasks did weigh heavily on the government, this is
only another way of saying that in practice it gave far greater
priority to administrative continuity and orderliness than it did
to social and economic change.

The question also arises whether the creation of a grassroots
political organization of the kind needed to initiate radical
socio-economic change was a realistic objective in Papua New
Guinea. There is no doubt that, for reasons already explored in
this book, the forces for change were pitifully weak, and the
pressures seeking a continuation of the expensive administrative services supplied by Australia to a considerable minority
of the population were by contrast strong. In the absence of a
serious attempt by the government to mobilize for change, one
can only suggest that the logical line for it to have taken if it
had really wished to transform Papua New Guinean society

212

would have been to try to promote and consolidate unity and common purpose among those significant mass organizations which did exist and showed some disposition to break with the colonial past: Pangu Pati, the Mataungan Association, Napidokoe Navitu on Bougainville, the Highlands Liberation Front, the Kabisawali Movement on the Trobriands Islands, possibly even Papua Besena. We may readily concede the weakness in vision, political awareness, and organization of all these groups, but we have no sure way of knowing how they would have responded to decisive, inspiring and above all dedicated leadership from the government. We have even less grounds for determining what new forces might have emerged under the stimulus of a government-led offensive against the pillars of neo-colonialism and emergent capitalism. We do know, however, that Somare and his colleagues settled, with barely a whimper, for a conservative parliamentary alliance and a bureaucratic system.

The most fundamental ideological issue for the government was its future relationship with Australia, but there is no evidence that it ever saw its situation in those terms. Government advisers were intent upon securing as large an aid package as possible for as long a term as possible, freed from formal ties to specific projects and Australian procurements. In this they were largely successful by 1974. From that time onwards, their major preoccupation has been to find alternative sources of foreign aid and investment to compensate for the eventual phasing out of Australian aid. Nothing in the reference to self-reliance in the Eight Aims appears to have suggested to any member of the government that the acceptance of an amount of aid from one source which in 1978 still amounted to almost 40 per cent of the total Papua New Guinea budget inescapably represented a neo-colonialist relationship of a particularly intense kind, and one incompatible with the government's declared aims. No Papua New Guinean appears yet to have seen the inner connection between the emasculation of the Eight Aims and the Australian aid relationship. It is nevertheless real and intimate.

The literature on foreign aid is now sufficiently detailed to

213

demonstrate that there is no such thing as aid without strings. This holds for the case of Australia and Papua New Guinea. As an economist familiar with Papua New Guinea's aid problems has noted,

> [her] heavy dependence on aid leaves her exposed to fluctuations in the Australian economy and changes in policy. A foretaste of this was given in January 1971 when the Australian PM cut the grant to Papua New Guinea slightly in order to curb inflationary pressures in Australia. [The same thing occurred again in 1974 — RM.] This extraordinary action indicates both the expendability of aid commitments in response to political pressure — in this case to give evidence of government austerity — and the extent to which the government considers Papua New Guinea to be integrated with Australia (Langmore, 1972: 8).

It is of course impossible to determine to what extent Australia's control of Papua New Guinea's purse strings has been used to put pressure on the Papua New Guinean government to change or modify specific policies, but the then Chairman of Pangu, Moi Avei, found it more than a coincidence that the announcement of the Australian grant for 1975 followed a few days after the Somare government rejected its own board of inquiry's proposals for the rationalization of selected imports, on the grounds that they would harm 'traditional suppliers' of the commodities involved.

But direct pressure is a crude device seldom required in these kinds of relationship. If the Somare government knows in advance from its close links with Australian officials what is acceptable to them and what is not, and if it is relying upon a definite minimum of Australian aid to finance its programmes, then it is not likely to bite the hand that feeds it unless it has definite options to fall back on. To push the argument back one step further, the government will only have such options in mind if it has already developed an alternative development strategy that can dispense with at least some part of the Australian grant and risk the future of the aid relationship.

In the end, then, everything — except in highly exceptional circumstances — hinges not so much upon formal provisions in aid agreements of this close kind, but upon the relative strength and independence of outlook of the participants.

Australia did not need to fear for its interests in Papua New Guinea once it was clear that in accepting continued Australian aid on a large scale, the Somare government also accepted the continuance of their special relationship and the structures which defined and articulated it. The failure to develop the Eight Aims into a serious alternative socio-economic strategy did ensure this, and it is intriguing to note that it was in 1976 — the year that the Eight Aims were definitely if not officially buried — that Australia for the first time departed from its practice of guaranteeing its grant to Papua New Guinea only one year ahead and made a five-year commitment amounting to $A930m.

Well before that, however, other governments and international funding agencies had learned to live with and adjust to radical-sounding national aims so long as they still allowed room for the multinationals to operate profitably. Tanzania itself is a case in point; the World Bank recognized the acute ambivalence (to say the least) in the country's attitude towards foreign capital, and financed projects which will help enlarge Tanzania's dependence upon the world capitalist system. The Bank itself, after all, has taken up the rhetoric of self-reliance and equality in an effort to keep distortions in the economies of Third World debtors within bounds, encourage financial economies in them, and shore up crumbling regimes.

For several years, then, the government propagated the Eight Aims while it preoccupied itself with the multitudinous tasks of fashioning a governmental system able to carry on the Australian pattern of growth and open it up to some degree of indigenous participation. By 1974, the general lines of government economic policy had been clarified, and there was no longer any doubt which way the country was to go. As a government economist explained it in 1975:

Mr. Somare's Government inherited a large administration, financed largely from external grants and loans, that provided a range of services of varying usefulness to part of the population. The new government faced the awful choice of rejecting the whole colonial experience as a mistake, dismantling most services, and moving quickly towards financial self-reliance, or of modifying and seeking to extend the most valued services to areas which did not have them. By choosing to improve and extend services, the new government was bound to seek an accommodation with foreign governments on longterm aid and with foreign companies on major resource investments (Garnaut, 1975: 8).

The following year, the then Associate Director (later Director) of the Central Planning Office attempted to justify the abandonment of the central goal of self-reliance:

For the following reasons, the Papua New Guinea government now accepts that self reliance politically and economically may be an unrealistic policy to pursue at this point in time:
(a) that its major revenue earners such as coffee, copper and cocoa are closely tied to the international market process;
(b) that over 40 per cent of Papua New Guinea's budget is still being subsidized by the Australian budget;
(c) that Papua New Guinea's rich natural resources need external sources of capital and technology for development.

Therefore, the government now accepts that self reliance means the achievement of fiscal self reliance through the controlled flow of foreign capital and through foreign aid ... This 'compromise' policy has led the government to recognize that there are two underlying alternatives for self reliance:
(a) to completely sever relations with, and dependence on, the outside world and the international economy; or
(b) to accept economic growth through the effective but decreasing utilization of overseas aid and capital.

The Government has chosen alternative (b) for future self-reliance (Lepani, 1976a: 11-12).

Mr Lepani's apologia for government policy will not wash. The impediments which he lists merely define the conditions within which a policy of self-reliance would have to be framed; they would undoubtedly create major difficulties, but it has not been established that they would render such an aim impossible. The alternative he poses for the country's strategy are false ones: advocates of self-reliance do not argue for complete severance of relations with the outside world, but rather for the reduction of dependence to a point where it cannot determine the major guidelines of national development. Finally, in describing the government's 'compromise' as a form of self-reliance, and claiming that it is planning 'decreasing utilization of overseas aid and capital', he is refusing to face up to realities. Papua New Guinea's reliance on outside loans and investment is increasing and, within present policy lines, must continue to increase, as has been shown in Part One.

So far, the strategy is creating no insuperable problems for the government, thanks to the scale of Australian aid, copper revenues, high coffee prices, and the general acceptance of the ideology of 'bisnis' in the community. But some at least of the government's advisers recognize that the long-term prospect may not be so rosy. Economically, it faces 'the immense cyclical problem of a government that derive[s] all its domestic revenue from the volatile income of export-oriented resource projects and a large village population that derive[s] almost all its income from volatile world commodity markets' (Garnaut, 1975: 8).

Even limited forms of nationally controlled economic growth will not be easy to accomplish. As Lepani notes,

> because of the nature of Papua New Guinea's geography (high transport costs) and the small size and distribution of its population, the limitations on diversification of economic activity and import substitution are probably even more acute than in most small economies. Present import consumption patterns, in keeping with our very open economy, reflect the demand for luxury goods exerted by the expatriate sector, a consumption pattern which is being followed where possible by the urban indigenous sector (Lepani 1976a: 45-6).

While abandoning the Eight Aims in fact, members and agencies of the government continue to treat them as the guidelines of economic policy. How much of this rhetoric is deliberate deception, and how much is self-delusion, it is hard to say. The term self-reliance itself has undergone a subtle transformation. In the speeches of Julius Chan (Minister of Finance until 1977 and then deputy Prime Minister) and documents put out by the Central Planning Office, the term is almost always prefaced by an adjective, so that it now reads *fiscal* self-reliance, and this rendering has become so widespread that many commentators (including Garnaut and Lepani above) treat it as if it were the original and central concept. But fiscal self-reliance, it need hardly be stressed, implies merely the ability to meet government expenditures from internal revenue sources, and hence can be achieved despite overwhelming dependence upon foreign investment. There is in fact a substantial political advantage for the government, at least in the short term, in retaining the rhetoric of self-reliance. While pursuing an utterly and increasingly dependent policy itself, it can (and does) deflect pressures from the regions and rural areas for greater services and infrastructure by urging upon them the holy imperative of 'self-reliance'. If some group of villages needing a feeder road to market its cash crops appeals for government assistance, the reply comes back, 'Be self-reliant; build it yourself'. At the same time, the government proceeds with its urban development schemes and large-scale projects financed by overseas capital and lending agencies. Self-reliance, then, has become a slogan expressing the government's dual economic policy: dependent high-cost projects for the enclaves, urban areas and resource centres, and financial stringency for the rural areas.

Along with the abandonment of the strategy of self-reliance has gone a similar weakening of other objectives enshrined in the Eight Aims. The policy of giving priority to the rural areas, for example, is difficult to reconcile with the emphasis on making major resource projects attractive to investors; it is equally at odds with the interests of the government or bureaucratic groups which are attracted to the easy profits to be garnered in the urban service sector. Mr Somare was the first to confess an inclination to switch priorities to the urban sector. Answering a question put to him at Honiara (Solomon Islands) about the government's plans to stop urban drift, he said:

> I had in mind in my country to form some kind of organization, like youth organizations, where we can take people in ... In the past, I have planned for rural development; now I am thinking of changing my attitude and going in for industrial development, so that we will have industrial development and agricultural development, so that we can provide job opportunities for young people ... I think we are going to find

218

(a job) problem because we spend almost 50 per cent of our expenditure on education. And once you educate people, you have to provide jobs for them. So, I have reconsidered the position of having to have a lot of young people going out, and I think the only way to get them to have employment is by encouraging industrial development. Industrial development in forms of encouraging investment, so that industries can be built in the country. (NBC Broadcast, 1 October, 1975.) Minor changes have been made in the text to eliminate clumsy formulations — Mr Somare was speaking off the cuff. Note that the proportion of government revenue he claims is spent on education is grossly inflated.)

Mr Somare's statement flew in the face of a good deal of expert evidence that Papua New Guinea is not likely to attract significant investment in labour-intensive industries, and that such industrial expansion as does take place in a dependent economy tends to exacerbate rather than solve the problem of urban unemployment, by encouraging disproportionate immigration to the towns from rural areas. In the light of the developments already taking place at that time in the urban sector, it is not unlikely that Mr Somare was in fact rationalizing the interest of the urban middle classes in expanding *their* opportunities, rather than those of the unemployed. In any case, his explicit downgrading of rural development was politically inept, and unauthorized by Cabinet, and hence was quickly hushed up.

Public commitment to priority for the rural areas is a political necessity imposed by the electoral power of the big peasantry and its clientele, and the strength of regional interests generally. Consequently, government statements have continued to stress that income from major resource projects will be used primarily for rural development, and a good deal of financial juggling has gone on in an effort to maintain the belief that this is in fact happening. However, in a document presented to the House of Assembly accompanying the 1976-77 Budget, the then Minister for Finance, Julius Chan, allowed a peep into the real trend of public expenditure. After pronouncing the ritual obeisance to rural development — 'the main thrust of the Government's programmes must be to provide economic opportunities in rural areas' — this document then conceded that 'the largest proportionate increase of expenditure for 1976-77 by a small margin will occur in expenditures related to modern sector development' (*Programmes and Performance*, 1976-77: 7-9). A similar trend is evident in loans policy; between 1968 and 1977, Development Bank loans for industrial and commercial purposes increased by roughly 4000 per cent, while loans to agriculture rose by less than 400 per cent (*National Public Expenditure Plan*, 1978: 71).

Another passage in the same document indicates one reason why urban development is bound to predominate over rural development. It states (page 98):

> The policy of the Office [of Business Development] is to promote business and industry in rural areas where possible ... Nonetheless it is inevitable that most business opportunities will occur in urban areas and that Papua New Guineans will expect assistance in taking up these opportunities. Consequently much of the Office's activity has been in urban areas.

If the government is going to allow market forces to determine the priorities in this field, as this passage and its practice strongly suggest, then there is no doubt that the urban bias will continue and intensify. Capitalist development invariably favours the city over the countryside, for the obvious reason that economic opportunity, wealth and political power all tend to concentrate at the points where the market in fact assumes its most powerful form. The real promotion of rural development, on the contrary, assumes a conscious struggle with the centripetal forces of capitalist development and, if it is to be ultimately successful, a break with capitalist forms of property altogether.

There is no doubt at all that government statements considerably understate the urban bias of present Papua New Guinea government policy. It would be a painful and laborious process to document this in detail, but a number of economists working for the government have conceded the point privately. One small illustration may serve to nail the point, since it concerns a government fund which is explicitly and distinctly earmarked for the assistance of village self-improvement projects. The Village Economic Development Fund, as it is called, has the following stated aims: 'to assist in the establishment of commercial enterprises owned and operated by PNG groups [ie., village groups] where the benefits would accrue to all members of the group' (Papua New Guinea, *Auditor-General's Report*, 1974-75). Part of the fund was used to subsidize an aircraft company, Independent Air Transport, based on Wewak. The Office of Information, in announcing this fact, claimed that people from the East Sepik Province, Star Mountains area and Telefomin had put money into the business, thereby suggesting some (albeit tenuous) link to village self-improvement (*Our News*, 15 September 1976). A search of the company records of the venture, however, disclosed that the overwhelming majority of shares were held by a group of public servants employed on the Ok Tedi project and an Australian entrepreneur. Like the annual budget speeches, the 1978 National Public Expenditure Plan (pp. 105-7) promises to reverse the bias of expenditure to urban centres, but the Plan's vague and insubstantial proposals augur no improvement for rural areas.

Another unannounced casualty among the Eight Aims is the objective of regional equalization, regarded in 1972 as necessary to overcome the imbalance created by the colonial administration's concentration upon those areas where economic returns were most assured at least expense. Now that the Somare government has in effect restored colonial policy by seeking maximum growth through foreign inputs, the provinces which have the greatest immediate resource potential are likely to receive the greatest allocations for infrastructure and services. Another factor enters into the picture, however, which was not present in the colonial era. The Papua New Guinea government has to make its programmes fit political as well as economic necessities, and this involves a much more complicated exercise in which funds for the regions are allocated with both resource-based growth and election prospects in mind. One writer has argued that pressure from the more powerful regional groups has brought about a 'redirection of development resources towards the most favoured areas [which is] masked by the slogans of the government's new developmental policies' (McKillop, 1976b). This is certainly true in the case of Bougainville and Papua, and Berry, in a recent study, could find no support in the available figures for any suggestion that Development Bank loans, or the Rural Improvement Plan, or the Works Program, showed any bias towards the less developed provinces (Berry, 1977: 152-4).

Opposition spokesmen were not slow to suggest another kind of political influence at work when the East Sepik Province — the Prime Minister's home base — became the recipient of a massive K8.3m development grant late in 1976, mostly financed by the Asian Development Bank (*Post Courier*, 1 November 1976).

The general enlargement of regional inequality through preference in fund allocations is so marked, however, that it suggests a more general bias to urban enclaves and potential exporting areas. In the 1976 works allocations, for example, the four most favoured provinces were allocated K28.94 per head of population, while the ten least favoured received only K15.79 per head. This could be justified in terms of stated policy if the preference were being shown to the least developed areas, but this was clearly not the case. Thus the Central and National Capital provinces — Port Moresby and its hinterland — receved K1.4m more than the total allocation for all other Papuan provinces including the Southern Highlands. These two, together with the Eastern Highlands and East Sepik, received considerably more than the combined allocation to the more neglected regions of New Ireland, Manus, West Sepik, Western Highlands, Milne Bay, Gulf and Western (*Parliamentary Debates*, 10 August 1976).

Arrangements for the financing of provincial governments are certain to skew growth still further towards the more favoured provinces. Central government unconditional grants will be based on a sum sufficient to maintain the level of services operating in each province in 1976-77, which of course confirms existing inequalities. In addition, provinces will receive an amount based upon the value of their overseas exports, and royalties from resource extraction, and will be allowed to tax items such as retail sales, land, entertainment, licences, and personal income: all measures tending in the same direction of enlarging existing inequalities. There will be provision for supplementary grants on terms not defined when the National Public Expenditure Plan was published in February 1978, but in any case the amounts involved will be small. The Plan document concludes that 'the equalization of opportunity in the less developed provinces will take a long time' (NPEP: 86), but the more reasonable conclusion would be that it will recede further and further into the distance under present policies.

Decentralization — another of the Eight Aims — has had a more chequered history, because it is on this issue that the central government comes into most direct conflict with regional interests. To date, the focus of contention has been on provincial governments and the powers to be invested in them. When the Constitutional Planning Committee in 1973 first proposed a system of provincial government with substantial powers delegated by the central government, resistance at the centre was slow to manifest itself, but by the end of 1973 both Cabinet ministers and departmental heads had become alarmed at the prospect and sought to water down the proposals. At this stage, the whole issue became embroiled in the struggle over Bougainville secessionism, and the future of provincial government was deferred, pending the outcome of that struggle. Bougainville's eventual agreement with the central government in July 1976 ensured that provincial government would be introduced, and that it would involve some measure of financial and administrative autonomy, at least for those provinces such as Bougainville itself and the Gazelle where there exist movements with sufficiently capable leaders, backed by enough economic resources, to take full advantage of the measure. For the country as a whole, however, it is by no means clear yet that provincial government is going to further decentralization in any substantial way, or that the central government and bureaucracy will not succeed in reasserting effective centralized control (Conyers, 1976).

The only one of the Eight Aims which may be said to have been wholeheartedly pursued by the Somare government is that which provides for the creation of business opportunities for nationals. In the absence of indigenous entrepreneurial classes, the Somare government has extended the role of the state in the economy, both directly through state acquisition of interests in major industries, and indirectly through the promotion and subsidization of aspiring indigenous businessmen and investors. Significantly, however, the edge of its economic activities has not been turned against foreign business in Papua New Guinea. Plantations have been bought up on behalf of local residents, but no other section of foreign business has been touched against its will. The characteristic features of government policy are twofold: to establish partnership between the state and private investors on the one hand, and foreign enterprise on the other; and to finance the entry of Papua New Guineans into fields vacated or never exploited by colonial interests.

This activity has not been resisted by metropolitan or multinational capitalist interests, and in fact most of the directions taken by the government were charted by the Australian administration itself in the late 1960s out of a realization that future relations with the ex-colony would require a degree of participation by the embryo capitalists emerging in Papua New Guinean towns and rural areas. In this, it was merely following an established trend among the multinationals and industrial powers, who see in joint ventures and various other forms of partnership with interests in the host countries a relatively inexpensive means of tying the post-colonial state and strategic groups in the society to their own interests, obtaining guarantees of co-operation in their ventures, and reducing the risks of radical political measures being taken against them.

As is already obvious in Papua New Guinea, the indigenous groups and the state come to identify their future with that of world capitalism and take over its concept of development. But neither the state nor the urban educated and big peasant groups are motivated or equipped to establish and develop productive enterprises which will contribute to the greater independence of the country or its productivity. Overwhelmingly, they buy into existing businesses established by Europeans, or found new ventures in partnership with foreign capital —

usually low-risk ventures in the major urban centres and predominantly of a service nature.

In one respect, it is true, the Somare government has responded to pressure to follow a policy more consistent with the communal elements in Papua New Guinea's heritage. It has provided a legal structure and loan provisions applicable to group-based enterprise, including that based upon village initiatives. A good deal has been made of this innovation, particularly by government supporters with a neo-traditionalist bent, but a recent study has shown not only that individual enterprise remains by far the greatest recipient of public and private loans, but that even many ostensibly group projects are no more than shadow forms behind which the big peasant operates to subordinate his dependents (Fitzpatrick & Southwood, 1976).

## Foreign policy*

By contrast with socio-economic policy, Papua New Guinea's foreign policy has not undergone a process of evolution from the early days of the accession of the Somare government. While a considerable initiative in economic affairs was exercised by the new government from 1972, foreign policy remained under the control of Australia until the grant of independence in September 1975, and the Papua New Guinea government had no power to plot a course different to that pursued by the metropolitan power. Even today, foreign policy remains an area of low priority for the government; nevertheless certain definite orientations emerged during 1976, and these have proven to be remarkably in accord with the dependent outlook of the government in other spheres of policy-making.

Sir Maori Kiki, Minister for Foreign Affairs and Trade until 1977, adopted the term 'universalistic' to describe Papua New Guinea's foreign policy. From statements by him and other Foreign Affairs spokesmen, the term appears to mean that

* The material in this section is based on the writer's notes taken at a seminar on international relations convened by the Papua New Guinea Department of Foreign Relations and Trade on 16-19 July 1976.

Papua New Guinea proposes to treat all nations (except those practising apartheid and similar racialist policies) in a strictly even-handed manner, declining to take sides in international disputes or ideological quarrels. As testimony to the consistency of this policy, Sir Maori has emphasized that Papua New Guinea sought to negotiate diplomatic relations simultaneously with East and West Germany, North and South Korea.

Sir Maori insisted that universalism was not equivalent to non-alignment, by which we are given to understand that Papua New Guinea will not join any non-aligned blocs which seek to define Third World interests *vis-à-vis* the industrial powers. Indeed, Mr Somare has gone so far as to say that Papua New Guinea does not consider itself a part of the Third World, but rather a member of a 'fourth world' consisting of the countries of the South-west Pacific, including Australia and New Zealand. Again, Sir Maori defined the aim of the policy as one of 'making friends with all, and enemies of no one'.

Behind the considerable confusion these statements convey, there do exist a number of definite indicators pointing to Papua New Guinea's view of its place in the world. There is, in the first place, a decided reluctance on the part of the country's policy makers to make choices in international relations; a disposition to conceive relationships in terms of entanglements and obligations, rather than opportunities and benefits, and therefore to keep them to a minimum. This is clearly linked to the second stance, which treats Australia (and, to a lesser extent New Zealand) as constituting now and for the future Papua New Guinea's solid and reliable patners and friends, by comparison with which the rest of the world is regarded as vaguely but perceptibly dangerous and threatening, not by reason of any designs on Papua New Guinea, but rather because it may thrust its problems and conflicts under the noses of a country which would rather not have to think about them. Papua New Guinea is prepared to recognize a wide range of countries, but it would like to let it go at that. Whatever else this policy entails, it constitutes a dependency syndrome with a vengeance.

The *realpolitik* of the foreign policy, if it may be described as such, is a marked tendency to view international relations exclusively in terms of their economic implications. The main object of foreign policy, it has been argued, is the attraction of foreign aid and investment to Papua New Guinea on the most favourable terms obtainable. At this point in the analysis, the coherence of the orientation becomes discernible: the Australian connection is crucial, according to Foreign Affairs spokesmen, because Australian aid provides the financial security on the basis of which resource bargaining can most profitably be carried on. Having a guaranteed budget support, Papua New Guinea does not have to go begging to investors and importers of raw materials, but can hold out for the best available terms. In this respect she is in a decidedly more advantageous position than most Third World countries, and hence it is not in her interest to promote political relations with them which might harm her special relationship with Australia.

In this light, the rather obscure and convoluted phrases in which Papua New Guinea's foreign policy is cast reek less of confusion than of a patent self-interest premissed on the goodwill and backing of her former colonial master and present patron, Australia.

There is room to doubt that the policy will produce very tangible results, even in economic terms. To date, Papua New Guinea has not succeeded in gaining terms for the sale of her resources visibly in advance of those prevailing in the international market. Australian aid may compensate to some degree for other weaknesses in Papua New Guinea's politico-administrative system when it comes to resource bargaining, but in the long run the country may do better to concentrate on remedying these deficiencies rather than relying so heavily upon the real or presumed strength of a tie with a country whose interests as a resource supplier can easily conflict with her own (as happened on a number of occasions in the colonial past). Papua New Guinea after all is a relatively small supplier by world standards, and the great and urgent need for resource development which government strategy has created is easily discerned and capitalized upon by the hungry sharks of the international capitalist system.

The major criticism of Papua New Guinean foreign policy, however, turns on its complete neglect of the political dimension. The government talks and acts as if the country faces no conceivable problems on this front, but it knows better, even if it does not want to face up to them. The most obvious point of weakness lies along Papua New Guinea's common border with Indonesia. Without venturing into detail, it is apparent to any close observer of this scene that it presents a number of ticklish problems that are not going to evaporate in the near future. Indonesia's obsessional anti-communism and phobia about internal and regional security recently provoked one crisis in nearby East Timor; West Irian, with its unhappy population, a small but persistent guerilla movement operating on the border with Papua New Guinea, and a strong reservoir of sympathy among the political public of Papua New Guinea, represents another trouble spot. Papua New Guinea's leaders are counting on the situation remaining under control, but foreign policy should never base itself on a 'best case' forecast. They are also relying on Australia backing them up in the event of trouble with Indonesia, but if that trouble comes in the form of a limited 'confrontation' by Indonesia in response to what she regards as Papua New Guinea's failure to co-operate in border control, Australia may see her wider interests in terms distinct from those of Papua New Guinea's leaders (Mortimer, 1976).

Political considerations, therefore, strongly point to the desirability of Papua New Guinea diversifying her international relations by seeking closer relations with countries which have shown some interest in opposing Indonesian expansionism. The most likely candidates for such a role are the countries in the Organization for African Unity and the socialist states of Asia.

Such a re-orientation of Papua New Guinea's foreign policy would of course have implications for her foreign economic relations as well. She could hardly expact to gain sympathy for her border dilemma from these countries while pursuing a markedly pro-Western and self-seeking policy in the resources sphere. Any such change would entail risks, which Papua New

Guinean leaders are only too clearly reluctant to take; but can any observer claim that her present policy is devoid of risks for her future?

## The bureaucracy

The increasingly conservative bent of the Somare government's policies finds its appropriate reflection in the adoption of more conservative techniques of state rule. At the outset of its career, a new style of government breaking with the stifling bureaucratic centralism of the late colonial period was promised, alongside the new socio-economic policies epitomized in the Eight Aims. The government, it was said, would work closely with the people, promote and support their organizations, consult with them, bring officials within their reach and control, dismantle and reorganize the top-heavy public service. For a time, between 1973 and 1975, Prime Minister Somare supported efforts by the more radical members of Pangu's executive to permit public servants to join political parties, in the hope that this would make them more responsive to popular and governmental wishes.

Like the Eight Aims, reform of the state apparatus has become a dead letter. Open government has been replaced by closely guarded deals and operations, and the watchword of decision-making, expressed in slogans posted up in all government offices, is secrecy. After endless conferences, seminars and workshops on governmental reorganization, procedures and structures remain as complex as ever, and new offices and bureaus proliferate almost overnight. The public service has been confirmed in its 'independence' after a behind-doors struggle within Cabinet, when the Peoples Progress Party aligned itself with departmental heads to block reform, and the Waigani bureaucrats have set out to insulate themselves as securely from public scrutiny and influence as the colonial masters they now look back on as mentors.

Two international consultants, highly experienced in the administrative systems of post-colonial countries, said of the public service of Papua New Guinea in 1974: 'In our experience of political systems in Asia, Africa and the Caribbean, we have not come across an administrative system so highly centralized and dominated by its bureaucracy' (cited in Ballard, 1975 : 9). This heavy structure is the most obvious administrative legacy of late colonialism, and especially of the attempt by Hasluck and his successors to keep a tight rein from Canberra upon all aspects of economic and social policy during the 1950s and 1960s. That the Somare government is perpetuating many of the same bureaucratic features is shown by the growth in the size of the public service since it assumed office in 1972 and the plethora of new tasks it has entrusted to the bureaucrats. In 1972, the public service proper numbered 21 586 persons; by 1976, according to the Chairman of the Public Services Commission, the number had grown to 30 000, in addition to which 10 000 people were employed by the Teaching Services Commission, 30 000 by statutory authorities and 8000 in the defence and police forces, making a grand total of 70 000 people in professional or semi-professional government employment (*Post Courier*, 22 November 1976). The salience of the state sector in the economy is emphasized by the fact that in 1973 some 85 per cent of the professional and semi-professional manpower, and 60 per cent of the technical manpower, were employed in the public sector (PNG Department of Labour Manpower Unit, *Statistics on Monetary Workforce by Sector*, 1973).

The cost of administration to the country is enormous. In the 1975-76 Budget, for example, 68 per cent of government expenditure was on administrative and other non-economic services, an amount which exceeded total internal revenue by K50m (Lepani, 1976). Salaries and emoluments accounted for 63 per cent of total departmental spending (*Programmes and Performance*, 1975-76: 5), and 38 per cent of total receipts. (*Parliamentary Debates*, 10 August 1976).

One factor which enhances both the power and the cost of the bureaucracy is the carryover from the colonial era of the whole panoply of public service rights, career patterns, salary-determining structures and the like from its Australian counterpart. As a result the Public Service Association is the single most powerful pressure group in the country, and one

230

which is determined to defend tenaciously its status, privileges and relatively high incomes.

As a body, the public service hierarchy is intensely conservative. One reason for this is that by its nature, the Australian administration in which most of the present senior Papua New Guinean public servants were trained, and on which they base their outlook, was never permitted to take any action of any account without reference to Canberra. As a consequence, 'the PNG government inherited no policy-making and co-ordinating machinery. It also inherited an exceptionally large and costly staff with limited experience in taking initiative or in innovating outside Australian precedents' (Ballard, 1975: 1).

Like the politicians, senior bureaucrats are becoming addicted to a style of living and behaviour based on that of their colonial predecessors, but now increasingly influenced by the resident expatriate community and the international business executives and consultants with whom they associate in Port Moresby and other major centres in the country. They aspire to (if they have not already obtained) an expensive well-furnished European house surrounded by a high wire fence as protection against urban vagrants, the latest Japanese car, servants, European-style education for their children, and frequent overseas trips on some (usually vague and untended) government business. The international jet tour, in particular, has become a major symbol of status and cosmopolitanism, and the ministers and departmental heads whose jaunts have become a public scandal have been frenetically aped by parliamentarians, local councillors, middle public servants, students, and small-scale entrepreneurs.

Since the official incomes of senior public servants cannot stretch to all these amenities, all except the fortunate few whose stake in traditional forms of wealth is sufficiently large to accommodate their ambitions tend to opt for one of two major forms of income supplementation, or a combination of the two. The respectable avenue is the so-called 'business venture', which is usually nothing more venturesome than buying a block of flats or houses, or purchasing an interest in a successful European enterprise. Loans to upper-bracket bureaucrats are almost as readily available from public and private lending agencies as they are to the politicians, and foreign business interests are only too happy to facilitate partnership with an official who can lend national credentials to the firm and possibly assist it in more tangible ways.

The interlocking of politician, bureaucrats and foreign interests in business binds the three groups together as constituents in an emerging class structure. So far as the public servant is concerned, his class identity shapes the performance of his office, often in crucial ways. Service to the people may be the rhetorical watchword of the bureaucrat, but in these circumstances it cannot but be filtered through a consciousness which is partly that of employer, intimate of foreign business, associate of political leadership. The interests and lifestyle of the bureaucrat encourage him to look with contempt and distaste upon the ignorant, the uneducated, the poor and the 'kanaka' — in other words, the vast mass of his countrymen. Individual sympathies and sensitivities notwithstanding, the structural tendency of the bureaucrat's position can only be to reinforce the class alliance between the urban petty bourgeoisie, the rich peasantry, and the international capitalist.

From engagement in business as a supplement to and accessory of public service income, a growing number of public servants take the longer step to the abuse of office for personal gain. At the very top of the administrative ladder, we would expect to find arrangements being made between bureaucrats and foreign business to facilitate the operations of the latter, often at the expense of official regulations. From time to time, guarded references to such practices are made, particularly focusing on forestry deals involving Japanese interests (Garnaut, 1975: 17). However, these arrangements are notoriously difficult to confirm, and a government whose own hands are not clean is loath to probe too far. One paradoxical result of the official silence is that corrupt practices which may only affect a minority of senior public servants gradually come to be regarded as the norm by a poorly informed populace, with devastating results on public confidence and civil service morale.

Alongside this covert activity there has developed a disposition to loot the public purse directly. Reports of the Parliamentary Public Accounts Committee in 1975 and 1976 referred to considerable discrepancies and unexplained items in departmental finances; the Public Prosecutor in 1976 claimed in his annual report that 'theft and fraud within the Public Service is costing more than K2million a year' (*Post-Courier*, 6 September 1976); and the Ombudsman Commission in the same year stated that corrupt activities 'such as free overseas trips, generous entertainment and dinners are already upon us', adding that it had heard of 'Ministerial staff being allowed to attend university on virtually a fulltime basis, or engaging in outside activities, or looking after Ministers' private business interests, or collecting political party funds' (*Post Courier*, 24 November, 1976).

The level of corruption by officials is still low by world standards, as one would expect at this early post-colonial stage. Some officials and experts believe, or affect to believe, that it will be controlled as more efficient accounting procedures are brought into effect. Comparative experience suggests, however, that the social and political climate is the decisive factor in the growth of corruption — it is in fact one of the most graphic indicators of the impact of underdevelopment upon neo-colonial administrative structures — and from that standpoint the forecast for Papua New Guinea cannot be optimistic.

Having been obliged by its own policies and political weakness to rely more and more exclusively upon this bloated, costly, conservative and corruptible machine to enforce its control and carry out its programmes, the Somare government now finds that the monster is resistant even to those modest administrative reforms which it feels obliged to attempt in order to meet political pressures being made upon it. An instance of this occurred when a group of departmental heads showed their intense opposition to the Bougainville settlement and the introduction of provincial government, decisions which the government itself only reluctantly adopted in order to resolve the issue of Bougainville secession. Expressing the frustration he felt in carrying through the policy, the Minister

for Provincial Affairs (Mr Oscar Tammur) gave vent to his ir-
ritation in a public outburst in the press:

> There is practically nothing the Minister can do if the public service
> chooses to adopt 'go slow' tactics. There has been no disobedience of in-
> structions, there has been no failure to perform one's duties. All that has
> happened is that endless allegedly insoluble problems appear, staff is in-
> sufficient, the workload becomes too great etc ... Inevitably the Ministry
> backs off because it does not have the experience, expertise and con-
> fidence to oppose the public service when confronted with complicated
> technicalities and sophisticated arguments as to why its policies cannot
> be implemented ... whenever small changes are proposed, the sacred
> doctrines of procedures, seniority, permanency and security are held up
> as unalterable laws ... many senior public servants today, having been
> trained and having gained their experience in (the colonial) machine, are
> reluctant to institute changes because 'the road you know is always
> preferred to the one you don't, and power once tasted is very sweet'
> (*Post Courier*, 13 September 1976).

Other instances of tension in the partnership between the
government and the bureaucracy have been publicly aired,
especially on occasions when the government has felt obliged
to move someone from outside the public service into a key
post either to overcome bureaucratic obstruction or lethargy,
or to serve better the political interests of a particular minister
or group of ministers.

In defending its corporate interests against the government,
and establishing its ascendancy over it, the bureaucracy has a
number of key advantages. It is aware of the weakness of the
government, which stems not only from the inexperience which
Mr Tammur emphasized, but above all from the fact that the
government basically accepts the bureaucratic model of administration. Having sprung in the main from the ranks of the
colonial administration themselves, and having cut their
political teeth on the issues of public service localization and
rates of pay, the ministers are naturally responsive to the
preoccupations of the bureaucracy, and the mutuality of their
outlooks is reinforced by the existence of strong family,
business and associational ties between them. Their strongest
bond, however, is their common interest in preserving the cen-

234

tralized system of power they have inherited and expanded, and using it for their own aggrandizement.

The bureaucracy has a powerful corporate structure and spirit to pose against the government's organizational weakness, its shaky position in parliament, its internal divisions and its incompetent members. If that were not enough, the departmental heads can call (and have called) upon regional sentiment at times to buttress their opposition to policies of which they do not approve. The entrenched Papuan contingent from Central Province, which in 1975 held no less than 40 per cent of the executive positions in the public service, has been particularly adept at using the spectre of Papua Besena as a threat with which to ward off government moves antipathetic to its interests (McKillop, 1976b).

In the final analysis, the government, having discarded the option of popular democratic rule based upon the Eight Aims, cannot dispense with the bureaucracy. The same does not hold for the public service which, in alliance with one or more ambitious individuals with political appeal, and the defence forces, could quite conceivably oust the parliamentary system and take the authoritarian road when the time seemed ripe. Would the armed forces respond to such a proposition?

A favourite child of the colonial power, Papua New Guinea's Officer Corps have had showered upon them facilities and equipment unmatched in any other institution in the country. Within the well-appointed barrack communities which insulate them from the wider society, officers comprise a select élite trained to command, to accept deference, to exert discipline, to conceive of themselves as the reserve saviours of the nation. Still highly dependent upon Australian army experts, equipment, and technical services, the armed forces have nevertheless produced a crop of self-confident, tough and ebullient commanding officers. Though the army, like many of its counterparts in the Third World, enjoys boasting of its civic action projects and self-reliance farms, the officers live comfortably when they are not on exercises or border patrols. They too have followed the bureaucratic style by investing in business. Comprising only two battalions, the armed forces are too small to be of much use against Papua New Guinea's only potential enemy, Indonesia, but large enough to play a decisive role in internal political control. At the time of the Bougainville troubles, there were contingency plans for the armed forces to go in and hold key installations; rightly or wrongly, their officers believe they could have accomplished their tasks successfully within a matter of hours.

The officers have a number of grievances. They resent budget cuts imposed during the economic crisis; they complain that they are not consulted on policy issues which affect them; and they are indignant at what they claim is government failure to back them up against the Indonesians on border control problems. They are politically knowledgeable, both in the general sense of taking part in regular seminars and lectures on world politics, and in the particular sense of having a pretty good idea of what goes on among the politicians. Their attitude towards the government is ambivalent; on the one hand, they still regard it as promoting national unity, a cause which they probably hold to more strongly and with less qualification than any other segment of the élite; on the other hand, they are cynical about government expediency, compromises and addiction to self-interest. There is little doubt that in a situation of breakdown or political crisis, the army leaders would be prepared to step in and rule through the bureaucracy. Their background suggests that in that event their impulses would be more oppressive than reforming in character.

## Prospects

There is nothing singular in the manner in which Papua New Guinea has been integrated into the world capitalist system following formal independence; the pattern is all too familiar in the Third World. Among the distinctive features of her case, however, the one that stands out is the absence of any sustained or coherent opposition in the country to the neo-colonialist economy and state. The basic features of government ideology are shared in practice by virtually all organized groups within the country, and, apart from regional challenges, the Somare-led coalition has so far faced only one national political attack of any importance.

The occasion for this one departure from the consensual character of Papua New Guinea politics was the establishment in 1972 of an all-party Constitutional Planning Committee by the House of Assembly under the chairmanship of Father John Momis, the regional member for Bougainville. (Father Momis was nominally deputy for Somare, but in practice headed the Committee.) A Roman Catholic priest whose views reflect influences from Julius Nyerere, aspects of progressive Catholic social policy and traditional Papua New Guinean egalitarianism, Fr Momis succeeded brilliantly for a time in welding the CPC into a pressure group promoting a more militant brand of nationalism than that represented by the government and a stricter adherence to the stated government aims of self-reliance and equality. By publicizing its discussions and proposals, the CPC managed to spark something of a debate among the educated upon the country's goals and the kind of moral principles that ought to govern political institutions, and it succeeded against government resistance in incorporating into the Constitution and organic laws some useful checks on government power and some commitment to decentralization of government. It failed in its major objective of fashioning a constitution in line with 'Melanesian values', however, and the final product of its labours represented no more than a complex lawyer's gloss on the Westminster system.

The major effect of the CPC's work was to provoke a bitter conflict between its members (and particularly John Momis), and the government, centred on the terms for granting citizenship to non-indigenes and the establishment of provincial governments. Ironically, in view of Momis' early championship of national unity, his disillusionment with the government led him to throw his weight behind the secessionist movement in his native Bougainville. At the same time, however, he and other members of the CPC formed a Nationalist Pressure Group in Parliament and initiated moves to form an anti-government alliance among dissidents on Bougainville, the Gazelle peninsula, the Trobriands Islands, the Highlands, and

Papua. These were groups which had in common a kind of regional proto-nationalism, an antipathy to continued white influence on the government and some experience of grass-roots organization and developmental effort.

The challenge was short-lived, however. No common programme emerged to hold together groups with diverse interests and outlooks, and Momis failed to provide the rebels with any clear leadership or guidance. While it lasted, though, it generated some strong attacks on the government's dependent attitude to Australian and foreign business, particularly from Mataungan leader John Kaputin and Bougainville leaders Momis and Leo Hannett. How much of this sprang from thwarted ambition and regional resentment against the central government, rather than any basic disagreement with government policy, is another question. Kaputin, for instance, while consistently seeking to restrict European enterprise where it competes with Papua New Guineans' activities, and fulminating at the deference to Australian advice evident in Port Moresby, is the advocate of a home-grown capitalism which essentially takes the wider context of the world capitalist system for granted. As the manager of the Mataungan-based New Guinea Development Corporation, with assets of over half a million kina, he has become increasingly absorbed in the profitable opportunities for investment in Port Moresby real estate and service industries on behalf of himself and his corporation (Kaputin, 1975b). Leo Hannett, the stormy petrel of Bougainville nationalism, is likewise head of the Bougainville Development Corporation, which derives most of its substantial income from providing services to the mining corporation upon whose management expertise it relies.

All in all, the so-called 'radicals' among Papua New Guinea's leaders, with the possible exception of Momis, go no further than seeking a more assertive and dignified relationship with foreign interests. From time to time, educated leaders who have identified themselves with their local communities have emerged, initiated local development projects based on concepts of self-reliance and cultural revival, and criticized the government for its neglect of popular participation and rural development. In virtually every case, however, these emergent leaders have fallen victim to the lure of 'bisnis' or political ambition and been absorbed into the system. Perhaps the best known, and certainly among the most able and sophisticated in his grasp of the skein of community development action, was John Kasaipwalova, founder and leader of the Kabisawali Movement in the Trobriands Islands. Kasaipwalova's career is almost a caricature of the lost local leader: from apostle of the virtues of village self-reliance and self-improvement, he became successively manager of small urban retail outlets in Port Moresby; a campaigner for a luxury tourist hotel in the Trobriands; a would-be millionaire with aspirations to open branches in Tokyo and New York; and a substantial investor in Port Moresby service industries in partnership with a Singapore-based entrepreneur. Like a number of other local development group leaders, Kasaipwalova found it difficult to draw a strict line between his community's interests and his own personal ones, and in 1977 he served a seven-month prison sentence for the diversion of funds allocated to his area before being freed on appeal.

The government's neo-colonialist strategy, therefore, appears immune to ideologically-based opposition until the strategy itself produces sharper class contradictions. In the meantime, however, conflicts of interest among the indigenous beneficiaries of the neo-colonialist order are becoming more manifest. The tension between the urban-based politico-bureaucratic groups and the big peasantry has been reflected in stronger challenges form a new parliamentary Opposition headed in 1978 by Iambakey Okuk, an aggressive rural capitalist form Chimbu Province.* The basic conflict between these two groups, of course, centres upon the distribution of the government cake between the major coastal centres and the rural areas and Highlands towns.

The introduction of provincial government may give the big peasants added leverage upon the government, since in most cases they should be able to dominate the provincial assemblies

---

\* Now called Simbu Province

and administration. On the other hand, by making some provision for independent revenue-raising by provincial governments, the government will undoubtedly use its own debauched slogan of self-reliance to deflect demands for services back upon the provinces and local councils, as it is already doing with local pressures for roads, schools, medical services and the like. But the rising tide of regionalism is to hand for the big peasantry to use in its fight for greater wealth and power, and this is likely to prove a decisive test of the government's political capacity. When the present coffee export boom collapses, as has begun to happen, the already high incidence of lawlessness and disorder in certain regions could prove beyond the government's capacity to control.

Urban tensions are also mounting steadily. Port Moresby and other large urban centres have a severe dose of what are called 'law and order' problems, exacerbated by a constant migration of job seekers from rural areas, many of them unemployed, living in shanties around the main suburbs, and spawning gangs of young 'rascals' which are becoming increasingly daring and antagonistic towards the wealthier groups, both white and black.

All projections point to an intensification of the unemployment problem, and its extension to more highly educated groups. The Government White Paper in 1976 predicted that 'by 1981 it is likely that 40 per cent of adult males will be without formal wage employment' in the urban areas (*Post-Courier*, 9 November 1976), and in Papua New Guinea there is no tradition of informal survival occupations such as exist in most of the Third World; these must develop, but without prior experience and skill, and facing administrative harassment carried over from colonial days, they are likely to lag well behind the need.

In the middle educational bracket, it has been estimated that 'by 1984 ... 50,700 primary and secondary school leavers will be competing for the 7000 jobs available in semi-skilled categories in formal wage employment' (Lepani, 1976: 40). Still higher, the prestigious and well-paid positions in the public service are being rapidly filled by young or comparatively young men who will before long be defending them tenaciously against still younger, better qualified (in academic terms) and disgruntled aspirants.

It is doubtful that the kind of government and government system Papua New Guinea now has will be able to cope with the conflicts which seem bound to rend the society. In the absence of forces capable of successfully steering the country in a socialist direction, the most likely outcome is that the two most strongly organized, authoritarian institutions in the country — the bureaucracy and the armed forces — will combine to take affairs out of the hands of a failing government presiding over a disintegrating nation. Our study of these institutions does not suggest that they will provide the country with anything better; if anything, their rule will be characterized only by greater repression and ruthlessness in the service of their own ambitions and those of neo-colonialist mentors. Again, the story is all too familiar — an object lesson in the power and historical force of the imperialist system.

## Conclusion

There are close similarities between the evolution of the post-colonial state in Papua New Guinea and that of its counterparts in Africa at a comparable stage in their elaboration. The following description of the structural characteristics of many African states shortly after independence, for example, echoes the themes which have been stressed in this chapter:

> The absence or incoherence of an independence ideology and development programme was the first major reason for the decline of the independence parties. The second was the shift of gravity from party organization to state, from the ways of popular mobilization to the methods of the administrator ... The state asserted itself over the party, not the other way about. Once again, as in colonial days, bureaucratic methods dominated over the political ... On the whole government continued to function much as it had done during the colonial period, as a centralized and hierarchical system of administration (First, 1970: 119-20).

241

## As for structure, so for function:

> The first phase of independence was characterized by the efforts of the power élite to use the state not only as an instrument of political domination but also as a source of economic power, in the interstices of the economy unfilled by external control. Possession of government and the resources of the state proved the decisive means. For the state in Africa is the main source of domestic capital and its accumulation. The state plays the major role in economic activity and development. The state is the principal employer of labour, the chief dispenser of jobs, benefits, patronage, contracts, foreign exchange and license to trade. Manipulation of the offices and resources of the state by the power elite proved the shortest cut to wealth. It was political power that made possible the creation of economic power, not the other way about (First, 1970: 101).

Even some of the detailed mechanisms adopted by what is here termed 'the power élite' in Papua New Guinea to facilitate their aggrandizement of power and wealth through the state structures are prefigured closely in one or more African countries. Thus:

> Sometimes the manipulation was a party-managed affair, as in Nigeria, where each of the major Southern parties had its bank, business and financial structures, to make money for the politician-businessman and provide money for the parties themselves (First, 1970: 101-2).

Hamza Alavi (1972), noting the similarities in the political and bureaucratic structures in so many post-colonial societies, has sought to define and analyse their structural characteristics in more general terms. Founding his argument on the colonial experience of Pakistan in particular, Alavi has drawn attention to three features of the post-colonial state which, he argues, differentiate it from the classical capitalist state and help to explain the inordinate role it plays in social control. In the first place, he claims, the state in post-colonial society is overdeveloped by comparison with the size of the economic base. The colonial powers established an apparatus designed to destroy the independence and vitality of all indigenous social classes in the colony, necessarily a major undertaking which required a powerful military and bureaucracy in particular. The

242

post-colonial society inherits and tends to perpetuate these institutions and their established practices.

Taking issue with Alavi, Colin Leys (1976: 42), while conceding that the state often tends to expand rapidly after independence, cites figures suggesting that central government expenditures in post-colonial societies nevertheless remain relatively small by comparison with those of industrialized states.

There is no doubt, from the figure we have already cited on the size and costliness of the Papua New Guinean public service, that in the late stages of colonialism, and certainly in the post-colonial period, the state in Papua New Guinea did become (and remains) overdeveloped in relation to the scale of economic activity. However, the peculiar Australia-Papua New Guinea relationship has to be borne in mind when assessing the general significance of this fact. As we have mentioned more than once, Papua New Guinea was Australia's only colony, and one small in size and adjacent to the metropolis. This enabled and encouraged Australia to invest rather large sums in aid to the colony when she could afford to do so, and it is aid alone which built up and sustains the unusually large bureaucracy in Papua New Guinea.

Obviously, a good deal more research is needed to clarify the differences in the size of the colonial and post-colonial states, and the significance of the issue. The Papua New Guinea case draws attention to some of the variables that operate, but surely does not exhaust them. Generalizations need to be tested against a good deal of specific historical experience before we can arrive at more firmly grounded hypotheses.

Neither of the other two points advanced by Alavi is particularly new or striking. He points to the enhanced economic role played by the state in post-colonial societies, seeing it as a consequence of the weakness of indigenous entrepreneurial classes and a means by which the political legatees of the colonial order entrench themselves and begin to convert themselves into a ruling class. Our study of post-colonial Papua New Guinea has confirmed the universality of this tendency, which however has previously been analysed in some depth by First and other writers.

Finally, Alavi emphasizes the ideological role of the post-colonial state, by which it seeks to legitimate itself, establish the hegemony of the ruling groups, and assert the primacy of national power. This has long been recognized as a pronounced feature of state activity in newly independent countries. In his influential essay on the subject, Clifford Geertz argued that ideology served more than a political function in new states; it created 'cultural maps' which enabled people faced with entirely new problems and fears and uncertainties to chart their futures with some degree of confidence and security (Geertz, 1964). However, once again Papua New Guinea seems to be one of the exceptions. Ideological activity has not been a prominent feature of Papua New Guinean politics, and, apart from the short-lived and low-key attempts to popularize the Eight Aims, the state has assiduously avoided resort to ideological appeals. Now that reliance upon bureaucratic techniques of political management and manipulation have become routine, it is unlikely that the present group of leaders, at any rate, will make much use of expressive ideology to consolidate their power.

In explaining the low level of ideological activity in Papua New Guinea, we are once more compelled to point to the lack of nationalist consciousness which has characterized the country, and the consequent weakness of political parties, popular mobilization, and anti-imperialist sentiment. By slipping into bureaucratic conservatism so quickly, the state eschewed the path of ideological mobilization around national goals in favour of methods of manipulation, management and top-level negotiation. In all likelihood, ideology will gradually emerge, not as a weapon of the state, but as a weapon against it, wielded both by regional interests and class interests opposed to its strategic objectives or the manner in which it pursues them.

# Notes

## INTRODUCTION

1  Though it receives some attention in Brookfield (1972). This book, while purporting to be based upon underdevelopment theory, is however essentially liberal in outlook.

2  For a cogent critique of this academic ideology, see A.G. Frank (1969).

3  The classification should not be seen as a rigid and unchanging one. The place of different nation states within and among the categories can and does change, as this book demonstrates. In fact, analysis of the reasons for such changes is one of the most interesting aspects of underdevelopment theory.

## 2  THE PLANTATION SYSTEM

1  Although political change came in German-ruled New Guinea from 1915 onward, when Australia assumed control and Australian commercial interests inherited the German-owned enterprises, the real changes of *economic* significance in both colonies occurred after the 1939-45 War. I am grateful to Donald Denoon for clarifying this perspective.

2  The twenty-year depression in the sugar market beginning in the mid-1880s may have been a significant factor in the ease with which blackbirding was abolished from Papua and New Guinea. The subsidies from the Australian Commonwealth Government for transforming the sugar industry were important (see Docker, 1970).

3  This consideration of hierarchies can be extended further within the colonial economies themselves wherein the mining and coastal plantation regions dominated the labour exporting regions and the 'subsistance sector' (see Frank, 1969; and below).

4  In fact before the 1914-18 war, German shipping to a limited extent provided a slightly better service to Papua (Power, 1974: 161).

5  This is a small sum in absolute terms but when considered in relation to the small size of the plantation industry and the fact that 'in the twenty years up to 1939 about £40 000 had been spent on native education and agriculture', it was a substantial subsidy (Power, 1974: 213).

245

6   A similar situation existed in another ultra-periphery, colonial Nyasaland (Malawi), where: 'The land and labour policies of the early administrations were designed to encourage European settlers ... But they were also intended to protect African interests ... the resultant curbs on land alienation to Europeans and on methods of labour recruitment compared unfavourably — from the settlers' viewpoint — with the policies adopted in neighbouring territories' (Morton, 1975: 6).

7   As a separate pressure group, however, the Planter's Association was not very active since planters were well represented on the Legislative Council (Power, 1974).

8   The fact that the major export, copra, was not included in the preferential treatment arises from the position of Australia within the world system. The largest market for the colony's exports, and the most important supplier of imports, was Europe rather than Australia.

9   In 1924, the company producing copper near Port Moresby, New Guinea Copper Mines Ltd, was the largest single enterprise that Papua had ever boasted (Mair, 1948: 71).

10   Even today Papua continues to have an exceedingly limited road network, even by 'Third World' standards.

11   The New Guinea Kompagnie was closely linked with one of the largest private banking companies in Berlin. Through its founder, Adolf von Hansemann, a leading Berlin banker, the Kompagnie was also linked with the 'Long Handle Company' (Moses, 1969: 47).

12   If this point is perhaps being overemphasized it is because liberal Australian historians in PNG have tended to 'explain' the differences between the colonial experiences of Papua and New Guinea in terms of the differences in 'racial' or 'national' characteristics of the respective colonial masters, with Australians appearing more benevolent and wiser (see Burnet, 1967; Biskup *et al*, 1968). They miss the point that in the circumstances Australia was in, it would have been counter-productive, and perhaps impossible even, for the Australian colonial state to have been anything but paternalistic in Papua. For a relatively unbiased account of German colonialism in New Guinea, see Reed (1943).

13   Wage rates were also lower, compared to those in Papua, but not half of Papua's rate as claimed by Murray (Power, 1974: 172-3) and other Australian apologists. The *cash* component (equivalent of 5 shillings per month) was half that in Papua (10 shillings per month). The bulk of the wage in both colonies however, was paid in kind, which tended to be the bare minimum for subsistence. The 10 shillings per month cash wage in Papua was a carryover from the Queensland blackbirding days. Since the cost of imports in Papua was higher, the real value of this cash component was probably only marginally higher than that of New Guinea. In any event, even the money value of this 10 shilling wage was much lower than elsewhere in the colonial world.

14   Metropolitan aid to New Guinea varied from some £35 000 to £84 000 be-

tween 1900 and 1914. In Papua it increased from £15000 to £30000 (Burnet, 1967: 172-3). In the inter-war period, however, the economic foundation built in German New Guinea, and the development of gold mines, enabled Australia to rule New Guinea without any subsidy whatsoever. Papua on the other hand continued to receive Australian assistance at the rate of £40000 to £50000 per year.

[15] At the same time as Germany was establishing the mono-crop copra colony in New Guinea, German-ruled Tanganyika was being moulded to specialize in sisal production, again on plantations. This of course was a typical pattern of international specialization forced on colonial peoples (and resources) by metropolitan capitalism.

[16] A Royal Commission was appointed in 1919 to look into the future of German New Guinea. Hubert Murray, Lieutenant Governor of Papua, had wanted to see the two colonies merged into a single administration (under his leadership) but was overruled by the other two Commissioners, 'being safe men for the capitalists in general and Burns Philp, in particular' (Murray, quoted in Power, 1974: 167). Murray had advocated state ownership of the expropriated properties. The capitalist interests were naturally averse to this, just as they were to Murray's perceived 'pro-native' colonial policies in Papua.

[17] This company was formed in 1914 by a former employee of Burns Philp and, like BP, grew into a Pacific-wide multinational, with extensive interests in Australia and Fiji, as well as Papua New Guinea.

[18] This tendency of the large trading houses to grow by taking over the smaller individual enterprises had been a feature of western imperialism in the Pacific from the end of the nineteenth century. With the exception of the New Guinea Kompagnie which was a truly pioneering enterprise, large companies always tended to follow and buy out the pioneering small-scale establishments. Often the smaller enterprises would become indebted to the trading houses and pass into the latter's ownership in hard times. Burns Philp particularly had been growing in this manner in Papua as well as Queensland; and Steamships, a very small shipping enterprise, arrived in Port Moresby in 1920 and grew by buying out other smaller enterprises during the 1930s. The company purchased its first plantation, a 2300-acre property valued at £78000, for a price of £875 in 1934! (Nicklason, 1967: 242).

[19] Burns Philp thus acquired a monopoly over shipping in New Guinea as well as Papua. It benefited greatly from this position, particularly during the five years when the Australian Navigation Act was in force in Papua and New Guinea. It had an edge over other plantation companies due to this shipping monopoly; and many of the smaller planters in effect become its mere agents (see Brookfield, 1972).

[20] The volume of production in Papua rose from some 4080 tons in 1920 to 13400 in 1940. However 12800 tons were already reached in 1929. Most of this increase is therefore accounted for by the maturation of plantings carried out by 1920.

21  The precise amounts of peasant output for 1940 are unknown (both Mair and Reed claim that the statistics are not available). Shand (1969: 287) ventures the figure of 3-4 per cent for 1934. While this may be correct it would not be typical, due to the effects of the depression in the 1930s (see below).

22  BDG was floated with authorized capital of Can$4 000 000. In 1930, 476 000 shares at $5.00 each were paid up, giving a total of $2 130 000; Australian shareholders predominated in the company's ownership.

23  Indeed even the cost structures and fares for air transportation within PNG are among the highest in the world in the 1970s.

24  In addition to contributing to the balance of payments of Australia, New Guinea was subjected to a Gold Tax by the Commonwealth Government in 1939. This tax represented 172 per cent of the royalty paid by BGD in that year (Healy, 1967: 94-5).

25  New Guinea's exports increased from £A1.47m in 1928 to £A1.776m in 1934 and £A3.68m in 1940 (Burnet, 1967, Appendix A); gold accounted for more than half the value of exports from 1932 onwards. The number of people employed increased from some 30 000 to 43 250 in 1938 (West in Ryan, 1972: 845); and the 5 per cent royalty provided the colonial government with some 25 per cent of its total revenue (Healy, 1967: 94).

26  After 1941 the rate of return fell sharply but never went below 10 per cent right up to 1962. Total dividend payment up to 1962 amounted to some $34.00 per $5.00 share. Similarly, Guinea Airways, established in 1927 with paid-up capital of £20 000 netted a profit of £42 466 in 1929 and 1930; it paid out dividends at the annual rate of 40 per cent of share value in 1930 and 1931. Thereafter, due to the need for reinvestment for expansion, the dividend rate was 20 per cent per share up to 1937 (Healy, 1967: 76).

27  The slack demand for plantation labour during the 1930s and the interruption of World War II delayed the incorporation of this region until the late 1940s and 1950s.

28  The United States' South and Queensland are excepted since they were not separate colonies but peripheries within continental economies from which the plantation system was eventually ousted, and the economies integrated into a single progressive capitalism. Cuba has been an exceptional example of a plantation neo-colony attempting a strategy of socialist construction. While the mode of producing sugar has been transformed i.e. the plantation as an institution has disappeared, the economy has continued to rely heavily on sugar exports (see Beckford, 1972: Thomas, 1974).

29  Barnett (1976: 7, 8), borrowing from the *PNG Resource Atlas*, 1974, and a CSIRO report (1975) states that a total of 2 per cent of the land area falls within the category of 'land with very high capability' and probably only 12 per cent of the total land area would seem to be suitable for cash

248

crop agriculture of varying kinds'. Since almost all plantation land would be included in this latter category at least, the alienation of good land may be between 8 and 10 per cent. The alienated proportion of the best 2 per cent is likely to be much higher.

[30] These peripheries traditionally included the Sepik region, the Gulf and Western Papuan region and — in the post-war period — less well-off Highlands districts. In addition, the outlying areas within the plantation districts themselves tended to suffer 'backwash effects' in the same manner as did the regions which were net exporters of plantation labour. For a dynamic analysis of the underdevelopment of a labour-supplying region in colonial Tanganyika, see Wayne (1971).

[31] The sharp contrast between the 'domestic' orientation of the pre-colonial trading networks and the external orientation of the colonial shipping routes can be observed in the charts in Brookfield with Hart (1971: 321, 340).

# 3 THE TRANFORMATION OF PERIPHERAL CAPITALISM 1945-1978

[1] However, the terms of trade for the underdeveloped world as a whole tended to deteriorate, especially in the period 1954-70; and there was a long term *decline* in agricultural productivity which 'in the Afro-Asian countries [had] fallen by some 20 per cent between 1922-26 and 1968-72' (Bairoch, 1975: 195).

[2] This rapid growth in export performance and manufacturing output was, however, offset by an even faster growth in imports and indebtedness as a result of greater metropolitan investment and lending, stagnation in domestic food production and deterioration in the terms of trade. Thus the dependence of these countries upon metropolitan capitalism increased and the extent of their economic disarticulation became aggravated, in spite of their diversification into industrial production (see Ashworth, 1975, Bairoch, 1975).

[3] The Gazelle Peninsula, the area with the greatest plantation concentration, was heavily affected by the war (Brookfield, 1972: 93, 95).

[4] The estimated shortages of labour in the Territory as a whole amounted to 33 000 'units' in June 1948 and fell to about 2800 in June 1951 (Harris, 1971: 6).

[5] Although the employers were charged a fee for this service, the state operated the service at a loss, thus subsidizing the capitalist sector. In 1972-73 a loss of $A9.07 per 'unit of labour' was sustained by the state agency recruiting the labour (Collins, 1974: 24).

[6] These settlers included some of the gold prospectors and government officials who had pioneered the exploration of the Highlands during the 1930s. The coffee plantations turned out to be a large enough consolation prize for a few of them who built up, by the 1960s, significant plantation-commercial empires based in the Highlands region.

7    Little is known at present about the precise levels and mode of production on plantations bought by local groups and companies (few cases of single individuals buying up expatriate plantations are known). The transfer of ownership involves the local group putting up a deposit, on the strength of which a loan is obtained from the state-owned Development Bank, or one of several government agencies, or occasionally from the vendor. The Papua New Guinean government has made several requests to the Australian government for a special grant to effect a speedy acquisition of plantations, but so far in vain. To date, some 10-15 per cent of the 1200-odd plantation properties have been transferred to local business groups and companies, including corporations owned by provincial governments. Where the plantations involved have been senile or badly run-down, or if the particular product happens to be experiencing a trough in the world commodity markets, the new owners are likely to have to bear heavy debt burdens. Or conversely, these new owners may join the ranks of the emerging 'kulak' and rural capitalist classes. A simple, equitable and efficient tactic of doing away with the plantation mode of production, and localizing ownership of the assets, would have been simply to raise the legal minimum wage to a high enough level, whereby the majority would have been forced to close down and sell out (in a depressed, buyers' market). Rather unsurprisingly, this option was not taken up by the neo-colonial state, ostensibly because such a move would cause a drop in export production and large scale unemployment, as well as frighten away potential foreign investors. For an industry which has traditionally, and even today, depended upon *bonded migrant* labour, the unemployment argument is a laughable excuse (although in a minority of cases the problem would arise and could be dealt with relatively easily). The *possible* decline in output would only be temporary, and would, in any case, be more than compensated for by the saving of surplus at present transferred overseas. As regards investor confidence, once again the argument may be exaggerated. The modern, large-scale corporations view 'land reforms' as progressive rather than threatening to their interests.

8    These statistics are derived from IBRD (1965: 431, 434) and PNG Bureau of Statistics (August 1976). In view of overlaps, and the broad classifications of import and export items in official statistics, the amounts advanced here should be taken as approximations of magnitudes involved rather than as precise values.

9    It is easier and cheaper to buy Coca Cola in Port Moresby than young coconuts for refreshment: this in an ex-copra colony! Coffee drinkers in the Highlands region, where good quality *arabica* coffee is produced, drink the high-cost, Australian-processed, instant coffee which is an inferior drink. In April 1977, even without import duties, the retail price of Australian instant coffee was four times that of ground coffee from Goroka. Yet there were no government policies to promote the consumption of locally produced coffee and imported instant coffee continued to remain the most popular type of coffee consumed. Incredibly, Papua New Guinea has not yet even imposed tariffs on imported coffee and cocoa products. These anomalies exist at almost every level within the economy:

250

coconut cream sold in supermarkets is imported from Britain. A cooperative society producing peanut butter in the Markham valley imports peanut oil as an ingredient when peanuts have been one of the economy's exports. At a recently established soap factory in Lae only 16 per cent of the oil-based ingredient is locally produced in the form of coconut oil, the rest being imported in the form of tallow (personal communication, Chris Livesy, National Investment and Development Authority, December 1976); and so it goes on . . . .

10  Given the stranglehold these trading houses had, and continue to have, over the economy; their vertically-integrated operations; the export orientation of the transport, marketing, extension and research infrastructure; and the economic policies persued by both the metropolitan and colonial governments, it is simplistic to attribute the failures of import substitution to simple trade practices. However, from a Mission whose recommendations were overwhelmingly to further exports, even such an observation is valuable, though anomalous.

11  The number of expatriate public servants alone increased from just under 1000 in 1947 to about 6500 in 1972; the total public service employment increased from 7500 to 44 120 during the same period. In 1974 public service employment stood at about 50 000, and the total employment in the public sector as a whole, including statutory bodies, was about 64 300. The public sector therefore became the major employer in the economy, the number of its employees being roughly double that in the plantation sector in 1972 (Papua New Guinea, Central Planning Office, 1975; Department of Labour, 1975).

12  Dixon's calculations show a rate of growth of output, at constant prices, of about 17 per cent per annum. This compares with an average growth rate of industrial production in the 'Third World' as a whole of some 7 per cent (Bairoch, 1975; Ashworth, 1975). It should be remembered however, that PNG's high growth rate is upon a very small base.

13  With respect to African economies, see Arrighi (1967).

14  In 1973 the shares of wages/salaries and surplus were roughly 50 per cent each, being $A389.2m and $A398.4m respectively (Lepani, 1976: 5). The urban minimum wage rate began to increase rapidly from 1971 onwards, rising from $A8.00 to $A13.80 in 1973 and $A27.30 in 1976. At present, in money terms, the minimum urban wage is one of the highest among 'Third World' Countries. So is the cost of living, due to the highly oligopolistic structures of Papua New Guinean capitalism, the high cost of Australian manufacturing, and imported inflation.

15  The manufacture of beer, cigarettes, soap, ice cream, clothing (all five under oligopolistic control), cordials and aerated water, bakery products, and cheese snacks are the major consumer goods industries in PNG. In all cases the raw materials are invariably imported as is typical in much of the underdeveloped world. This arises both from the nature of the technology used as well as imported tastes. The only soap factory, built in 1976, for

251

example, cost $A700 000, employs 36 workers (working only one shift) and produces 180 tons of soap, to replace only a proportion of the imports. A UNIDO-sponsored team, investigating the possibilities for the development of small-scale industries, recommended the establishment of: a single toilet soap factory costing $A70 000 and employing 40 workers to produce 80 tons of soap per month to replace all imports (running at 482 tons in 1974); and 60 small units each costing $A1000, employing 4 workers, and producing 50 tons of laundry soap per year. The total capital cost with this option would have been $130 000 and would have employed 280 workers producing 330 tons of soap per month working a single shift per day (UNIDO, 1974: 84-7). Apart from providing more employment, this option would have meant a greater use of locally produced raw materials and, eventually, the possibility of domestic production of the capital goods as well.

[16] Some of this decline may be accounted for by the non-enumeration of the wage labour force on plantations transferred to national ownership. Given the small number of plantations involved, however, this error cannot be very significant (personal communication, Peter Williamson, PNG Department of Labour, December 1976).

[17] The level of the Australian subsidy declined in real terms by about 12 per cent in 1975-76 from the previous year (PNG Central Planning Office, 1975: 325). The latest agreement between the two governments has fixed the annual subsidy at $A180m up to 1981. Although supplementation over and above this sum is allowed for, it is unlikely that the real value of the subsidy will go any higher than this level, particularly in view of the very large devaluation of the Australian dollar announced in late 1976. Indeed there is a greater likelihood of the opposite.

[18] The share of copper ore in total exports of course fluctuates very widely according to the price of the metal in the world market. On average, however, copper exports are likely to continue to account for between 50 and 60 per cent of the total.

# 4 CONSOLIDATION OF THE NEO-COLONIAL ECONOMY

[1] Plywood, veneer, woodchips and wooden chopsticks are the major manufactured exports from PNG. Much of the output is produced at the plywood factory at Bulolo now owned jointly by a Japanese company and the PNG Government. It was established soon after the 1939-45 war ended, to supply an Australian market suffering acute shortages of timber at the time.

[2] In addition, PNG exported $A2.6m worth of rubber and imported $A6.6m worth of rubber products in 1975. It also imported $A1.68m worth of processed coffee, tea and cocoa products, a good proportion of the raw material contained in these imports typically originating from within PNG in the first place.

3   I am grateful to S. Ganguli for introducing me to this line of thought, practised in Chinese socialist construction.

4   The almost casual purchase of computers in PNG is something of a standing joke. The University of Papua New Guinea, for example, is one of the most 'capital-intensive' universities to be found anywhere in the world (although its 'capital:output ratios', at every level, leave much to be desired!)

5   In the absence of direct evidence the statement here is advanced cautiously. The only evidence of relevance known to the author are some nutrition studies (e.g. Lambert, 1976) and impressionistic works (Rowley, 1965, Reed 1943). It is indeed possible that the entry into export crop production by peasants was a desperate attempt to counter the decline in their productivity, as well as to satisfy the need for cash to pay taxes and to buy new products, in response to the demand created by peripheral capitalism.

6   One of the enterprises that the mining Company nurtured is the Bougainville Development Corporation Ltd, owned by the North Solomons provincial government. Its nine subsidiaries include shipping, air services, engineering, taverns, catering, laundry and timber logging. With a capital investment of $A200000 — almost all of it loan-financed — the corporation netted a total tax-free profit of about $A200000 in its first year of operation. By far the greatest part of this profit was generated by its two 'wet' canteens serving the mine workers. Among the corporation's stated policies is to invest 'in projects that cater for the basic needs of the Bougainville Copper Limited employees' (BDC Prospectus, 1976, quoted in Makis Uming 1976: 67)

7   This has fluctuated between $A33m and $A99m per annum over the last three years. In 1973, the first year of its operation, the mining company netted a profit of $A158m and paid out in cash dividends over $A80m. This compared with a paid up capital of $A134m, two-thirds of the project having been loan-financed. In 1974 the company made an even higher $A181m profit and paid in cash dividends nearly $A74. Within about 2½ years of the start of production, the company returned to stock-holders their total investment and an additional return of 16.5 per cent.

8   In 1974-75, government capital expenditures amounted to only $A33.1m as against current expenditures valued at $A341.0m. The percentage share of capital expenditures in the total actually *fell* from about 20 per cent five years ago to around 10 per cent currently.

# 5   CONCLUSION

1   Van Zwanenberg with King (1975: 299) notes a similar situation in East Africa: 'Apart from the introduction of the use of the imported [hoe], which was probably a small improvement on the older, locally produced hoe, the techniques of production were little affected by western science and knowledge. The old problems of drought and famine had in no way lessened and may in some instances have become greater'.

# 6   THE DEVELOPMENT OF AUSTRALIAN CAPITALISM

1   Blainey (1966: 149-50) believes that the convict system was 'vital to Australia', because it contributed to the strength of local manufactures and commerce and hastened the rise of a dynamic export economy. 'Without it relatively few people from the British Isles would have made the costly journey across the world in Australia's first half century.'

2   The Anglo Boer war, for example, 'evoked a larger and more spontaneous outburst of feeling than the ceremonies marking the proclamation of the Commonwealth or the opening of the first parliament. Over 300 000 people cheered the second South African contingent from New South Wales on its way as it marched through Sydney streets on 17 January 1900' (Meaney, 1976: 41).

3   The degree of unionization was soon high by international standards. For example, the percentage of unionists in the population, in 1914, in the United States was 2.48; Germany 3.20; France 2.60; Britain 8.92; and Australia 10.59 (Turner, 1965: 228).

4   By 1931-32 the tariff on British goods had been raised to 80 per cent above the pre-depression level (Schedvin, 1970: 8).

5   In consequence also of changing production decisions (whether, e.g., car bodies and/or engines are to be produced in South Africa or elsewhere rather than in Australia) by international corporations over which Australian industry has little or no control.

6   For example, in November 1976, the Australian Industries Development Association warned that there might soon be little manufacturing industry left, and that Australia might instead become 'a large land mass, [with] a rich endowment in natural resources but with a small population, affluent or otherwise, according to the vagaries of world prices for primary products' (*Post-Courier*, 17 November 1976: 20).

7   R.B. Joyce (1971) makes this point with reference to New Guinea, but it would seem to hold for the whole country.

8   The Chairman of the Government Parties' Parliamentary Defence Committee, Bob Katter (quoted in *Post-Courier*, 7 June 1976: 7).

9   Dr. Robert O'Neill, head of the strategic and defence studies centre, Australian National University (quoted in the Melbourne *Age*, 3 January 1977: 4).

10   Sir Maori Kiki, Minister for Defence, Foreign Affairs and Trade, is inclined to present this as the only undertaking PNG gives to Australia under the Agreement (*Post-Courier*, 19 November 1976: 9); however, given Australia's existing dominance it is the only one that would be required of the country.

# 9   THE FORMATION OF THE PEASANTRY

1   The problem has appeared with greater clarity in recent years. Alienated

land in the Western Highlands, for example, was estimated in 1976 to be over 20 per cent, most of which is in the area of greatest land use potential. Of late, 'a significant amount of land has been sold in a totally informal manner' to migrants from adjacent areas, and has brought prices 'in excess of K1,000 per hectare' (Western Highlands Province Development Study, 1976: 35). The basic elements in the changing relationship are the expansion of cash crop production, localized land shortages, and the emergence of a market for land (Shand, 1969: 310). The problem is considered further below.

2. A spectacular, contemporary example of the process at work was provided by Yano Belo, then Minister of Housing, and son of a 'big man', in September 1976, at Kagua. Belo and his brothers slaughtered what was reported to be (with almost certainly some hyperbole) approximately 3000 pigs and distributed them to people from all over the Southern Highlands. The Minister was 'dressed in all the adornments of a great traditional leader'; he hoped, it was said, to 'show his people just what sort of a leader he was', and he had felt, more specifically, that 'it was time his family moved back into an area which had been lost to the line in traditional fighting many years ago' (Carien Stocker, *Post-Courier* 24 September 1976: 5).

3. Standish quotes Hau'ofa to the effect that anthropologists have seriously underestimated the importance of the hereditary principle in PNG. This would appear to imply that the range of centralized political structures existing in the country was also ill considered.

4. Not least by academic observers. Brookfield (1972: 115) wrote that 'the initial object seems to have been to provide education in democratic processes ...'

5. The norms for the establishment of a Council, until 1960, were that an area should be economically developed and have a minimum population of 4000. As Simpson notes, Baluan had a population of some 1700 and little or no economic development or potential.

6. The character of the large volume of anthropological research has been described as 'infinitely detailed work on one or two communities which includes no attempt to generalise further afield' and is 'socially irresponsible' (Hinchcliffe, 1976: 2).

7. Finney has described the career of Bimai Noimbano whose growing wealth was based on the exploitation of the savings, unpaid labour, and other resources of clansmen and other followers but which collapsed on his sudden death leaving hundreds of dissatisfied claimants.

8. R.T. Shand (1969: 296) has said of the general situation in PNG that 'initially the administration favoured planting and ownership on a communal basis, but soon switched to encouragement of individual [family] ownership'. This does not weaken the statement by Bob McKillop who was, in any case intimately involved in extension work in the Eastern Highlands.

[9] On the question of precisely who was first accorded assistance, extension officers in Maprik, in the early 1960s 'selected one or more individuals in a village ... Sometimes these were the Administration representatives (luluai and tultul); in other instances they were simply individuals with initiative' (Shand and Straatmans, 1974: 139).

[10] Through the detailed political stratagems of Fenbury, and also with the general aim, in the words of Paul Hasluck, Minister for Territories, 1951-63, of ensuring that the transition to 'urban communities of landless wage-earners could be made without harm' (Hasluck, 1976: 131).

[11] Despite these various ministrations, Lowa was dissolved at the end of 1975, only to reappear as the Lowa Investment Corporation with interests in a number of enterprises in Goroka, in October 1976 (*Post-Courier*, 1 February 1977: 17).

[12] Auwo Ketauwo, a shareholder in Pacific Helicopters and chairman of directors of the Federation of Savings and Loans Societies, had earlier criticized the existing laws which left land lying unused because the local people did not have the money or wish to develop it (*Post-Courier*, 12 April 1976).

[13] Sinake defended the countryside against the towns when criticizing the revaluation of the kina by 5 per cent — 'the people of the rural area are supplementing the income of the people living in the town to this extent' — and also said that the Highlanders obtained the maximum disadvantage from government actions (*Post-Courier*, 8 September 1976).

[14] Votes were held by a few whites and Sinake, with thousands of non-voting indigenous members (personal communication from Peter Fitzpatrick).

[15] There is much support for Holloway's views. In the words of a church representative, "beer is the biggest item of business in Goroka now"; total Eastern Highlands' beer sales reached K800 000 in June and in July 1976 (*Post-Courier*, 30 September 1976). In the Western Highlands, malnutrition is 'definitely a serious problem' (Western Highlands Province Development Study, 1976: 86), and in Enga it is 'among the worst' in PNG (Harris, 1976: 5).

[16] In 1973, 'food and live animals' represented $47.7m, and 'beverages and tobacco' $5m. Of the total sum, $43m was imported from Australia, which is by far the largest supplier of food and beverages to PNG.

[17] The emergence of a distinct middle peasantry in the Kainantu area, centred politically on the Komuniti Kaunsils (Munare Uyassi, personal communication 1976), represents perhaps the appearance of a sector of rural society with some potentialities for organized, independent action in future.

[18] The then Minister for Transport, Iambakey Okuk, said in Mt. Hagen, in October 1975, that work under the control of the Plant and Transport Authority would be given to private truck-owners (*Post-Courier*, 27 October 1975), and the Minister for Finance, Julius Chan, stated in his 1976 budget speech that more government work would be given to private

enterprise (*Post-Courier*, 4 August 1976). Similarly, the national government's recent acquisition of Angco, one of the major coffee exporters in the country, was soon followed by assurances from the Prime Minister, Michael Somare, that 'Angco will not be given any special advantages' and that the government would continue to support the private sector in the marketing of coffee and cocoa (*Post-Courier*, 28 March 1977: 3).

[19] According to Sunaivi Otio from the Eastern Highlands, 'many parliamentarians like me do not have the [necessary] educational background', especially those who are traditional or business leaders from the Highlands, and he called on the educated elite to cooperate with them and to offer advice (*Post-Courier*, 31 January 1975). And Akepa Miakwe, when MHA for Goroka (now Unggai-Bena), initiated the establishment of the Eastern Highlands Leaders Association, which aimed, in his words, 'to unite both traditional and elected leaders with our young educated elite to work together and serve the people' (*Post-Courier* 1 February 1977: 17).

# 10 THE FORMATION OF THE WORKING CLASS

[1] Some of these figures are at best estimates and approximations. Daniel (1976: 6) has said that 'data for the years before 1966 (especially ... demographic and employment data) are in some cases non-existent and in most others of extremely doubtful accuracy'. 1966 was the year of the first complete census of the indigenous population of PNG.

[2] For example, 'expressed as a percentage of the average number of labourers in the Northern Division [of Papua] the death rate varied from about thirty per cent in 1898/99 to ten per cent in 1903/04, and even in later years it was probably never less than five per cent' (Nelson, 1975: 313).

[3] The Public Service Association of Papua New Guinea, *Submission to National Minimum Wage Enquiry* (n.d.: 5) offers an analysis strongly suggesting widespread breaches of the minimum wage laws in rural areas in the early 1970s.

[4] For example in New Guinea for the year 1959-60 there were 2286 such complaints and seven prosecutions (*Report on the Administration of the Territory of New Guinea for Years 1959-60*: 237-8 — hereafter referred to simply as *New Guinea Report*). In addition, labour laws were enforced ten times more against workers than against employers in New Guinea over the whole period up to and including the year 1950-51. Thereafter, with most of the penal sanctions against workers abolished at the end of 1950, convictions of employers decreased sharply. And at no time did a conviction for an offence under the labour laws hold much terror for an employer, for he was fined an insignificant amount and never imprisoned. (Conclusions derived from New Guinea Reports relating to a sample of half the total number of years of Australia's rule in New Guinea.)

[5] In New Guinea a worker could renew his contract for a further period before returning home. On the figures in the New Guinea Reports, the great majority chose not to do this.

6   To take one instance, the colonial administration basically only allowed the recruitment of 'single' men and this despite a professed concern with homosexuality on plantations and despite occasional pressures from employers to promote the recruitment of families. Provision was made for wives to accompany workers but was so hedged about and accompanied by greater obligations on employers that it was rarely used. Allowing families to reside near the work place would speed the dissolution of non-capitalist society and the creation of a permanent wage-labour force.

7   In justifying capital punishment, the relatively enlightened Murray wrote of Papua 'where a small white community is surrounded by a barbaric population hardly out of the stone-age' (quoted in Inglis, 1974: 109).

8   In 1945 the *Pacific Islands Monthly* was still surprised at a strike on a coastal ship whose crew, of 'untutored savages from Papua', had 'displayed a remarkable new fluency on the subject of wages and working conditions ...' (quoted in Martin, 1969: 138).

9   Australia's concern to prevent detribalization and the formation of a landless proletariat is referred to in Smith (1975: chapter 2) and by Paul Hasluck (1976: 131) who thought that 'we should be cautious about building up an urban proletariat or disturbing the attachment of people to their own family groupings, ... until we had some prospect that the transition to a different condition among various urban communities of landless wage-earners could be made without harm.'

10  By 1940 recruitment of indentured labour was close to saturation point, and this was followed by the unparalleled severity of the Australian war-time administration in labour matters.

11  This did not mean the abolition of all forced labour in PNG. Compulsory labour on the maintenance of roads and bridges continues today in the Southern Highlands.

12  Also private communication from officers of the Department of Labour, Port Moresby.

13  Hasluck said, 'I suggest that we will see the situation more clearly if we recognize the present measures as indicating the direction of changes which are just beginning and which will gather pace in the next ten years. What we do now is less for to-day than for the decade ahead of us' (House of Representatives, *Parliamentary Debates*, 15 August 1961: 11-12).

14  In reality both were successful efforts at colonial containment (Fitzpatrick, 1975, and Simpson, 1976).

15  The industrial relations law prohibits the organizing of a strike when an award applies as one would to most urban workers. Almost all other organized urban workers would be prohibited from striking by specific legislation covering their occupation such as the Public Service Act.

16  The secretary of the Bougainville Mining Workers Union, Tom Vevo, has

258

called for changes in the industrial relations legislation (*Post-Courier*, 12 November 1976: 4).

17 These official figures exclude such significant categories as military personnel and domestic servants, and their accuracy for some categories is doubtful.

18 The TA, at its foundation, not only had the sympathetic encouragement of the Director of Education of the time, but was also provided with an experienced, full-time organizer by the colonial state. Building upon an educated, 'professional' membership (who might be important influences in their villages), the TA was able to introduce the check-off system, by which union dues are automatically deducted from the employee's salary, thereby gaining a guaranteed income and an accurate listing of membership. It has established branches at the provincial and sub-provincial level, it has a full-time staff in Port Moresby headquarters, and a national executive elected annually by all financial members. The organization has regular contact on both a formal and informal basis with the bureaucracy at many levels, and when led by a vigorous president (for example, by Rose Kekedo in 1975) it is able to assert pressure nationally on a range of issues (Fandim, 1975).

19 The President of the Trade Union Congress, Tony Ila, has said that the Federation had no money because affiliated unions have not paid their fees (*Post-Courier*, 12 November 1976: 4).

20 The President of the then recently-formed Rural Workers Association of the Eastern Highlands, Paul Noibano, claimed in 1974 a membership of 120 (*Post-Courier*, 9 July 1974: 3).

21 Wright (1976: 6). The question is clearer and more important in advanced than in underdeveloped capitalism.

22 Van Onselen has written of the more exploitative situation in Rhodesia. However, there were parallels with PNG especially with regard to indentured labour.

23 The action began on 12 May, when about half of the total workforce marched towards the company pay office carrying placards which read: 'The Company does not abide by industrial agreements'; 'Give to God what is his and to the workers what is theirs'; and 'The Company tells lies to union officials'. The use of violence by the strikers — stoning buildings, commandeering bulldozers — and the arrival of police and their resort to the use of tear gas against the workers, seems to have occurred almost simultaneously, and was followed by the closure of the mine by the company (*Post-Courier*, 13 May 1975: 1, 4). The demonstrations continued the next day, as nearly 1000 women and children were evacuated in convoys from Panguna to Arawa. The 220 riot police rushed in from Rabaul and Port Moresby warned the strikers that 'they wouldn't get away with it', and poured dozens of tear-gas shells into workers' living quarters. During this time at least 700 mine-workers were arrested and another 300 apprentices were detained by police for questioning. On the morning of 14 May, following an early raid by police mobile units on, as it was put, 'one

of the last pockets of suspected resistance in Camp', scores of 'weary and hungry strikers came out of hiding from the hills surrounding Panguna and gave themselves up to police' (*Post-Courier,* 14 and 15 May 1975). On 18 May, about 700 of the arrested workers were released on the orders of the District Commissioner because police feared that the detainees being held, as it was described, in ' appalling condition in a makeshift detention compound', might attempt a mass breakout (*Post-Courier*, 19 May 1975: 1). Bougainville Copper officials estimated that it cost aboutK500 000 a day to close the mine, and set damage to plant at about K400 000 (Office of Information, *Newsletter*, 21 May 1975); no independent assessment of the damage has been made public.

24  The union called on the government to set a firm date for the nationalization of the Bougainville Copper mine; said that the government should insist that all positions of authority be opened to nationals with effective training plans; and declared that trade unions in PNG should broaden their outlook and objectives to include the main social, economic and political questions affecting the people, and not just aim for improvements in wages and conditions (*Post-Courier*, 21 September 1976: 4).

25  Most recently Jacob Lemeki took his own advice and accepted endorsement as a Parliamentary candidate from the People's Progress Party for the 1977 national elections (*Post-Courier*, 24 February 1977: 3). This was an interesting move for, while it is hard to make a precise judgement, the People's Progress Party, under its parliamentary leader, Julius Chan, is possibly the party with the strongest ideological commitment to capitalism in Papua New Guinea. Lemeki was elected and became Deputy Leader of the People's Progress Party.

26  That these wages are not exactly excessive is suggested by the fact that, e.g., in 1972, when the urban minimum wage for Bougainville towns was only $6.00 per week, a study of mine workers with families in Panguna concluded that the minimum weekly requirements of a household (of two adults and two children) would cost $32 per week. Similarly in Port Moresby, in 1974, when the urban minimum wage had reached $20 per week, a budget survey by the Housing Commission showed average weekly household expenditures by Commission tenants who were not in arrears with their rents of $44.68, and for those with rent arrears $42.08 per week (quoted in Daniel, 1976; 26-7).

27  It has accepted, among other things, that wage increases associated with the cost of living should be restricted to two-thirds only of the rise in the Consumer Price Index over the given period.

# 11  A NOTE ON THE FORMATION OF THE EDUCATED PETTY BOURGEOISIE

 * In this section there is a paucity of material: the government reports, the writings on 'industrial relations', and the anthropological monographs which assist the consideration of the working class and peasantries are not matched for the petty bourgeoisie.

1 'Very few even of the more efficient mission schools carried the pupils beyond the equivalent of the third or fourth standard of the Australian primary schools.' With complacent cynicism Hasluck also recalls the following: 'I saw more than one school where a dear earnest person who had been moved to bring the 'light of the gospel to the heathen' was conducting a school in a grass shed with practically no equipment of any kind and no idea of teaching except getting the children to imitate the sound of the Bible texts she recited or the Sunday school hymns she sang in a quavering treble' (Hasluck, 1976: 86).

2 As Hasluck himself said in 1962, 'Part of the difficulty we had was that very few even of the more advanced people at that time could learn readily from written material ...' (1976: 401).

3 The Bully Beef Club was a discussion group of administrators and parliamentarians out of which Pangu grew.

4 The reduction of the wages of national public servants to a level 'geared to the country's capacity to pay' (Hastings, 1973: 98) — that is to pay for a large indigenized bureaucracy.

5 It continues perhaps most clearly in the public discourse of university students which is characterized by frequent reference to themselves as the country's educated or intellectual elite.

6 I am grateful to Peter Fitzpatrick, who participated in discussion with a number of Bank officials on 15 December 1971, for this information.

7 Of the first national departmental heads 'all but one came from Papua and the Islands, including eight from the Central District alone' (Ballard, 1975: 27). For a consideration of inequalities in the education system see Weeks (1977), unfortunately published too late for inclusion here.

8 We may nevertheless agree with John Ballard (1976b: 1) that students 'contributed to the development of Papua New Guinea nationalism', while recognizing the weakness of the nationalist movement and all its offshoots.

9 He was then a member of the breakway Republic of the North Solomons, and head of the Bougainville Development Corporation which is in a dependent relationship with the mine (Makis Uming, 1976: chapter 4). For example, the career of John Kasaipwalova is referred to in the chapter on the post-colonial state.

## 14 THE POLITICAL PARTIES

1 A tendency common to colonial regimes (See G. Balandie 1972: 160).

2 Pangu was accused of being 'subversive' and was subjected to a strenuous anti-party campaign throughout the 1968 elections, so much so that in certain electorates Pangu was equated with a form of evil (Epstein et al, 1971).

3 A brief survey of educational and occupational backgrounds can be found in Hegarty (1972).

4 Damai is a pseudonym once used by Somare.

# Bibliography

Note: For more detailed information on and background to political and administrative developments between 1972 and 1976, the reader is referred to the regular half-yearly chronicles appearing in the *Australian Journal of Politics & History* and *Australian Quarterly* by David Hegarty and W.A. Standish respectively.

Alavi, Hamza, 1965    'Peasants and Revolution', in Ralph Miliband and John Saville (eds), *The Socialist Register*, London.
—— 1972    'The State in Post-Colonial Societies: Pakistan and Bangladesh', *New Left Review*, 74.

Amin, S., 1974    *Accumulation on a World Scale: A Critique of the Theory of Underdevelopment*, 2 vols, New York & London.

Anis, Pedi, 1974    'John Kaputin', *Yagl-Ambu*, 1, 3.

Arrighi, G., 1970    'International Corporations, Labor Aristocracies, and Economic Development in Tropical Africa', in R.I. Rhodes (ed.), *Imperialism and Underdevelopment: A Reader*, New York & London.

Ashworth, W., 1975    *A Short History of the International Economy Since 1850*, London.

Australian Department of Overseas Trade, 1976    *Annual Report, 1975-76*, Canberra.

Bairoch, P., 1975    *The Economic Development of the Third World since 1900*, London.

Balandier, Georges, 1972    *Political Anthropology*, Harmondsworth.

Ballard, John, 1972    The Politics of Localisation in Papua New Guinea, Australian National University, mimeo.
—— 1975    Public Administration, University of PNG, mimeo.
—— 1976a    Wantoks and Administration, Public lecture 26 May, and University Printer, University of PNG.
—— 1976b    Students and Politics in Papua New Guinea. Paper presented at the Institute of Commonwealth Studies, University of London, 1 December, mimeo.

Banaji, Jairus, 1973    'Backward Capitalism, Primitive Accumulation and Modes of Production', *Journal of Contemporary Asia*, 3.

Barnett, Tony, 1976    Land and People in Papua New Guinea, mimeo, Central Planning Office and United Nations Development Programme.

Beckford, G.L., 1972    *Persistent Poverty: Underdevelopment in Plantation Economies of the Third World*, New York.

Bernstein, Henry & Pitt, Michael, 1974    'Plantations and Modes of Exploitation', *Journal of Peasant Studies*, 1, 4.

Berry, Roger, 1977    'Some Observations on the Political Economy of Papua New Guinea: Recent Performance and Future Prospects', *Yagl-Ambu*, 4, 3.

Bettelheim, Charles, 1972    'Appendix 1: Theoretical Comments by Charles Bettelheim', in Emmanuel Arghiri, *Unequal Exchange*, New York & London.

Biskup, P., Jinks, B. & Nelson, H. N., 1968    *A Short History of New Guinea*, Sydney.

Blainey, Geoffrey, 1966    *The Tyranny of Distance*, Melbourne.

Boehm, E. A., 1971    *Twentieth Century Economic Development in Australia*, Melbourne.

Bolton, G. C., 1967    'The Rise of Burns Philip, 1873-1893', in A. Birch and D. S. Macmillan (eds), *Wealth and Progress: Studies in Australian Business History*, Sydney.

Bredmeyer, Theo, 1975    'The Registration of Customary Land in Papua New Guinea', *Melanesian Law Journal*, 3.

Brenchley, F., 1973    'The Stranglehold Australia has — and will keep — on PNG', *National Times*, Australia, 19-24 November.

Brett, E. A., 1973    *Colonialism and Underdevelopment in East Africa*, London.

Brookfield, H. C., 1961    'Native Employment in the New Guinea Highlands', *Journal of the Polynesian Society*, 70, 3.
—— 1972    *Colonialism, Development and Independence: The Case of the Melanesian Islands in the South Pacific*, Cambridge.
—— 1973    'Full Circle in Chimbu', in H. C. Brookfield (ed.), *The Pacific in Transition*, Canberra.

Brookfield, H. C. with Hart, Doreen, 1971    *Melanesia: A Geographical Interpretation of an Island World*, London.

Brown, Michael Barrat, 1974    *The Economics of Imperialism*, Harmondsworth.

Brown, Paula, 1966    'Social Change and Social Movements', in E. K. Fisk (ed.), *New Guinea on the Threshold*, Canberra.

Bundy, Colin, 1972    'Emergence and Decline of a South African Peasantry', *African Affairs*, 71, 285.

Bureau of Industrial Organizations (various dates). *Workers News*, Boroko.

Bureau of Statistics, Nov. 1975    *Papua New Guinea: National Accounts Statistics, 1960/61 — 1973/74*, Port Moresby.

Bureau of Statistics, March 1976    *PNG Statistical Bulletin: Private Overseas Investment, 1967/68 — 1973/74*, Port Moresby.

Bureau of Statistics, June 1976    *PNG Statistical Bulletin: National Accounts Statistics — 1974/75*, Port Moresby.

Bureau of Statistics, August 1976    *PNG Statistical Bulletin: International Trade, June Quarter, 1975*, Port Moresby.

Burnet, I. D., 1967    'The Economic Development of New Guinea' (M. Sc. Thesis, Cornell University.)

Butlin, N. G., 1964    *Investment in Australian Economic Development 1861-1900*, Cambridge.

Cabral, Amilcar, 1969    *Revolution in Guinea*, London.
—— 1969    *Our People Are Mountains*, London.

Castley, R., 1977    *Education Without Employment in Papua New Guinea*, Waigani: Manpower Planning Unit, Discussion Paper No. 6.

Central Planning Office, 1975    *Programmes and Performance, 1975-6*, Port Moresby.

Central Planning Office, 1976    *The Post-Independence National Development Strategy*, Port Moresby.

Central Planning Office, 1976a    *Programmes and Performance, 1976-77*, Port Moresby.

Clark, David, 1975    'Australia. Victim or Partner of British Imperialism?', in E. L. Wheelwright and Ken Buckley (eds), *Essays in the Political Economy of Australian Capitalism*, Sydney.

Clunies-Ross, A. & Langmore, J., 1973    *Alternative Strategies for Papua New Guinea*, Melbourne.

Cochrane, Peter, 1976    'Australian Finance Capital', *Intervention*, 6.

Cohen, Robin, 1972    'Class in Africa: Analytical Problems and Perspectives', in Miliband and Saville (eds), *The Socialist Register, London*.

Collins, G.D., 1974    An Appraisal of the Highlands Labour Scheme, Department of Labour and Industry, Port Moresby, mimeo.

Commonwealth of Australia, 15 August 1961    *Parliamentary Debates, House of Representatives*, 23rd Parliament, 3rd Session.

Conyers, Diana, 1976    *The Provincial Government Debate: Central Control versus Local Participation in Papua New Guinea*, Institute of Applied Social and Economic Research, Monograph 2. (Passages from this work appeared in the *Post-Courier* over eight issues during November 1976.)

Corris, P., 1973    *Passage, Port and Plantation: A History of Solomon Islands Labour Migration, 1870-1914*, Melbourne.

Crocombe, R. G., 1964    'Communal Cash Cropping among the Orokaiva', *New Guinea Research Bulletin*, No. 4, Port Moresby.

Currey, G. R. B., 1973    'The Definition of Development', in R. Mortimer (ed.), *Showcase State: The Illusion of Indonesia's Accelerated Modernisation*, Sydney.

Curtain, Richard, 1977    The Patterns of Labour Migration in Papua New Guinea with Particular Reference to the Sepik Area, Australian National University, mimeo.

Daniel, Philip, 1976    Wages and Employment in Colonial Papua New Guinea, University of Cambridge, Department of Applied Economics, mimeo.

Daro, Boio Bess, 1976    'The Papua Besena Movement: Papua Dainai, Tano Dainai, Mauri Dainai', Institute of Applied Social and Economic Research, Boroko, *Discussion Paper 7*.

Deech, Fran, 1976    'Trade Unions in Papua New Guinea', *Yagl-Ambu*, 3, 1.

Department of Labour, 1969    'The Supply of Agreement

Labour through the Highlands Labour Scheme, Konedobu, Port Moresby, mimeo.

Department of Labour and Industry, 1974    *Report of the (National) Minimum Wages Board*, No. 4, Port Moresby.

Dixon, R., 1974    Productivity, Growth in Secondary Industry in Papua New Guinea over the period 1960-73, A Report prepared for the Central Planning Office, Port Moresby, mimeo.

Docker, E. W., 1970    *The Blackbirders: The Recruiting of South Seas Labour for Queensland, 1863-1907*, Sydney.

Dupré, Georges & Rey, Pierre-Phillipe, 1973    'Reflections on the Persistence of Theory of the History of Exchange', *Economy and Society*, 2, 2.

Emmanuel, A., 1972    *Unequal Exchange: A Study of the Imperialism of Trade*, New York and London.

Epstein, A. L., 1969    *Matupit*, Canberra and London.
—— 1970    'Aspects of Political Development on the Gazelle Peninsula', Marion W. Ward (ed.), *The Politics of Melanesia*, Canberra and Port Moresby.

Epstein, A. L., Parker R. S. & Reay, Marie (eds), 1971    *The Politics of Dependence*, Canberra.

Epstein, T. Scarlett, 1968    *Capitalism, Primitive and Modern*, Canberra.
—— 1973    'Economy, Indigenous', in *Encyclopaedia of Papua New Guinea*, Melbourne.

Evans, D., 1972    'Australia and Developing Countries', in J. Playford and D. Kirsner (eds), *Australian Capitalism*, Melbourne.

Fandim, Tom, 1975    Papua New Guinea Teachers Association, Department of Political Studies, University of PNG, mimeo.

Finney, Ben R., 1973    *Big-Men and Business*, Canberra.

First, Ruth, 1970    *The Barrel of a Gun*, London.

267

Firth, S., 1972    'The New Guinea Company, 1885-1899: A case of Unprofitable Imperialism', *Historical Studies*, 15.

Firth S., 1973    'German Firms in the Western Pacific Islands, 1857-1914', *Journal of Pacific History*, 8.

Fisk, E. K. (ed.), 1966    *New Guinea on the Threshold: Aspects of Social, Political and Economic Development*, Canberra.

Fisk, E. K. & Tait, Marie, June-July 1972    'Less Aid for Niugini?' *New Guinea and Australia, The Pacific and South-East Asia*, 7, 2.

Fitzpatrick, Peter, 1975    'A New Law for Co-operatives', *Annals of Public & Co-operative Economy*, 46, 3.
——    'Really Rather Live Slavery: Law and Labour in the Colonial Economy of Papua New Guinea', in Wheelwright & Buckley, *op. cit.*

Fitzpatrick, Peter & Southwood, Julie, 1976    The Community Corporation in Papua New Guinea, University of PNG, mimeo.

Forge, Anthony, 1970    'Prestige, Influence and Sorcery: A New Guinea Example', in M. T. Douglas (ed.), *Witchcraft, Confessions and Accusations*, London.

Frank, A. G., 1969    *Capitalism and Underdevelopment in Latin America*, Harmondsworth.
—— 1969    'Sociology of Development and Underdevelopment of Sociology', in A. Frank *et al, Latin America: Underdevelopment or Revolution*, New York and London.

Gadiel, D., 1973    *Australia, New Guinea and the International Economy*, London.

Gammage, B., 1975    'The Rabaul Strike, 1929', *Oral History*, 3, 2.

Garnaut, Ross, 1975    *Neo-colonialism and Independence: Papua New Guinea's Economic Relations with Australia and Japan*, Boroko.

Geertz, Clifford, 1963    *Agricultural Involution*, Chicago.
—— 1964    'Ideology as a Cultural System', in David Apter (ed.), *Ideology and Discontent*, New York.

George, Margaret L., 1973    Australian Attitudes and Policies Towards the Netherlands East Indies and Indonesian Independence, 1942-1949, Ph. D. thesis, Australian National University.

Gerritsen, Rolf, 1975    Aspects of the Political Evolution of Rural Papua New Guinea, Research School of Social Sciences, Australian National University Seminar Paper.

Good Kenneth, 1975    'The Static Concept and Changing Reality of Tribe', *Australian and New Zealand Journal of Sociology*, 11, 3.
—— 1976a    'Class Formation in Colonial Situations: Some Definitions and Directions', *Australian and New Zealand Journal of Sociology*, 12, 3.
—— 1976b    'Settler Colonialism: Economic Development and Class Formation', *Journal of Modern African Studies*, 14, 4.

Gottliebsen, Robert, 2-7 August, 1976    'Why the Island Traders Prefer Nuts and Bolts to Cash and Wrap', *National Times*, p. 59.

Gregory, Chris, 1975    The Concept of Modern Monetary Sector as Engine for Development in Underdeveloped Dual Economy Countries, Seminar on Industrial Democracy in Papua New Guinea, University of PNG, mimeo.

Griffin, J. T., September 1975    'Ethnocentralism and Integration', *Meanjin*, 34, 3.

Gunther, Dr J. T., 1963    'From Stone Age to Parliamentary Government in a Decade', Appendix in Colin Simpson, *Plumes and Arrows*, Sydney.

Halliday, Jon, 1975    *A Political History of Japanese Capitalism*, New York.

Handbook for Industrialists, 1975    Port Moresby.

Hannett, Leo, J., 1972    'Niugini Black Power', in F. S. Stevens (ed.), *Racism: The Australian Experience*, 3, Sydney.

Harris, G. T., 1975    Labour Surplus Theories of Development: The New Guinea Experience, Economics Department Discussion Paper, La Trobe University.
—— 1976    *The Development of the Enga Province*, Report submitted to the Central Planning Office, Port Moresby.

Hasluck, P. M. C., January-February 1952    'A policy for New Guinea', *South Pacific*.
—— 1956a    Australian Policy in Papua and New Guinea, George Judah Cohen Memorial Lecture, Canberra, mimeo.
—— 1956b    Australia's Task in Papua and New Guinea, Roy Milne Memorial Lecture, Canberra, mimeo.
—— 1976    *A Time for Building*, Melbourne.

Hastings, Peter, 1973    *New Guinea: Problems and Prospects*, Melbourne.

Healy, A. M., 1967    'Bulolo: A History of the Development of the Bulolo Region, New Guinea', *New Guinea Research Bulletin*, No. 15, Port Moresby.

Hegarty, David, 1972    A Preliminary Analysis of the 1972 Elections in Papua New Guinea, University of PNG, mimeo.

Hegarty, David & Samana, U. U., 1976    'Issues, Expectations and Mobilization: The Lai Open Electorate', in David Stone, (ed.), *Prelude to Self Government*, Canberra.

Heron, L. R., 1973    *Economic and Business Structure in Papua New Guinea*, Melbourne.

Hinchcliffe, Keith, 1976    Anthropology and Economic Policy Making in PNG, Central Planning Office and United Nations Development Programme, Port Moresby, mimeo.

Hobsbawm, E. J., 1969    *Industry and Empire*, Harmondsworth.

Hollerman, L., 1974    'Foreign Trade in Japan's Economic Transition', in Frank, Isaiah (ed.), *The Japanese Economy in International Perspective*, Baltimore and London.

Howlett, Diana, 1973a    *Papua New Guinea: Geography and Change*, Melbourne, London and Ontario.

—— 1973b    'Terminal Development: from Tribalism to Peasantry', in H. C. Brookfield (ed.), *The Pacific in Transition*, Canberra.

Hudson, W. J. & Daven, Jill, 1971    'Papua and New Guinea Since 1945', in W. J. Hudson (ed.), *Australia and Papua New Guinea*, Sydney.

Hughes, Ian, 1975    The Use of Resources in Traditional Melanesia, Waigani Seminar, University of PNG, mimeo.

Hunt, Attlee, 1905    'Report on British New Guinea, 1905', *Commonwealth Parliamentary Papers*.

Inglis, Amirah, 1974    *Not a White Woman Safe*, Canberra.

Inglis, K. S., 1974    *The Australian Colonists*, Melbourne.

International Bank of Reconstruction and Development, 1965    *The Economic Growth of the Territory of Papua New Guinea*.

Jackson, R. T., Fitzpatrick P. & Blaxter, L., 1976    'The Law and Urbanisation' in Richard Jackson (ed.), *An Introduction to the Urban Geography of Papua New Guinea*, University of PNG, Department of Geography, Occasional Paper No. 13.

Jeffries, Richard, 1975    'The Labour Artistocracy?' *Review of African Political Economy*, 3.

Jinks, Brian, 1968    'The Establishment of Local Government in the Northern District', *Journal of the Papua New Guinea Society*, 2, 1.

Jinks, R., Biskup, P. & Nelson, H., 1973    *Readings in New Guinea History*, Sydney.

Joyce, R. B., 1971    'Australian Interests in New Guinea Before 1906', in Hudson (ed.), *op. cit.*

271

Kaplan, J. J., 1974 'Raw Materials Policy: Japan and the United States', in I. Frank, *op. cit.*

Kaputin, John, May-June 1975a 'The Law — A Colonial Fraud?', *New Guinea*, 10, 1.

Kaputin, John 1975b 'Rural Development — New Guinea Development Corporation', *Yagl-Ambu*, 2, 3.

Kay, G., 1975 *Development and Underdevelopment: A Marxist Analysis*, London.

Kerpi, Kama, 1974 Social Tensions and Clan Wars in Kup, University of PNG, mimeo.

Kiki, Albert, Maori, 1968 *Ten Thousand Years in a Lifetime*, Melbourne.
—— 1970 'Development of Trade Unions in the Territory', in Marion W. Ward (ed.), *The Politics of Melanesia*, Canberra and Port Moresby.

Korte, R., 1975 Food and Nutrition in PNG, Nutrition Section, Department of Public Health, Port Moresby, mimeo.

Lamb, Geoff, 1974 *Peasant Politics*, Lewes, Sussex.

Lambert, J. N., 1976 Trends in Food Consumption Patterns in Chimbu, 1956-1975, Nutrition Section, Department of Public Health, Port Moresby, mimeo.

Langmore, John V., 1970 'Recent Developments in Industrial Relations in Papua New Guinea', *Journal of Industrial Relations*, 12, 3.

—— August 1972 A Critical Assessment of Australian Economic Policy for Papua New Guinea Between 1945 and 1970, University of PNG, Economics Department, Discussion Paper 1.
—— 1973 'Labour Relations in Papua New Guinea 1970-72', *Journal of Industrial Relations*, 15, 2.
—— 1976 Wages, University of PNG, mimeo.

Lawrence, Peter, 1964 *Road Belong Cargo*, Melbourne.

Lawrence, P. R., 1975 'Plantation Sisal: The Inherited

Mode of Production', in L. CLiffe *et al* (eds), *Rural Co-operation in Tanzania*, Dar-es-Salaam.

LeBrun, O. & Geery, C., 1975    'Petty Producers and Capitalism', *Review of African Political Economy*, 3.

Legge, J. D., 1956    *Australian Colonial Policy*, Sydney.

Lepani, C., 1976a    Planning in Small Dependent Economies: A case study of Papua New Guinea, paper presented to Seminar on Planning in Small Dependent Economies, Institute of Development Studies, Sussex University.
—— 1976b    Workers' Organizations, University of PNG, mimeo.

Levin, J. V., 1960    *The Export Economies: Their Pattern of Development in Historical Perspective*, Cambridge, Mass.

Leys, C., 1975    *Underdevelopment in Kenya: The Political Economy of Neo-colonialism, 1964-1971*, London.

Leys, Colin, 1976    'The "Overdeveloped" Post Colonial State: A Re-evaluation', *Review of African Political Economy*, 5.

Loveday, P., 1976    'Voting and Parties in the Third House 1972-1975', in P. Loveday & E. P. Wolfers, *Parties and Parliament in Papua New Guinea 1964-1975,* IASER Monograph No. 4, Boroko, PNG.

Mair, L. P., 1948    *Australia in New Guinea*, London, reprinted Melbourne, 1970.

Makis Uming, Ephraim, 1976    The Impact of Bougainville Copper Limited Operations on Local Business on Bougainville: A Study of Underdevelopment, thesis for the degree of Bachelor of Economics, Department of Economics, University of PNG.

Mamak, A. & Bedford, R., 1974    *Bougainvillean Nationalism*, Christchurch.

Martin, R. M., 1969    'Tribesmen into Trade Unionists: the African Experience and the Papua New Guinea Prospect', *Journal of Industrial Relations*, 11, 2.

Marx, Karl & Engels, F., 1970    'Manifesto of the Commu-
nist Party', in *Karl Marx and Fredrick Engels, Selected
Works.*

McFarlane, Bruce, 1972    'Australia's Role in World
Capitalism', in John Playford and Douglas Kirsner (eds),
*Australian Capitalism*, Melbourne.

McKillop, R. F., 1975a    Problems of Access: Agricultural
Extension in the Eastern Highlands, mimeo.
—— 1975b    Coffee Industry, University of PNG, mimeo.
—— 1976a    Helping the People in PNG?, paper presented
at the Conference of the Sociological Association of Australia and New Zealand, La Trobe University.
—— 1976b    The Papuan Separatists as a Nonviolent Political Movement, mimeo.

McQueen, Humphrey, 1970a    'Laborism and Socialism', in
Richard Gordon (ed.), *The Australian New Left*, Melbourne.
—— 1970b    *A New Britannia*, Melbourne.

Meaney, Neville, 1976    *The Search for Security in the
Pacific 1901-1914*, Vol. 1, Sydney.

Meillassoux, Claude, 1972    'From Reproduction to Production: A Marxist Approach to Economic Anthropology',
*Economy and Society*, 1, 1.

Moore, Phillip, 1972    'Australian Capitalism Today', *Intervention*, 1.

Morauta, Louise, 1974    *Beyond the Village*, Canberra.

Mortimer, Rex, 1976    'Australia, Indonesia and Papua New
Guinea', *New Guinea*, 10.

Morton, Kathryn, 1975    *Aid and Dependence: British Aid
to Malawi*, London.

Moses, J. A., 1969    'The German Empire in Melanesia,
1884-1914: A German Self-Analysis', in *The History of
Melanesia*, collection of papers presented at the Second
Waigani Seminar, University of PNG and Australian
National University.

Murray, J. H. P., 1912    *Papua or British New Guinea*, London.
—— 1920    *Review of the Australian Administration in Papua from 1907 to 1920*, Port Moresby.
—— 1925    *Papua of Today*, London
—— 1931    *The Scientific Method as Applied to Native Labour Problems in Papua*, Port Moresby.

Myrdal, G., 1957    *Economic Theory and Underdeveloped Regions*, London.

Nelson, H. N., 1976    *Black, White and Gold: Goldmining in Papua New Guinea 1878-1930*, Canberra.

Nicklason, N., 1969    'The History of Steamships Trading Company', in *The History of Melanesia*, collection of papers delivered at the Second Waigani Seminar, University of PNG and Australian National University.

Nicolaus, Martin, 1970    'The Theory of the Labour Aristocracy', in Paul M. Sweezy and Harry Magdoff (eds), *Lenin Today*, New York and London.

Oliver, Douglas, 1973    *Bougainville*, Melbourne.

Oram, N. D., 1973    'Administration, Development and Public Order', in A. Clunies Ross and J. Langmore (eds.), *Alternative Strategies for Papua New Guinea*, Melbourne.
—— 1976    *Colonial Town to Melanesian City,* Canberra.

Papua New Guinea, March 1976    *Summary of Statistics*, Bureau of Statistics, Port Moresby, 1973/74.
—— 1974-75    *Government Auditor-General's Report.*
—— 1977    Central Planning Office, *Programmes and Performance, 1976-77*, Port Moresby.
—— 27 October 1976    Central Planning Ofice, *The Post-Independence National Development Strategy*, Waigani.
—— 1976    *Labour Information Bulletin*, Series 2, No. 1, Department of Labour and Industry, Boroko.
—— 1976    *Quarterly Summary of Economic Conditions*, Department of Finance, Waigani.

—— 1978    National Planning Office, *The National Public Expenditure Plan, 1978-1981.*

—— *n.d.*    *Labour Information Bulletin, No. 9*, Department of Labour and Industry.

Parker, M. L., 1973    *Papua New Guinea: An Inter-Industry Study.*

Parker, R. S., 1966    'The Growth of Territory Administration', in Fisk, *op. cit.*

Paterson, John, 1969    'New Guinea's Trade Unions', *New Guinea and Australia, the Pacific and South-East Asia*, 4, 1.

Patterson, G. D., 1968    *The Tariff in the Australian Colonies 1856-1900*, Sydney.

Phimister, I. R., 1974    'Peasant Production and Underdevelopment in Southern Rhodesia, 1890-1914', *African Affairs*, 73, 291.

Pim, Sir Alan, 1946    *Colonial Agricultural Production*, Oxford.

Poulantzas, Nicos, March-April 1973    'On Social Classes', *New Left Review*, 78.

Power, A. P., 1974    A Study of Development in Niugini from 1880 to 1940, M.A. Thesis, University of PNG.

Price, Richard, 1972    *An Imperial War and the British Working Class*, London.

Public Service Association, n.d.    *Submission to National Minimum Wage Enquiry*, Port Moresby.

Radi, Heather, 1971    'New Guinea Under Mandate 1921-4', in W. L. Hudson (ed.), *Australia and Papua New Guinea*, Sydney.

Reed, S., 1943    *The Making of Modern New Guinea*, Philadelphia.

Reno, P., 1970    'Aluminium Profits and Caribbean People', in R. I. Rhodes (ed.), *Imperialism and Underdevelopment: A Reader*, New York and London.

Robson, R. W., 1965    *Queen Emma*, Sydney.

Rokotuivuna, A. *et al.*, 1973    *Fiji: A Developing Australian Colony*, IDA, North Fitzroy, Victoria.

Rollins, C.E., 1970    'Mineral Development and Economic Growth', in R. I. Rhodes (ed.), *Imperialism and Underdevelopment: A Reader*, New York and London.

Rostow, W. W., 1960    *The Stages of Economic Growth*, Cambridge.

Rowley, C. D., 1958    *The Australians in German New Guinea 1914-1921*, Melbourne.
—— 1972    *The New Guinea Villager*, Melbourne, 1965, 2nd edition.
—— 1971    'The Occupation of German New Guinea 1914-1921', in W. J. Hudson (ed.), *Australia and Papua New Guinea*, Sydney.

Rowley, Kelvin, 1972a    'The Political Economy of Australia Since the War', in Playford and Kirsner (eds), *Australian Capitalism, op. cit.*
—— 1972b    'Pastoral Capitalism', *Intervention*, 1.

Rweyemamu, J., 1974    *Underdevelopment and Industrialisation in Tanzania: A Study of Perverse Capitalist Industrial Development*, Oxford.

Ryan, P., (ed.), 1972    *Encyclopaedia of Papua New Guinea*, 3 vols, Melbourne.

Sahlins, Marshall D., 1963    'Poor Man, Rich Man, Big-Man, Chief: Political Types in Melanesia and Polynesia', *Comparative Studies in Society and History*, 5.

Salisbury, Richard D., 1964    'Despotism and Australian Administration in the New Guinea Highlands', *American Anthropologist*, 66, 4.

Salisbury, R. F., 1962    *From Stone to Steel: Economic Consequences of a Technological Change in New Guinea*, Melbourne.
—— 1970    *Vunamami*, Melbourne.

Sandbrook, Richard, 1975    *Proletarians and African Capitalism: The Kenyan Case, 1960-1972*, Cambridge.

Sandbrook, Richard & Cohen, Robin, 1975    *The Development of an African Working Class*, London.

Saul, John, 1974    'The State in Post-Colonial Societies: Tanzania', *The Socialist Register*, London.

Schedvin, C. B., 1970    *Australia and the Great Depression*, Sydney.

Seddon, N., 1975    'Legal Problems Facing Trade Unions in Papua New Guinea', *Melanesian Law Journal*, 3, 1.

Shanin, Teodor, 1971    'Peasantry as a Political Factor', in T. Shanin (ed.), *Peasants and Peasant Societies*, Harmondsworth.

Shand, R. T., 1969    'Papua New Guinea', in R. T. Shand (ed.), *Agricultural Development in Asia*, Canberra.

Shand, R. T. & Straatmans, W., 1974    *Transition From Subsistence: Cash Crop Development in PNG*, New Guinea Research Bulletin No. 54, Port Moresby and Canberra, New Guinea Research Unit.

Shand, R. T. & Treadgold, M. L., 1971    *The Economy of Papua New Guinea*, Canberra.

Shineberg, Dorothy, 1967    *They came for Sandalwood: A Study of the Sandalwood Trade in the South-West Pacific, 1830-1865*, Melbourne.

Shivji, Issa, 1975    'Peasants and Class Alliances', *Review of African Political Economy*, 3.

Simpson, David, 1976    The Administration and Political Development of Local Government in PNG to 1964, unpublished B. A Honours thesis, Department of Political Studies, University of PNG.

Smith, D. W., 1975    *Labour and the Law in Papua New Guinea*, Canberra.

Somare, M., 1970    'Problems of Political Organization in Diversified Tribes in Papua New Guinea', in M. Ward (ed.), *The Politics of Melanesia*, Canberra.

Somare, Michael, 1975    *Sana — an Autobiography*, Port Moresby.

Sorrell, Geoff, 1972    'The Australian Arbitration System', in Playford and Kirsner (eds), *op. cit.*

Standish, Bill, October 1973    'The Highlands', *New Guinea*, 8, 3.
—— 1976    Researching Chimbu Politics, Research School of Social Sciences, Australian National University, Seminar paper.

Stevenson, Michael, 1968    'A Trade Union in New Guinea', *Oceania*, xxxix.

Stocker, Garien, 24 September 1976    'Pig Kill of Peace and Forgiveness', *Post Courier*.

Strathern, Andrew, 1971    *The Rope of Moka*, Cambridge.

Territory of Papua and New Guinea, 1970    *Report of Board of Inquiry, Investigating Rural Minimum Wages, Wage Fixing Machinery and Related Matters* (Cochrane Report).
—— 1970    *The Structure of Unskilled Wages and Relativities Between Rural and Non-Rural Employment in Papua New Guinea* (Isaacs Report).
—— 1961    *Legislative Council Debates*, Vol. VI, No. 3.
—— 1959-60    *Report on the Administration of the Territory of Papua and New Guinea*.

Thomas, C. Y., 1974    *Dependence and Transformation: The Economics of the Transition to Socialism*, New York and London.

Turner, Ian, 1965    *Industrial Labour and Politics*, Canberra.

UNIDO, 1974    'Potentialities and Programmes for Development of Small Industries in Papua New Guinea', 2 vols, Port Moresby.

Van Onselen, Charles, 1973    'Worker Consciousness in Black Miners: Southern Rhodesia, 1900-1920', *Journal of African History*, XIV, 2.

Voutas, A. C., 1970    'Elections and Communications', in M. Ward, *op. cit.*

Wallerstein, I., 1974    'The Rise and Future Demise of the World Capitalist System: Concepts for Comparative Analysis', in *Comparative Studies in Societies and History*, 16, 4.

Ward, R. G. & Lea, D. A. M., 1970    *An Atlas of Papua New Guinea*.

Wayne, J., 1975    'The Development of Backwardness in Kigoma Region' in L. Cliffe *et al* (eds), *Rural Co-operation in Tanzania*, Dar-es-Salaam.

Weeks, Sheldon G., 1977    The Social Background of Tertiary Students in Papua New Guinea, Education Research Unit Report No. 22, University of PNG.

West, R., 1972    *River of Tears: The Rise of the Rio Tinto-Zinc Mining Corporation*, London.

*Western Highlands Province Development Study*, 1977 Compiled for the Melpa Area Authority by the Dept of Provincial Affairs, Mt Hagen, and the Central Planning Office, Port Moresby.

White, R. C., 1964    'Social Accounts of the Monetary Sector of the Territory of Papua New Guinea, 1956-57 to 1960-61', *New Guinea Research Bulletin*, 3, Port Moresby.

Williamson, P. G., 1977    'Is there an Informal Sector to just Poverty?', *Yagl-Ambu*, 4, 2.

Willis, Ian, 1974    *Lae: Village and City*, Melbourne.

Wilson, K., 1975    'Socio-economic Indicators applied to PNG' *Yagl-Ambu*, 2, 1, Port Moresby.

Wolf, Eric R., 1966    *Peasants*, Englewood Cliffs, New Jersey.

—— 1971    *Peasant Wars of the Twentieth Century*, London.

Wolfers, E. P., 1970    'A Short History of Political Party Activity in Papua New Guinea', in Marion Ward (ed.), *The Politics of Melanesia*, Canberra.

Wolpe, Harold, 1975    'The Theory of Internal Colonialism: The South African Case', in Ivar Oxaal, Tony Barnett and David Booth (eds), *Beyond the Sociology of Development*, London and Boston.

Woolford, Don, 1973    'The United Party', *New Guinea*, 8.
—— 1974    'Blacks, Whites ... and the Awful Press', *New Guinea*, 8, 4.

World Bank, 14 July 1976    *Papua New Guinea: Economic Situation and Development Prospects*, Report No. 1150, PNG.

Worsley, R. J., 1966    *The Developing System of Industrial Relations in Papua New Guinea*, University of New South Wales.

Wright, Erik Olin, 1976    'Class Boundaries in Advanced Capitalist Societies', *New Left Review*, 98.

Yoshino, M. Y., 1974    'Japan as Host to the International Corporation', in I. Frank, *op. cit.*

Zable, A., 1972-73    'Neo-colonialism and Race Relations: New Guinea and the Pacific Rim', *Race*, XIV, 4.

Zwanenberg, R. M. A. van with King, Anne, 1975    *An Economic History of Kenya and Uganda, 1800-1900*, London.

# Index